Witnesses to the Kingdom

Jon Sobrino

Witnesses to the Kingdom

The Martyrs of El Salvador and the Crucified Peoples

ORBIS BOOKS

Maryknoll, New York 10545

Founded in 1970, Orbis Books endeavors to publish works that enlighten the mind, nourish the spirit, and challenge the conscience. The publishing arm of the Maryknoll Fathers and Brothers, Orbis seeks to explore the global dimensions of the Christian faith and mission, to invite dialogue with diverse cultures and religious traditions, and to serve the cause of reconciliation and peace. The books published reflect the views of their authors and do not represent the official position of the Maryknoll Society. To learn more about Maryknoll and Orbis Books, please visit our website at www.maryknoll.org.

Library of Congress Cataloging-in-Publication Data

Sobrino, Jon.
    Witnesses to the kingdom: the martyrs of El Salvador and the crucified peoples/Jon Sobrino.
     p. cm.
    Includes bibliographical references (p.)
    Contents: Archbishop Romero—Maura, Ita, Dorothy, and Jean—Companions of Jesus—From a theology of liberation alone to a theology of martyrdom—Jesuanic martyrs in the Third World—The Latin American martyrs—The crucified peoples—Monsieur Romero, a Salvadoran and a Christian—Archbishop Romero, requirement, judgment, and good news—The legacy of the martyrs of the Central American University—Archbishop Romero and the faith of Ignacio Ellacuría.
    ISBN 1-57075-468-3 (pbk.)
     1. Christian martyrs—El Salvador. 2. El Salvador—Church history. I. Title.

BR1608.E25S63 2003
272'.9'097284—dc21

2003048220

Contents

Introduction: Jesuanic Martyrs and the Crucified Peoples

Part One
MY MEMORY OF THE MARTYRS

1. Archbishop Romero   11
   Some Personal Recollections

2. Maura, Ita, Dorothy, and Jean   54

3. Companions of Jesus   58
   "Something Terrible Has Happened"   59
   Who Were They?   63
   Why Were They Killed?   71
   Who Killed Them?   77
   A New Idea of a Christian University   83
   Their Church   86
   Their Theology   90
   Their Legacy   93

Part Two
THEOLOGICAL REFLECTION

4. From a Theology of Liberation Alone
   to a Theology of Martyrdom   101
   Prior Reflections   101
   Importance for the Theological Task   104
   Importance for Systematic Theology   107
   Importance for Basic Theology   115
   Importance for Spirituality   116

5. Jesuanic Martyrs in the Third World   119
   The Need to Historicize the Traditional Conception
   of Martyrdom   120

The "Jesuanic" Conception of Martyrdom   122
The Jesuanic Martyrs and Theology   125
The Crucified People: Reference Point of the Jesuanic
    Martyrs   131

6. **The Latin American Martyrs**   134
   Challenge and Grace for the Church
   The Need for a Challenge to Today's Church   134
   Incarnation: "Overcoming Unreality"   138
   Mission: "Salvation of the Reality"   142
   Cross: "Bearing the Burden of Reality"   146
   Resurrection: "Letting Reality Carry Us"   149

7. **The Crucified Peoples**   155
   Yahweh's Suffering Servant Today
   The Crucified Peoples: A Horrifying Fact   155
   The Crucified People as Yahweh's Suffering Servant   157
   The Salvation the Crucified Peoples Bring   159

Part Three
THEIR LEGACY

8. **Monseñor Romero, a Salvadoran and a Christian**   167
   Monseñor Romero Was, Like Jesus, "Real" in His
       Incarnation within the True Reality of El Salvador 169
   Monseñor Romero, Like Jesus, Fulfilled His Mission,
       Which Was the Evangelization of an Entire Nation,
       of All of Reality   172
   Monseñor Romero Bore the Burden of Reality:
       Like Jesus, He Died on the Cross   175
   Monseñor Romero Accepted the Burden of Reality
       and Experienced the Grace of Living as if Already
       Participating in the Resurrection   176

9. **Archbishop Romero: Requirement, Judgment**
   and Good News   179
   Monseñor's Presence in This Anniversary   180
   Monseñor's Identity: Identification with the People
       and with His God   181
   The Real Tradition of Monseñor: To Carry
       On His Work and His Cause   185
   Archbishop Romero: Prophecy, Judgment,
       and Good News   193

10. The Legacy of the Martyrs of the Central
    American University   195
    The Incarnation Which Humanizes: Coming to Be
        in the Real World   196
    The Heart Which Is Moved to Mercy   197
    The Truth Which Defends the Victims   198
    Structural Mercy: The Paths of Justice   200
    Enduring Mercy: The Greatest Love   201
    The Joy of the Beatitudes   202
    The Faith Which Walks Humbly with God
        through History   203
    Martyrdom: A Cry Which Continues to Resound   205

11. Archbishop Romero and the Faith of Ignacio Ellacuría   208
    Struggling with God   209
    Facing the Mystery of God with Archbishop Romero   211
    Carried by the Faith of a Crucified People   213

Part Four
EPILOGUE

A Letter to Ignacio Ellacuría (1990)   219

Letter to Ignacio Ellacuría (2001)   222

Notes   225

Introduction

Jesuanic Martyrs and the Crucified Peoples

When Orbis Books encouraged me to publish a selection of articles about martyrdom, I accepted with pleasure. Not so much because these are my own reflections, but because it is a way to keep alive a deep and massive, human and Christian reality that may otherwise be lost to memory. In the last thirty or forty years, thousands of human beings in the Third World—especially in El Salvador and in Latin America—have died as Jesus did (we call these Jesuanic martyrs), and tens of millions have died and are still dying as the suffering servants of Yahweh (we call these the crucified people). What we are forgetting even more is that those thousands and millions of people are precisely the ones who have best shown us the need for compassion and salvation; they are also, paradoxically, the ones who have best expressed compassion and salvation in their own lives.

But this, which we consider a central reality in our world, is not real to the affluent societies. Certainly it is not considered in the process of globalization, nor is it real to most churches and theologies, although there are some exceptions. Their excuse seems to be that martyrdom, in Latin America for instance, is seen as a thing of a happily forgotten past. Besides, keeping alive the subject of martyrdom is seen as masochistic, as a glorification of suffering that verges dangerously on sacrificialism. Martyrdom has negative connotations in today's climate. Indeed, certain forms of terrorism have been described as martyrdom, although they involve self-immolation for a cause judged noble and liberating, in order to produce death to the enemy. So some people conclude that it is best not to speak of martyrdom.

The usual way of silencing martyrdom is by relegating it to the past, in purely chronological terms. So publishing a book today about the martyrdom of the last few decades is a way of overcoming the silence, of reclaiming what has happened in our recent past as something that remains central in our time. That was the valid and necessary reason for the Old Testament cry of "Hear, O Israel," which raised the past and the people's memory into central categories, *a priori*. Historical experience also reaffirms it, *a posteriori*. That experience shows that undervaluing the past and our memory makes it easier to conceal the present reality and to diminish the future, with its promise and hope. Remembering the past does not necessarily mean

1

getting tied down to it; it means drawing on the life-giving sap that has nourished the best and deepest roots of our life and history, and can also nourish our growth.

And when we find martyrdom in the past, then we have found something central to all human history, certainly to Christian history. "Do this in remembrance of me," Jesus said in his time of martyrdom. Of course those words must be historicized over the years, but we cannot ignore them, distort them, or reduce them to a mere cultic phrase that no longer communicates an historical reality, without renouncing the life-giving blood of the first Christian martyr (although not the first martyr in human history). The fact that Jesus' Last Supper happened in the past does not diminish its importance as the fundamental expression of what it means to live and die a human being.

In short, the reason for this book is our refusal to let the martyrs die forever, to kill them again in a different way. Archbishop Romero, the martyrs of El Mozote, the countless unknown martyrs whose names have been shamelessly taken from them in Africa and so many other places—we need them as much as we need air to breathe. For that reason, no matter how these reflections are received, I believe that going back to the martyrs is in itself an important, humanizing task. That, at least, is the hermeneutical presupposition behind this modest book.

Taking the martyrial reality seriously is fundamental for society and the Church, but also for theology, although I fear that—with some honorable exceptions—theology has not taken it as seriously as it deserves. Theologians today may have heard of Archbishop Romero, for instance, but I do not believe they have gone very deeply into the theological meaning of martyrial reality, and its impact on the method and content of theology.

Certainly there has been important theoretical progress regarding the concept of martyrdom. We see it in the often-repeated comment by Karl Rahner in 1983: "Why should a Monseñor Romero, for example, fallen in the struggle for justice in society, a struggle that grew out of his deepest Christian convictions, not be considered a martyr?" We have gone beyond *odium fidei* to *odium iustitiae* as a formal element of martyrdom. But we can safely say that, in general, today's theologians have little interest in going beyond an historical analysis of the concept of martyrdom, which offers some novelty, to confront its reality.

This is not to deny the importance of historical concepts of martyrdom, but the concepts by themselves do not have the energy that leads to understanding. I believe a qualitative leap is needed, motivated by the martyrial reality of our own time and not by concepts alone. It requires us to ponder the reality of what is happening, not only the accuracy or inaccuracy of the concepts. And, yes, it also means expressing in concepts and words the weight of the reality of the millions of people massacred as servants of

Yahweh, and the reality of the thousands of witnesses to the greatest love, who like Jesus gave their lives freely and gratuitously, in order to bring them down from the cross.

I believe the failure to confront the martyrial reality theologically will lead to serious consequences for church life and also for theology. One of these is that by not taking this reality seriously we may come dangerously close to docetism. To theoretical docetism, which, without saying so, transforms real misery and death into mere (albeit macabre) illusion, and looks elsewhere for true reality; to praxic docetism, which honors petty, minimal efforts to give life to the crucified ones as if those efforts were serious, responsible praxis; and to affective docetism, shallow tears and laments that push aside true, serious, committed compassion (although it may tolerate an occasional protest).

In short, we must take the martyrial reality seriously. But that reality is also something to think about, that moves us to thought, moves us to theological conceptualization. From that reality, as we have lived it in El Salvador and its neighbors, especially Guatemala, we have tried to develop a concept of martyrdom that goes beyond earlier concepts, and above all, that does justice to reality. In the process we have discovered two new things that we think are worth considering.

The first is to understand, in the context of Jesus' life and death, the martyrial death of the active martyrs whose lives were taken violently and unjustly. They are the ones we call Jesuanic martyrs. They are the martyrs of the kingdom, of humanity; it happens in the Church and may also happen elsewhere. I shall not go into this here, for it is very present in the book.

The other discovery is a question about the majorities of people who die innocently and defenselessly, as a result of everyday injustice or of massacres: are they also martyrs, and in what sense? I shall say more about this here, for I believe the question is not often seriously discussed. By way of answer, let me cite the fundamental ideas from an article I have recently written on the subject (*La utopía de los pobres y el reino de Dios*, RLT 56 [2002], pp. 154–161).

There are poor and victimized majorities in the world whose lives are filled with misfortune, and which end in the slow death of poverty or the violent death of massacres. But what is important in this context is not whether we call them martyrs or not. The more serious problem is that they have no names. They were anonymous in life but also in death, including the massive, cruel, innocent, and unjust death that comes from war, genocide, and terrorism, in the usual sense, and above all, at the hands of the State.

With all due respect, most of the North American victims in Viet Nam have names, names that are even engraved on monuments; the same will probably be true of the World Trade Center victims in New York and the Pentagon victims in Washington. But the victims in the Third World have no names, not even a date. New York has a date: 9/11 (September 11, 2001) is universally familiar. But 10/7 (October 7, 2001), when the bombing of Afghanistan began, does not; there is no date for the poor countries. Forced anonymity—a massive, routine, and still common reality—is a quintessentially ungodly act, for God moves us to "give names." It would be a scandal anywhere, but especially for those who call themselves democratic and Christian. Yet it is a reality. We have lived it in El Salvador and in Central America, and it is also happening in the African Great Lakes region. There the immense majority of victims no longer have names, in fact and (almost) under law, because they are not "rich" but "poor." They are Salvadorans, Haitians, Rwandans, Congolese. The western world does not care about their names. They are poor people.

Something similar may happen in the Church and its theology to those who die from unjust poverty—although we hope not so cruelly, and we hope things may be changing in this regard. It may even happen, less understandably, to the victims of massacres. There are among us thousands of men and women, young and old, innocent and defenseless, victims of persecution and repression; they have been massively and cruelly murdered, often simply for possessing "subversive" materials (Archbishop Romero's homilies, the Bible), or for living in or near guerilla-controlled territory, or for giving humanitarian assistance (food, medical care) to rebels or sometimes to government soldiers. In some places there have been concerted efforts to remember and honor their names; that is to the credit of the local communities. But in general, and in official circles, we still do not know what to do with them, what to call them, in order to express the Christian dignity of their deaths.

In ecclesial and theological circles we have no name for those human beings and Christians whose deaths were historically cruel—and were illustrious deaths in Christian terms, thinking of the servant of Yahweh, however scandalous it may be to say so. There has been progress toward an understanding of "active martyrs," such as Archbishop Romero, but the church is still ignoring the most painful reality: these massive deaths. At first we called them "passive martyrs," to draw a parallel and to point out that they had done nothing to "deserve" death. In this sense it is worth remembering that the Church has considered describing the death of soldiers and combatants as martyrdom, but it does not know what to do with innocent victims, with the exception of the "slaughter of the holy innocents" that is still remembered as a tragic, decorative theological element in the stories of Jesus' infancy.

But there has been a miracle. The most important thing Archbishop Romero did as a pastor, and Ignacio Ellacuría as a theologian, was to notice this situation—which might be called an anomaly or a scandal, depending on one's point of view—and heal the sin of forgetfulness and ingratitude. They gave names, "titles of dignity" as they were called in ancient christology, to these massacred majorities. They called them "the suffering servant" (Isaiah 52:13–53:12), "Christ crucified in history," "the crucified people." Setting aside the problem of language—setting aside the difficulty of using analogy to understand these majorities "canonically" or at least "theologically" as martyrs—they got down to the important point: These victims were like Christ at the culminating moment of his crucifixion.

So the victims now have a Christian name. We call them "the suffering servant of Yahweh," "Christ crucified in history." From this standpoint it doesn't matter that we are using the term "martyrs" in an analogical sense; it is a powerful way to honor the Christian excellence of their deaths. But perhaps we may think, without excessive boldness, about the need for another step forward. Comparing the deaths of these majorities with those of the Jesuanic martyrs, and even with Jesus' death, these are less about the praxis of defending the poor and the active struggle against the anti-kingdom; they are also less about faithfulness under persecution and about facing death freely, since they often did not have even the possibility of avoiding death. But the deaths of these majorities are more expressive of historical innocence, because they had done nothing to "deserve" death except to be poor. They had made no bitter prophetic denunciations, for instance, and they are more expressive of defenselessness, because they had no physical way of avoiding death. Above all, they are the best expression of the fact that these majorities are unjustly bearing the burden of the sin that destroyed them bit by bit in life, and wiped them out forever in death. And let us remember that these are large majorities of humanity.

These majorities, oppressed in life and massacred in death, are the best expression of the overwhelming suffering of the world. It is they who, without intending it and without knowing it, are completing in their flesh "what is lacking in Christ's afflictions." They are the *analogatum princeps* of the crucified ones in this world, on whom God gazes with infinite tenderness whether we call them martyrs or not. Yet they are surrounded by an inhuman and anti-Christian silence, which coexists "elitistically," so to speak, with the praise rendered to the great saints. A Francis of Assisi or an Archbishop Romero would be the first to raise vigorous protests against that separation.

Finally, these suffering and crucified majorities are the reason why there are Jesuanic martyrs. The latter are killed, as Jesus was, for defending the victims.

This new way of thinking about martyrial reality—looking at the Jesuanic martyrs and the crucified people together, attributing logical priority to the latter over the former—seems fruitful to us, primarily as a way of being honest with reality and overcoming the docetism we mentioned earlier. It can also be useful for theo-logy, because it leads us to the ultimacy of reality and thus to the ultimacy of God, including of course the question of theodicy. It leads us to Christo-logy, for just as Christ helps us to understand the Jesuanic martyrs, they in turn—within the hermeneutic circle—help us to understand the life and death of Jesus. And it also leads us to ecclesio-logy, since on the one hand the Jesuanic martyrs can be described as primordial witnesses to the faith, and on the other, the crucified people are the primary addressees of ecclesial mission.

Let me close with a word about the structure of the book. The first part is a collection of personal memories of the martyrs who were very close to me: Archbishop Romero and my Jesuit brothers. It also includes a brief article about Maura, Ita, Dorothy, and Jean, which will have special meaning for U.S. readers: these martyrs are women and religious sisters from the United States. Their martyrdom is a symbol of cruelty in its crudest form, but also of innocence, tenderness, and love for the "least of these" in our country. As I have said before, they symbolize the best that the United States has given to El Salvador.

The second part is comprised of theological reflection. It goes more deeply into the fundamental points mentioned in this introduction, and discusses the martyrs' specific, irreplaceable benefit to everyone who seeks to be moved by reality. Particular attention is given to their role as challenge and grace for the Church.

The third part gathers the martyrs' legacy, especially that of Archbishop Romero and the Jesuits of the UCA (Central American University). The point here is that the martyrs have left us something important, but that it depends on us to receive it, to let ourselves be graced by them, and to use their legacy productively.

Let me also say a brief word about the method, if we can call it that, of these reflections. That is best explained by telling how I began to write about the reality of martyrdom.

Rutilio Grande, my friend and Jesuit brother, was assassinated on March 12, 1977. Monseñor Romero had just become the archbishop. In view of the repression that was already occurring against the peasants, and now Rutilio's assassination, he asked me to write something on the persecution of the Church from a theological perspective. I remember that I couldn't find anything written elsewhere that would illuminate the persecution and deaths in El Salvador. Those first reflections were later published in my book, *The True Church and the Poor* (Orbis, 1984, pp. 228–252).

The point is that I started early to theologize about persecution, martyrdom, and victims, and that this was a great challenge to my theology. It wasn't easy, therefore, to cite and copy other works; one had to look reality in the eye, and from that experience to reread Scripture, especially the life and death of Jesus and of the servant. To me "reflection" meant "rumination," in a pre-Socratic way, in the presence of reality.

Finally, my years of experience in El Salvador have opened me—I hope—to a grasp and understanding of martyrial reality in many other countries of Latin America, Africa, Asia, the Balkans, and so on. The circumstances are different, but there are commonalities among them. Along the way I became convinced that there is nothing more ecumenical than martyrdom: It is the suffering that comes to bloodshed, and the service that comes to the greatest love.

Martyrdom expresses the universality of negativity, suffering, cruelty, injustice, and death. But it also, and especially, expresses the universality of the positive: compassion, mercy, generosity, justice, and love.

I believe that in places like El Salvador it is easy—easier, at least—to understand the active and passive victims in other places, to let ourselves be affected by them, to venerate them, to be grateful for their generosity and innocence—and to dedicate our lives to making salvation possible for them in this world.

Jon Sobrino
San Salvador
September 2002

Part One

MY MEMORY OF THE MARTYRS

Chapter 1

Archbishop Romero

Some Personal Recollections

I

My first personal encounter with Archbishop Oscar Romero took place on March 12, 1977. In the afternoon of that day, Father Rutilio Grande, S.J., and two *campesinos,* a boy and an old man, had been murdered near El Paisnal. A few hours later, in the Jesuit house at Aguilares, a large number of persons had gathered—we Jesuits, other priests, sisters, and hundreds of *campesinos,* all come to weep for the two murdered *campesinos* and for Rutilio, the priest who had proclaimed to us the good news of the gospel.

We had been awaiting the arrival of Archbishop Romero, installed as head of the Archdiocese of San Salvador less than three weeks before, on February 22, and of his auxiliary, Bishop Rivera. The bishops would lead our concelebration of the first eucharist in the presence of the remains of the three murder victims. But it was growing late, and the prelates had not yet arrived. The people were beginning to show a certain impatience and uneasiness, especially now that night was falling. So Father Jerez, Provincial of the Jesuits of Central America, decided to begin the celebration of the eucharist without them; and all except myself—I no longer remember why—began to move toward the church, which was attached to the house. Suddenly there was a knock at the door. I went to the door, opened it, and there stood Archbishop Romero and Bishop Rivera. The archbishop looked very serious and concerned. I greeted our visitors, and without another word led them to the church.

This was my very first personal contact with Archbishop Romero. It was of course a very brief, purely symbolic encounter. But the occasion rendered it one of immense personal significance for me. At the moment, obviously, all our thoughts were on Rutilio and the two *campesinos,* the murder

Originally published in English in Jon Sobrino, *Archbishop Romero: Memories and Reflections* (© 1990 by Orbis Books).

victims. It had occurred to all of us what might be in store. True, the repression of the *campesinos* had been mounted long since. And a number of priests had been arrested and expelled from the country. But for a priest to be murdered in El Salvador was unheard of. Now it was no longer merely the rules of fair play that were being broken; treachery itself had taken hold. Anything could happen in the country if the powerful had dared to murder a priest. And 1977 would indeed prove a difficult year for *campesinos*, priests, and us Jesuits. Two months after Rutilio's murder, the three remaining Jesuits in Aguilares were expelled from the country. On June 20, all of us Jesuits received death threats.

Uppermost on our minds that night, then, was the dead body of Rutilio. But I was also mightily struck by the serious, preoccupied face of Archbishop Romero. Here was an ecclesiastic of whom I had heard only that he was very conservative, and not really very courageous. And here he was, beginning his archiepiscopal ministry not amidst a series of solemn celebrations, but awash in arrests, torture, the expulsion of priests, and now, suddenly, the blood of Rutilio Grande, one of the priests with whom he had been on the most familiar terms. Who could have foretold that the growing repression of *campesinos* and laborers, which the Salvadoran bishops, at the insistence of Bishop Rivera in particular, had so courageously denounced in their message of March 5, would so quickly come to this?

From that night on, my mental image of Archbishop Romero's serious, concerned face when I opened the door was like a magnet to me, attracting me to him and overwhelming me with the idea that I must somehow help him. Actually, the preconception we had had of him had already been somewhat modified, as in the course of the clergy meetings of the closing days of February, where he was introduced as our new archbishop; at that time he had asked our help in the serious difficulties he was sure to encounter. My decision to try to help him was an enthusiastic one, then, and it was shared by many. It was also something we all perceived as a matter of urgency, since we all expected things to get very difficult in the immediate future, and we knew that we would do much better if we faced them united as a church rather than in a state of separation and division. And so there had already been a noticeable change in the relationship between Archbishop Romero and ourselves. But that night of March 12 sealed that relationship.

To tell the truth, the change was a surprising one. For one thing, my little contact with him had been rather tense since I had returned to El Salvador in 1974. And the one thing I knew for certain about Archbishop Romero was that he had been a very conservative auxiliary, much under the influence of Opus Dei, and an adversary of priests and bishops who had accepted the Medellín line; sometimes he had gone to the point of accusing these bishops and priests of "false ideology." He also regarded several Salvadoran Jesuits as "Marxist" and "politicized," and these were precisely the persons under whose guidance I was taking my first steps as a Jesuit and theologian after a seven years' absence from the country.

The first time I ever laid eyes on Archbishop Romero, if my memory serves me correctly, was in 1974, at the seminary of San José de la Montaña, where I was giving a talk to priests and seminarians on the historical Jesus and the Reign of God. In the front row, to my right, sat Archbishop Luis Chávez, along with Bishop Rivera, his auxiliary, and Bishop Romero, then likewise his auxiliary. What impressed me that evening about Bishop Romero was that, apparently, at least, he was there only out of a sense of duty to his archbishop. He never raised his head to look at me all during the time I spoke. It was as if he wished to show that he did not endorse what I was saying, but, precisely, was keeping his distance from it. In a word, I must have been another of those "Marxist priests." And I, for my part, was convinced that Bishop Romero was exactly as he had been portrayed.

My worst suspicions were confirmed on August 6, 1976, when our country celebrated its patronal Feast of Our Lord Jesus Christ the Divine Savior, and the customary Solemn High Mass was celebrated in the Metropolitan Cathedral of San Salvador. In those years a well-known priest or ecclesiastic would be invited to pronounce a solemn homily on that day, in the presence of all of the bishops, government officials, the diplomatic corps, and so on. It was an important address, then. It certainly had been in 1970 (if I may be permitted a little digression), when the homilist had been Father Grande, so respected and loved in the archdiocese, and a candidate for appointment as rector of the seminary. Rutilio had divided his homily according to the three words on the Salvadoran flag: *Dios, Unión, Libertad*—"God, Unity, Freedom." His homily consisted of a resounding denunciation of the condition of the country. With the latter two elements in the Salvadoran motto missing, said Rutilio, so was the first! As there was no unity or freedom among us, we were without God. This had caused a great deal of surprise, and a great stir. And Rutilio had not been appointed rector of the seminary.

In 1976, then, the homilist chosen for the occasion had been Bishop Romero, then bishop of Santiago de María. I did not attend the Mass that August 6, but a few hours after its conclusion a fellow priest brought me a tape of the homily. I turned on the recorder, and chills went up my spine. Bishop Romero's first point was a criticism of the christologies being developed in El Salvador—"rationalistic, revolutionary, hate-filled christologies." Bishop Romero had begun his homily with a virulent criticism of my own christology!

Understandably, then, many of us priests and others were anything but enthusiastic over the prospect of Bishop Romero's succeeding Archbishop Luis Chávez. Chávez had been a pastoral bishop, very close to the people, and we had been on very good terms with him. To my mind the ideal candidate would have been Bishop Rivera. But it was not to be. Returning to El Salvador on a flight from Mexico City on February 8, I saw a large photograph of Bishop Romero on the cover of a Salvadoran magazine. The new archbishop of San Salvador was Bishop Romero. Bad times in store, I thought. I wondered if Archbishop Romero would have the courage to denounce repression, or if on the contrary he would abet it—if he would defend the threatened *campesinos* and priests, or leave them in the lurch. A few days later I received a post card from a Mexican Jesuit that might as well have been a letter of condolence. As a matter of fact, we all thought we faced a very bleak future. Fortunately, we were all mistaken.

The things I am recounting now, of course, seemed of scant importance that night of March 12. The homily of August 6 was the furthest thing from either of our minds, Archbishop Romero's or my own. But in thinking it over afterwards, it seemed to me that that first, silent greeting had been a kind of reconciliation with Archbishop Romero—the beginning of a new ecclesial relationship and a new friendship. I know that many of my colleagues thought the same, and we were all glad. Some people think that the only thing forward-looking priests, liberation theologians, and base communities are after is tactical relations with the hierarchy. But this is not true. For all of us it is a joy to live in the church as brothers and sisters, including and especially—when it is possible—those brothers of ours who are also our bishops.

But about that same time, another thought began to haunt me. I knew that Archbishop Romero generally had the humility and delicacy to apologize for behavior he regretted. He had come to a base community to ask forgiveness, years after the fact, for what he had said to them in 1972, when he practically justified the militarization of the national university and the ensuing repression. He had also asked forgiveness of a fellow Jesuit of mine who had been rector of the seminary when the bishops—among them, most definitely, Archbishop Romero—decided to take the seminary away from the Jesuits. This was typical of his humility and delicacy. I do not know why, but for some reason I was obsessed by the notion that one day Archbishop Romero would feel badly for his attacks on me, and apologize. Happily, I never spoke of this. If I had, I think I should have been even more haunted by the idea. At all events, one day—I think it was toward the end of April 1977—Archbishop Romero saw me in a corner of the cathedral and came to speak to me. "Thank you," he told me, "for your reflections on the church. I think it helped a great deal." He was referring to the dossier he had taken to Rome to explain the situation in our country and the changed behavior of the church after Rutilio's death. I had done some of the work on the theological part of the report. Actually there was no need for Archbishop Romero to thank me or any of the many others who had placed ourselves at his service. But I certainly appreciated the gesture. It meant a kind of ecclesial acceptance of what we were doing. Especially, it was a demonstration of confidence. Archbishop Romero always had this delicacy. Whenever I had helped him in some way, in publishing the documents of Medellín and Puebla, for example, or with any theological reflections I might write for his use, Archbishop Romero would send me a letter or little note of thanks.

II

But to go back to that night of March 12: after Mass, Archbishop Romero asked us priests and sisters to remain in the church. Some of the *campesinos* stayed too, and naturally we made no discrimination. And we held a planning session right then and there, in the late hours of the night, without waiting for the next day or a night's rest. Archbishop Romero was visibly agitated. He seemed to be laboring under the responsibility of having to do something and not knowing exactly what to do. After all, the problem facing him was unheard-of. And the question he asked us was elementary. What should we and could we do, as church, about Rutilio's murder?

Agitated, perturbed, still he was ready to do whatever would be necessary, and I could see this. He must have been afraid, however. The hour had come in which he would have to face up to the powerful—the oligarchy and the government. I shall never forget how totally sincere he was in asking for our help—how his words came from the heart. An archbishop was actually asking us to help him—persons whom a few weeks before he had regarded as suspect, as Marxist! This gesture of dialogue and humility made me very happy. And I reflected that, while the tragedy of that day seemed such an inauspicious beginning for Archbishop Romero in his new, archiepiscopal responsibility, actually it could be a most auspicious one. The seed of a united, determined, and clear-sighted church, a church which would one day grow to be so great, had been sown. I felt great tenderness for that humble bishop, who was asking us, practically begging us, to help him bear the burden that heaven had imposed on him, a far heavier burden than his shoulders, or anyone else's, could ever have borne alone.

I also felt, or seemed to surmise, that something very profound was transpiring deep within Archbishop Romero. Surely he was uneasy. But in the midst of his uneasiness in those first moments, with all of his hesitancy about what to do, I think he was forming the high resolve to react in whatever way God might ask: he was making an authentic option for the poor, who had been represented, a scant hour before, by hundreds of *campesinos* gathered about three corpses, helpless in the face of the repression they had already suffered and knowing full well that there was more to come. I do not know whether I am correctly interpreting what was actually transpiring in Archbishop Romero's heart at these moments, but I believe he must have felt that those *campesinos* had made an option for him—that they were asking him to defend them. And his response was to make an option for the *campesinos*—to be converted and transformed into their defender, to become the voice of the voiceless. I believe that Archbishop Romero's definitive conversion began that night.

Actually Archbishop Romero did not particularly like to hear his change referred to as a conversion. And he had a point. He used to recall his humble origins. He had never known anything like wealth or abundance. His family had led a life of poverty and austerity. And of course it was universally acknowledged that his life as a priest and bishop had been one of outstanding virtue. In his own way, he had been open to the poor. He had defended them in Santiago de María at a moment when they were suffering cruel repression. No one, then, regarded Archbishop Romero as an evil, irresponsible, or deceitful person. Even in his most conservative period, his ethical stature encouraged his subordinates to feel free to speak with him of the most delicate matters. I believe, then, that Archbishop Romero had always had a heart that was pure, and an ethical reserve that not even his conservative ideology, or the backward, reactionary behavior of a goodly part of the national hierarchy to which he belonged, could succeed in stifling. What had happened is that his inner personhood had been divided in two. In his heart he maintained authentic religious ideals, and accepted the directives of Vatican II and Medellín in principle. But he interpreted the novelty of the council and Medellín from a very conservative posture, with fear of anything that might possibly immerse the church in the conflictive, ambiguous flesh of history. It was this interior division, I believe, that dissolved that night, and I believe that this phenomenon can be called a conversion—not so much in the sense of ceasing to do evil and beginning to do good, but in the sense of grasping the will of God and being determined to implement it, and this in the spirit of deep, radical change. The will of God must have looked very different to Archbishop Romero that night in the presence of those three dead bodies and with hundreds of *campesinos* staring at him wondering what he was going to do about what had happened.

Whether one actually calls it a conversion or not, the radical change that took place in Archbishop Romero on the occasion of Rutilio's murder was one of the most impressive things anyone around him, including myself, had ever seen. He was fifty-nine years old at the time, an age at which people's psychological and mental structure, their understanding of the faith, their spirituality, and their Christian commitment have typically hardened. Furthermore, he had just been named an archbishop—the highest level of responsibility in the institutional church, which, like any other institution, necessarily has a strong instinct for continuity and prudence, not to say out-and-out retrenchment. Finally, historical circumstances were scarcely favorable. Archbishop Romero was altogether aware, from the outset, that he had been the candidate of the right. He had known the cajolery of the powerful from the start. They would build him a magnificent bishop's palace, they told him, and they hoped he would reverse the line taken by his predecessor, Luis Chávez y González. But Archbishop Romero changed, and changed radically. He refused the beautiful palace and went to live in Divine Providence Hospital, in a little room next to the sacristy. Thus not only were the powers cheated of their hopes for a nice, pliable ecclesiastical puppet, but the new archbishop was actually going to oppose them somehow. In store for him, of course, if he did so, was the wrath of the mighty—the oligarchy, the government, the political parties, the army, the security forces, and later, the majority of his brother bishops, various Vatican offices, and even the

U.S. government. In the balance of forces operating in the background of his conversion, Archbishop Romero had in his favor a group of priests and nuns, and, especially, the suffering and hope of a whole people. Against him was everyone with any power. Evangelically, then, the balance of forces was in his favor; but naturally speaking, it was against him. If Archbishop Romero set out on new paths, at his age, in his place at the pinnacle of the institution, and against such odds, then his conversion must have been very real. It must have reached the deepest corners of his being, shaping him for good and all, and leading him to the sacrifice of his life. His external change in behavior—an undeniable change, acknowledged by all—must have been the result of a very deep, very real interior change.

What was the cause of Archbishop Romero's conversion? I have been asked this question countless times. I have no "objective," psychological answer, nor did I ever speak of this with him personally. It is not easy to plumb the depths of another, and of course it would be presumptuous to claim to be able to. Still I should like to set forth my own view of Archbishop Romero's conversion, be it only to show that the interior change of which I speak actually did take place, and that his external behavior is not to be ascribed to any sort of "manipulation."

I believe that the murder of Rutilio Grande was the occasion of the conversion of Archbishop Romero—as well as being a source of light and courage to follow his new paths. Archbishop Romero had known Rutilio, and held him in such high regard that he invited him to serve as master of ceremonies at his episcopal consecration. He did not, however, approve of Rutilio's pastoral ministry at Aguilares. It seemed too political to him, too "horizontal," foreign to the church's basic mission, and dangerously close to revolutionary ideas. Rutilio had been a problem for Archbishop Romero, then. In fact he was an enigma. Here was a virtuous, zealous, deeply believing priest. Yet this admirable priest's approach to the pastoral ministry was one which, at least in Archbishop Romero's eyes, was simply incorrect and mistaken. It was this enigma, I think, that was solved the day Rutilio died. I think that, as Archbishop Romero stood gazing at the mortal remains of Rutilio Grande, the scales fell from his eyes. Rutilio had been right! The kind of pastoral activity, the kind of church, the kind of faith he had advocated had been the right kind after all. And then, on an even deeper level: if Rutilio had died as Jesus died, if he had shown that greatest of all love, the love required to lay down one's very life for others—was this not because his life and mission had been like the life and mission of Jesus? Far from being a deluded, misled follower of Jesus, Rutilio must have been an exemplary one! Ah, then it had not been Rutilio, but Oscar who had been mistaken! It had not been Rutilio who ought to have changed, but himself, Oscar Romero. And Archbishop Romero translated these reflections, which theoretically could have remained in the state of pure ratiocination, into a decision to change—a determination to live and act as Rutilio had, and above all, as Jesus had. In the presence of Rutilio's dead body, Archbishop

Romero had felt what St. Ignatius Loyola felt in his contemplation on sin, when in the eyes of his imagination he stood before Christ crucified. There the question comes thundering in, down to the deepest recesses of one's being: "What will I do for Christ?" I believe that it was Rutilio's death that gave Archbishop Romero the strength for new activity. It "shook him up," as we say. Now Rutilio's life gave Archbishop Romero the fundamental direction for his own life. Of course, Rutilio had been a simple missionary priest, and not archbishop of San Salvador, and could not have given examples of the concrete expressions of this new fundamental direction that would be appropriate for the archbishop of San Salvador. It was up to Oscar Romero to find these concrete expressions himself, in function of his particular, critical historical circumstances. Archbishop Romero's conversion used to be referred to in those days as "Rutilio's miracle."

A second thing that must have had a prompt impact on Archbishop Romero in those first days was the different reactions of various elements in the church. He was well aware that his appointment had not been well received by priests who practiced a more forward-moving pastoral ministry, by the base communities, or by anyone whose work was one of consciousness-raising and liberation in the spirit of Medellín. He knew it had filled these persons with fear. He also knew of the jubilation that his appointment had inspired among comfortable Catholics—those who had been known to connive with the power groups that had attacked and calumniated his predecessor, Archbishop Chávez—and even among a little group of priests who had cozied up to those power groups. And so Archbishop Romero must have been very surprised when, in those first, so difficult days, when he saw that he was going to have to take real risks, the first group rallied to him and the second abandoned him. In the hour of truth, those whom he had regarded with suspicion, had attacked, and even out and out condemned, were with him. The others, whom he had regarded as devout and orthodox, so prudent and "nonpolitical," apparently so faithful to whatever the church had to say, left him in the lurch, as Jesus' disciples had their master, and promptly began to criticize, attack, and disobey him, thereby showing their true colors: their apparent loyalty to the hierarchy did not go so far as to agree with their archbishop when he said things no longer to their liking, or when their particular interests were somehow threatened.

I believe that all of this gave Archbishop Romero a great deal of food for thought. Not that everything the forward-looking priests did was perfect. But at least they were persons of far more truth and Christian love than were others. Whatever might be the theological and political ideas of the former—Archbishop Romero clearly saw—at least they were determined to stand up for him in his denunciation of the barbarity of his country, which showed that they were honest about the tragedy of Salvadoran reality, unlike the others, who ignored it and attempted to make excuses for it. And they were willing to run personal risks, speak out, make public denunciations, although now this would mean that they would be branded as unpatriotic and un-Christian, arrested, and even murdered. Archbishop Romero found this minimal truth and commitment in a good-sized group of priests and nuns, and did not find it in the other little group. The latter fell silent, and attempted to justify its silence, as Archbishop Romero himself had done some months earlier, with an appeal to the "good of the church." By way of one tragic example, we might recall the circular letter of Cardinal Mario Casariego of Guatemala to his priests, in which he said that it was Rutilio Grande's own fault that he had been murdered, that he had been meddling in matters that were of no concern to him, and that the priests of Guatemala would do well not to follow his example.

This kind of reaction had a great impact on Archbishop Romero. I recall how, one evening a few days after Rutilio's murder, at YSAX—the archdiocesan radio station, which was to become so well-known for its rebroadcasts of Archbishop Romero's homilies, as well as for having been repeatedly dynamited—he showed me a letter he had received. Written on elaborate stationery, with a floral motif if I remember correctly, it had been sent by someone who had been close to Archbishop Romero, but who now expressed surprise at the change that had come over him, and disapproval of his new behavior. Archbishop Romero showed not the slightest perturbation, I recall, but simply murmured to me: "Opus Dei." What I think he was saying is that here was someone who had no more understanding than he himself had once had.

Thus what the two sides did or did not do in those days helped Archbishop Romero acquire a clearer view of things, and this in turn helped him change. In sum, we might say: in times of national crisis, you cannot simply keep repeating that you are a Christian, and forget about history. You cannot hide in a "Christianity" that will exempt you from the obligation of being a citizen of your country. Those who had simply abandoned El Salvador to its fate under the pretext of being Christians no longer shed any light as far as Archbishop Romero was concerned. Those who had made an option for their country, by telling the truth, by denouncing atrocities, by making a commitment to justice—albeit with limitations and exaggerations—now became Archbishop Romero's guiding light.

A third factor in Archbishop Romero's conversion—the definitive factor, the one that kept him faithful to God's will to the end—was his people, a people of the poor. The poor very promptly showed him their acceptance, support, affection, and love. Surely he did not expect this when he was appointed archbishop. But the poor certainly hoped for an archbishop such as he proved to be. And the fact is, as I have already remarked, that in El Salvador, as in so many other places in Latin America, before the church made an option for the poor, the poor had made an option for the church. They had found no one else to defend them, not in the government, not in the armed forces, not in the political parties, and not in private enterprise.

While Archbishop Romero was taking his first steps, making his first denunciations, making his first visits to the base communities, the poor fairly swarmed around him. He took them to his heart, and they were there to stay. And they took him to their own hearts, where he has remained to this day.

I do not propose to belabor this abundantly acknowledged, public, point. I only wish to add that Archbishop Romero must have found in the poor what the prophet Isaiah contemplated in the Suffering Servant of Yahweh, and St. Paul saw in the crucified Christ: light and salvation. The suffering of the poor must have shaken Archbishop Romero to his depths as he watched their oppression swell to such intolerable proportions. The poor were effectively calling for his conversion. But in offering him light and salvation, they also facilitated that conversion. And Archbishop Romero recognized this. For me there is no doubt that this is Archbishop Romero's last secret, and I shall reveal that secret. In one of his most felicitous expressions, in words of the kind that cannot be invented, but can only come from the heart, he said: "With this people, it is not difficult to be a good shepherd."

III

In the immediate aftermath of Rutilio's murder, the archdiocesan chancery, indeed, the whole archdiocese, saw moments of great perturbation and turmoil—moments that marked out for Archbishop Romero a path he would walk to the end without ever looking back. He understood very soon that, as archbishop, he must clarify for the people the nature of the church—explain its prophetic denunciation and its defense of the poor. And in his very first year among us he wrote two pastoral letters on the church.

Archbishop Romero put these great convictions, that had begun to come together in his mind, to work. During those same first days he published a series of communiqués denouncing the repression of the people and the persecution of the church, it was the Catholics of the wealthy plantations who hypocritically complained that they would be deprived of the opportunity to hear Mass and fulfill their Sunday obligation! It seems not to have occurred to them that they could attend Mass more easily than anyone else—simply by driving to the cathedral—although, admittedly, they would have had to stand among the poor in the sun for three hours. But even Archbishop Romero had had his doubts at first about the single Mass. He was convinced that something dramatic had to be done to stun the country and shake it from its apathy. But he had a theological scruple, which he formulated at our meeting with characteristic sincerity. "If the eucharist gives glory to God," he asked, "will not God have more glory in the usual number of Sunday Masses than in just one?"

I must confess that my heart sank to hear him. Here was a theology straight out of the dark ages. But in thinking it over afterwards, and on the basis of all his actions, I finally came to interpret Archbishop Romero's words correctly. He was only showing his deep, genuine interest in the things of God. His theology was questionable. Beyond question, however, was his profound faith in God, and his surpassing concern for the glory of God in this world.

With the same frank attitude with which Archbishop Romero had propounded his own difficulty, others of us explained our theological reasoning to the contrary. A lengthy discussion ensued. Finally Father Jerez spoke up: "I think Monseñor is absolutely right to be concerned for the glory of God. But unless I am mistaken, the Fathers of the Church said, '*Gloria Dei, vivens homo*'—the glory of God is the living person." Father Jerez's intervention decided the issue for all practical purposes. Archbishop Romero seemed convinced, and relieved of his scruple. And he decided on the single Mass for that particular Sunday.

At the moment, I thought only that Archbishop Romero had made a lucid, courageous pastoral decision. But afterwards I thought what it must have meant for him to accept such a novel formulation of what the actual "glory of God" is. At stake had been nothing less than his personal understanding of God—his faith in God. It was not a mere matter of a new theological formulation. It was a matter of a new understanding of God. And Archbishop Romero had accepted that new understanding. Tirelessly he would repeat that nothing was more important to God than the life of the poor. When he went to Puebla, he met Leonardo Boff there, and told him: "In my country, people are being horribly murdered. We must defend the minimum gift of God, which is also the maximum: life." He himself reformulated Saint Irenaeus's aphorism, the one Father Jerez had cited, as, "'*Gloria Dei, vivens pauper*'—the glory of God is the living poor person." Conversely, he railed against the idols—those false, but real, divinities that deal in death, the deities that call for victims because they live on their blood as the only means to their own survival.

I believe that Archbishop Romero, at the age of fifty-nine, not only underwent a conversion, but had a new experience of God. Never again would he be capable of separating God from the poor, or his faith in God from his defense of the poor. I believe he saw in God the prototype of his own option for the poor, and that that prototype demanded he put his option into practice. But I think his experience also enlightened him as to who God is. Why was he never shocked by new formulations of God's identity? He assimilated concepts like "God of life, God of the Reign, God of the poor," and so on, altogether naturally. He was particularly fond of the Gloria of the *Misa Salvadoreña*, which sings the praise of the God of life and condemns the gods of power and money.

However, this costly, gladsome discovery of the God of the poor never induced Archbishop Romero to disparage in the least something I think must have been a constant in every aspect of his life: the mystery of God. From his new starting point in the poor, Archbishop Romero discovered that God is theirs—their defender, their liberator. Among the poor he discovered that God is God become small—a suffering God, a crucified God. But this also led him to sound the depths of the mystery of an ever greater, transcendent God, the last reserve of truth, goodness, and humanity, on whom we human beings can rely. I do not know whether Archbishop Romero knew the words from Irenaeus that immediately follow those cited by Father Jerez. "*Vita autem hominis, visio Dei,*" Irenaeus continues: "And the life of the human being is the vision of God." But whether he knew the words or not, he communicated their content. Personally, I was profoundly struck—and I have tried to convey it in my writings—by his faith in God, his absolute conviction of God's reality, his utter conviction that the mystery of God is salvific for human beings, that it is good that there is a God, that we should be glad there is a God. On February 10, 1980, in a situation that had become chaotic, in out-and-out confrontation with the government, the army, the oligarchy, and the United States, Archbishop Romero was once more the courageous, implacable prophet, speaking of the things of this world and coming out in defense of an oppressed people. But in the same homily, and just as naturally as he had pronounced his historic denunciations, he spoke the following words: "Tell me, beloved brothers and sisters, that the fruit of today's sermon will be that each of us will encounter God, and that we shall live in the glory of his majesty and our littleness! . . . No human being has self-knowledge without having encountered God."

To be able to utter these words is to have had a profound experience of God. In God's name Archbishop Romero defended the life of the poor. And when he sought to give all of us the best he had to give, he gave us simply God.

The God of the poor and the mystery of God are what Archbishop Romero made present to all who were willing to listen. In El Salvador he restored respect for God. The poor listened to him, of course—what else is left to them, frequently, but their faith in God? But nonbelievers listened to him, as well—those who at least respect God's name. And doubters listened to him, with gratitude that he was shedding light on something that had become darkness for them.

Thanks to Archbishop Romero, our country never hears the fateful reproach so frequently addressed to God's people in Holy Scripture: "On your account the name of God is blasphemed among the nations." But there is more. Italo López Vallecillos, the celebrated Salvadoran author, now deceased, once told me: "I have always pondered the mystery of God. When I was small, it was my grandmother who got me to think about it. Now this mystery has become present to me in Archbishop Romero."

IV

It was this immense faith of Archbishop Romero's, ever ancient and ever new, that was in gestation during those days. No one ever dared ask him, "In what God do you believe?" But the question arose spontaneously when

Archbishop Romero conceived the notion of having just one Mass in the archdiocese, in the Metropolitan Cathedral, on the Sunday following Rutilio's death. His decision to schedule the single Mass was the expression of a new faith. No matter that, on the surface, it might have seemed only a courageous pastoral decision to some, a political provocation to others.

But that decision also meant a first serious confrontation between Archbishop Romero and certain echelons of the church institution. And he suffered from this confrontation throughout his three remaining years.

The commotion occasioned by his announcement of the one Mass that Sunday was such that he decided to pay a personal visit to the apostolic nuncio to explain his action. He invited several priests to accompany him, and I was among their number. The nuncio was not in, and we were received by his secretary. It was obvious from the outset that the secretary was annoyed about the single Mass, and he made no effort to conceal his annoyance, although he was a simple monsignor and was addressing the archbishop of San Salvador himself. And so I experienced a little of the authoritarianism so frequently present in "curias" of all kind, civil and ecclesiastical, and their lack of understanding of the suffering of the people—or even that of an archbishop overwhelmed by heavy responsibilities. Rarely, I think, have I felt such indignation as I felt at that moment.

The secretary began by saying that the pastoral and theological argumentation in favor of the single Mass was good. I think he even said that it was very good. This surprised me, since in my naiveté I did not see how such laudatory words could be reconciled with his visible annoyance. "But," he added, "you have forgotten the most important thing."

I could not think what "the most important thing" might be, apart from, precisely, pastoral or theological considerations. But the monsignor went on, solemnly: "You have overlooked the canonical aspect." I could scarcely believe my ears. Nor could anyone else. I remarked that nothing was more important than the body of Christ, and that this body was being bled dry in our country; that nothing was more important for the church at this moment than to denounce repression and give the people some hope; and that canonical considerations are secondary in a spiritual emergency. And I reminded him of what Jesus had said about the "sabbath being for man." All was in vain, however, and we had to abandon all levels of the discussion except the canonical. Fortunately, some of the priests with us were able to show the nuncio's secretary that Archbishop Romero had acted correctly even from the standpoint of canon law. I do not think the monsignor was actually convinced, but at least it ended the discussion.

It was a long, unpleasant hour. What impressed me most, however, was that Archbishop Romero was perfectly silent all through the meeting. It was as if he were absent from all of this nit-picking, thinking more of Rutilio's corpse, murdered *campesinos,* and the people's fear and sorrow. At the end of the meeting, however—without raising his voice, and without entering into any discussion of the arguments—he said something like: "Our country is in a very dangerous, extraordinary state. The church must make some equally extraordinary response in terms of denunciation and evangelization. I am responsible for the archdiocese. We shall have the one Mass." That was all that he said. And we left the nunciature. I was still very perturbed. Archbishop Romero radiated serenity and peace. "They do not understand," he told me laconically.

On Sunday, March 20, we concelebrated the only Mass in the archdiocese that day, and it was an unprecedented pastoral success. Cathedral Square was packed. Tens of thousands prayed, sang, received communion, and took courage, the courage of Christian faith and hope. Before Mass several of us heard confessions. A number of penitents told me that this was the first time in a number of years that they had come to confession, and that they had felt the need to come back to God after what had happened to Rutilio. Even in terms of the traditional criterion of number of confessions, the single Mass was a magnificent pastoral achievement. But the nunciature never understood.

This Mass was the beginning of Archbishop Romero's long Calvary of hierarchical misunderstanding and rejection. True, in May 1977 the Salvadoran bishops published a message that could still be interpreted as an expression of support for him. But from that moment on, at any rate, he had nothing but difficulties with the Salvadoran bishops and some of the Vatican offices. Of the former, only Bishop Rivera remained loyal to him.

It is difficult to see how anyone of good will and sound judgment could question Archbishop Romero's loyalty to the church, Vatican II, Medellín and Puebla, the teachings of the popes, and the social teaching of the church. His homilies and pastoral letters draw so abundantly on all of these fonts. One of his greatest joys was to be able to go to Rome to see the Holy Father, tell him about the situation in the country and the Salvadoran church, and receive from him direction and encouragement, or admonitions if need be. He prized his communion with Rome very highly. I recall his jubilation on his return from his first visit to Paul VI, who had squeezed his hands and said, "*Coraggio!*" (Courage!). He also returned satisfied with his second visit to John Paul II, although, as he recounts in his diary, the first one had saddened and disappointed him: apparently misinformed, the Holy Father had failed really to understand him very well. I personally believe that John Paul II evolved in his estimation of Archbishop Romero. At all events, he eventually praised him, publicly, as a pastor and martyr who had given his life for the love of God and the service of his brothers and sisters.

Throughout the course of Archbishop Romero's three years at our head, he likewise had to face the opposition of the Salvadoran bishops themselves, who criticized him both in public and in harsh private reports to the Vatican. At Puebla, Bishop Aparicio publicly accused us Jesuits of being part of the cause of the violence in the country (and this in the presence of Father General Arrupe), and then declared to certain journalists that Archbishop Romero was acting irresponsibly and endangering the entire church, by

bringing it into confrontation with the government—adding that he was doing all of this out of vanity, in the hope of becoming "the Latin American
Jimmy Carter"! The Vatican sent Archbishop Romero three apostolic visitors in the course of a year and a half—to the astonishment of Salvadorans,
who wondered when even one apostolic visitor would be sent to another
diocese that had drawn up no pastoral plan, or whose bishop had publicly
endorsed the acts of a criminal army.

In Rome, Archbishop Romero's relations with Cardinal Baggio were
very tense. The cardinal spoke to him of the possibility that an apostolic
administrator, with full powers, might be appointed for our archdiocese.
Whereupon Archbishop Romero only asked that this be done in a dignified
way, to spare the people any suffering, although he added that he did not
think it would be the thing to do. On one occasion Cardinal Baggio received
him in his study with: "You are in bad company," and showed him a book
he had on his writing stand. The book, published by the University of Central America, contained Archbishop Romero's Third Pastoral Letter and
Bishop Rivera's first. On the cover were the names of Ignacio Ellacuría,
T. R. Campos, and Jon Sobrino.

And so Archbishop Romero discovered—unfortunately, when he least
expected it—the limitations, intrigues, and pettiness of the church institution. It was extremely painful to him that, with his country screaming in
agony, and with priests being murdered, the church institution offered him
not support but opposition—that with the Reign of God itself at stake, the
concern of the Salvadoran bishops was that nothing untoward befall the institution. This caused him a great deal of suffering, and in his last months he
felt a real distaste for the meetings of the Salvadoran Bishops Conference,
where two completely different languages were spoken.

During the last retreat he was ever to make, a month before his assassination, he wrote out, in his own hand, a list of the things that most concerned him, and that he had spoken to his spiritual director, Father Azcue,
S.J., by way of part of his preparation for a spiritual conference. One of the
concerns he listed was "my clashes with my brothers in the episcopacy." He
must have emerged from his talk with Father Azcue much heartened, since
he then wrote:

> The following consideration has given me a great deal of confidence.
> They criticize my pastoral actions. Very well, then what alternative do
> they propose? And this reflection has confirmed my conviction that the
> only important thing is the radicality of the gospel—something not
> everyone can understand. I can give in on incidental points, but I can-
> not yield when what is at stake is a radical following of the gospel. This
> radicality has always been met with opposition—and painful division.

In the midst of his suffering, Archbishop Romero found strength and relief
in his faith. He was also buoyed up by the people's immense affection for

him. Finally, he was consoled—as he recounts in his diary—by his conversations in Rome with Cardinal Pironio and Father Arrupe ("a saint," the diary calls the latter), as well as with Cardinal Aloísio Lorscheider on the occasion of the latter's visit to El Salvador. But the cross weighed very heavy on him. We could see this quite clearly at Puebla.

I went to Puebla, as did other theologians and social scientists, in order to be able to follow this important conference more closely, and to speak with the bishops who had asked our help. (We had not been invited to participate officially.) One evening our group met with a considerable number of bishops, who had come to our quarters to confer on certain theological matters. Together we considered the main themes of Puebla, together we dined, and together we prayed. Archbishop Romero was there. He looked happy, and was obviously enjoying himself. Lecture halls were not the "natural place" for someone like him. He liked being among the *campesinos,* and at Puebla he felt more at ease with journalists, speaking with them about El Salvador, than in the corridors of Palafox Seminary with its atmosphere of church politics and diplomacy. Toward the end of our meeting, someone suggested that the bishops at Puebla—whoever among them might so desire—send joint letters of encouragement and support to the bishops of the most afflicted churches of Central America: those of El Salvador, Guatemala, and Nicaragua. The letters to El Salvador and Nicaragua were written, and several bishops signed them. The Guatemalan bishops present at the meeting judged it more prudent to decline this public demonstration of solidarity. I remember how moved Archbishop Romero was, by everything, by the fellowship and communion of the meeting, by the sincerity of our discussions, by the atmosphere of faith and church, and especially by the affection and solidarity of his fellow bishops. Almost in tears he said, "I felt like a brother among my brother bishops."

V

These are my principal recollections of Archbishop Romero in his first months as our ordinary, together with some observations on the later course of events in his life. In sum, I think Archbishop Romero underwent a process of conversion, and that, relatively quickly, he found the new route that he would travel to the end. I do not actually know how much time it took him to find this new road. I do not know whether his conversion was like St. Paul's, sudden as a fall from a horse, or like the more gradual experience of a discernment of the movement of spirits, of which St. Ignatius Loyola tells. But a very few months after his appointment, Archbishop Romero had become a very special bishop, Christian, and Salvadoran.

In a brief time, Archbishop Romero had to learn to make important decisions on his own responsibility. He had to learn to maintain a dialogue with his priests. He had to learn serenity, lest he do things that would make the situation worse. He had to learn boldness, in order to be able to confront and denounce the powerful. He had to learn to give the people hope, and to receive from them their suffering, their faith, and their commitment. Within himself, he had to learn his faith in the God of the poor, who was also the God greater than all else, greater than his earlier ideas of God, and greater than the church itself, which was gradually becoming his cross. He had to learn that there is nothing more important than the Reign of God— that there was nothing more important than life, hope, love, and a communion of sisters and brothers. He had to learn that the church's place is among the suffering poor. The church must be immersed in the reality of the crucified peoples. The church must become a genuine Servant of Yahweh, as he would later say. Thus Archbishop Romero had to learn not only to give, but to receive light and salvation from these crucified peoples. And he learned all these things.

I never spoke of these matters with Archbishop Romero. But I suppose that his apprenticeship, like that of Jesus, must have been a painful one. I believe that Archbishop Romero wrestled with God as Jacob did, and lived out in the desert, like Jesus. More than once he must have asked God to let some chalice pass, and must have stood before God with the groans and lamentations of the true priest of the Letter to the Hebrews.

But I also could see that his conversion was a source of an immense peace, an immense freedom, and an immense joy. Here was someone who was rather shy by nature, in poor health so that he had always been forced to take an occasional physical and psychological rest cure, and who was now suddenly transformed into a strong person. I do not recall his having been ill at all during these years, or that he had to go anywhere for a psychological rest. His work load had increased immeasurably, but he fled none of the countless demands of his new task. He refused no request. On the contrary, he always seemed excited by new things to do, new projects, new topics for his pastoral letters. Sister Teresa, now deceased, his guardian angel in the little hospital, would see his light on in the late hours of the night and beg him not to work so hard. Archbishop Romero would answer simply that he had not yet said his rosary. It was no use trying to persuade him to slow down. Archbishop Romero had suddenly become an indefatigable laborer, and his store of energy was the astonishment of one and all.

I believe that the gospel he rediscovered in those days was not only a demand made on him, but a source of his strength, as well. Never did I hear him bewail his sufferings or complain about the amount of work he had to do. As he walked with the people in the strength of the gospel, and as the people walked with him, he performed his archiepiscopal ministry admirably to the end—which came at the altar of his chapel in the little hospital.

And he performed it joyfully. Of all the people I have ever known, Archbishop Romero is the one who best exemplifies Karl Rahner's words of genius: "The gospel is a light burden in the sense that the more one bears it, the more one is borne by it." Conversion placed a terrible burden on

Archbishop Romero's shoulders, but lo and behold, the burden became light, and gave him courage, energy, freedom, and joy.

VI

Three months after his appointment, Archbishop Romero had become a different bishop. He had changed. Repression and terror raged on all sides. In May 1977 the situation of the country actually took a turn for the worse, and persecution of the church became institutionalized. On May 1 a young Jesuit was arrested, then a week later turned over to his provincial and Archbishop Romero. The archbishop gave him a cup of coffee and refused to sign a statement that he had not been mistreated. On May 11 Father Alfonso Navarro was murdered. Again there was a huge Mass, and a major homily by Archbishop Romero. The situation in the country, he said, was like a caravan lost in the desert, and a bedouin would come along and show the travelers the right way and they would put him to death. On May 19 the army went to Aguilares, expelled the three remaining Jesuits, desecrated the church and sacristy, and declared a state of emergency. No one might enter Aguilares, not even the apostolic nuncio. And many *campesinos* were killed.

Repression and persecution increased rapidly, but Archbishop Romero already had a very clear notion of what he was to do. His attitude was one of determination, and his priests were remarkably receptive to his leadership. All this stood him in good stead on June 19.

After a month of the state of emergency, the army simply drove the people out of Aguilares. Archbishop Romero decided to go there at the first opportunity, denounce the atrocities that had been committed, and try to inspire a threatened, terrorized people with hope. A good many of us went along with him. It was a day I shall never forget.

The opening words of his homily are etched forever in my memory. "I have the job of picking up the trampled, the corpses, and all that persecution of the church dumps along the road on its way through." I thought: What a new, what a tragic, and what a perfect definition of the episcopal ministry! Only years later would Archbishop Romero reduce his celebrated "ministry of accompaniment" to theoretical expression. This was the day he formulated it in its maximal concretion, as he also did toward the end of his life, in February 1980, when a journalist asked him what the church would do if a war broke out. He answered that he would stand his ground "even if the only thing I could do was collect dead bodies and grant absolution to the dying." In these words, the option for the poor, so resoundingly demanded at Puebla, received profound, radical expression, and was shown to be worlds apart from anything like casual, empty chatter. And I thought: It's true, then. Archbishop Romero has made an option for his suffering people.

In his homily that day he also uttered a prophetic denunciation of those who "have transformed a people into a prison and a torture chamber." As well as I can remember, this was the first of so many homilies that, by their content, their courage, and the power of their expression showed the world that Archbishop Romero was a prophet in the strict, most authentic sense. Years later, in 1980, a scripture scholar, José Luis Sicre, an expert on the Old Testament prophets, told me: "I doubt that there have been more than a dozen authentic prophets, in the biblical sense, in the course of history—Amos, Isaiah, and so on. One of them is Oscar Romero."

Archbishop Romero's homily also provided a good example of his habit of thanking everyone who helped him and who rendered service to the church. He thanked the Jesuits for the work of Rutilio Grande and his fellow priests. And he thanked the Oblates of the Sacred Heart—the sisters who had had the courage to take charge of the parish of Aguilares when no priest dared work there any longer.

I also recall—and for me, this was the most striking thing in his homily—the great love Archbishop Romero showed for those *campesinos* of Aguilares, those suffering, terrified people, who had experienced such awful things over the previous month. How could they be helped to maintain their hope? How could they be given back at least their dignity in suffering? How could they be told that they were the most important thing to God and the church? Archbishop Romero put it this way: "You are the image of the divine victim 'pierced for our offenses,' of whom the first reading speaks to us this morning." You are Christ today, suffering in history, he told them. And in another homily, given toward the end of 1979, which I also remember very well, again speaking of the Servant of Yahweh, Archbishop Romero said that our liberator, Jesus Christ, so "identified with the people that scripture scholars do not know whether the Servant of Yahweh in Isaiah is the suffering people or Christ come to redeem us." To tell afflicted *campesinos* that they are Christ today in history, and to tell them that sincerely, is the most radical way a Christian has of restoring to them at least their dignity, and of helping them maintain their hope.

At Aguilares, Archbishop Romero went on: "We suffer with those who have suffered so much. . . . We suffer with the lost—those who have had to run away and who do not know what is happening to their families. . . . We are with those who are being tortured. . . ." I am with you, Archbishop Romero told the people, and they knew he was telling the truth. This miracle does not happen every day. But it happened here. The *campesinos* of Aguilares came into Archbishop Romero's heart and stayed there forever. And Archbishop Romero entered the hearts of all poor, simple, and suffering Salvadorans, and he is there today.

Archbishop Romero genuinely loved his people. He *only* loved them. He did not do as others, who, while loving the people, seek also their own personal, partisan, church interests. Archbishop Romero's love for his people caused him to relativize all else beside. As a result he could risk all that was not love for his people, even the institutional element in the church, even his own life. This is what has made Archbishop Romero such a source of hope, courage, and comfort for all suffering Salvadorans.

After Mass we held a procession of the Blessed Sacrament. We processed out into the little square in front of the church to make reparation for the soldiers' desecration of the sacramental Body of Christ and the living Body of Christ, the murdered *campesinos*. Across the square, in front of the town hall, were armed troops, standing there watching us, sullen, arrogant, and unfriendly. As the procession drew near the town hall we stopped. We were uneasy. In fact, we were afraid. We had no idea what might happen. And we all instinctively turned around and looked at Archbishop Romero, who was bringing up the rear, holding the monstrance. "*Adelante* (Forward!)," said Archbishop Romero. And we went right ahead. The procession ended without incident. From that moment forward, Archbishop Romero was the symbolic leader of El Salvador. He made no such claim. He had sought no such thing. But this is the way it was. From now on, Archbishop Romero led us, marching at our head. He had been transformed into the central reference point for the church and for the country. Nothing of any importance occurred in our country over the next three years without our all turning to Archbishop Romero for guidance and direction, for leadership.

As I have said, that day was very important for me personally. I saw Archbishop Romero transformed into a giant, while I was like a dwarf. I have already recounted how I tried to cooperate with him in every way, from the very start, placing my knowledge and my time at his service. What else could I have done in such tragic moments, with a recently appointed archbishop overwhelmed with his new responsibility and asking for help with such humility? But I have to confess that in those first weeks I thought that it was I who was helping him, and he who profited—that my theological ideas were surely more useful to him than his could ever be to me. And I doubt that I was the only one to feel that way. It was not a matter of trying to manipulate him. We only wanted to help him. Besides, Archbishop Romero very promptly demonstrated his evangelical autonomy. But the fact remained that our job was to help Archbishop Romero. Then came that day at Aguilares, with the Mass and procession, and I began to see things in a very different light. It was not I who was helping Archbishop Romero, but he who was helping me. It was not I who would be teaching him, but he who was teaching us. Archbishop Romero had already outdistanced us along the pathway of our pilgrimage—not by virtue of his formal authority as our archbishop, but on the strength of his evangelical and Salvadoran behavior. I hope that this does not sound like false humility. Archbishop Romero asked us to help him in a thousand ways. He expected us to help him. And we did. I think that we were very helpful to him. But when it came to basics, he had outstripped us. No longer was he the freshly appointed, nervous, overwhelmed archbishop. Now he was the trail-blazer, marching at our head, and in the most fundamental matters.

And I recall the impact Archbishop Romero had on my theology that day. His celebration of the eucharist at Aguilares was a revelation to me. Besides being the eucharist, it was also—although neither he nor I thought of it in this way at the time—a lesson in theology. Not that anything was added to the traditional themes of the eucharist: thanksgiving, the word, the sacrifice, the presence of Christ, the offering, the community, and so on. And of course all of these theological themes were extremely familiar to me in their theoretical form. But Archbishop Romero developed them *in actu,* with a truth and creativity that taught me more about the eucharist than I had learned in all my long years of study. From that moment on, Archbishop Romero became a source of inspiration to me even in the area of theology, as I explained in my address on the occasion of the posthumous conferral on him of the honorary doctorate in theology by the University of Central America.

In all sincerity, and with all gratitude, I must acknowledge that Archbishop Romero's life, work, and word—a word spoken from deep within that life and that work—have been my theological light and inspiration. I do not think that, without Archbishop Romero, I could ever have achieved a satisfactory theological formulation of things as basic as the mystery of God, the church of the poor, hope, martyrdom, Christian fellowship, the essence of the gospel as good news, or even of Jesus Christ, whose three years of life and mission, cross and resurrection, have now been illuminated for me by Archbishop Romero's three years as archbishop. Archbishop Romero also made me realize the importance of using current reality as a theological argument. I shall spare the reader any lengthy theoretical discussion here, and simply observe that while, as every theologian knows, in order to do theology one must use Scripture, tradition, and the magisterium, I began to realize that one must also use reality to explain theological content. What is hope? What is martyrdom? What is a bishop? What is prophecy? Archbishop Romero and others—as part of the reality around me—have shed light on these things for me.

I spoke with Archbishop Romero a number of times on theological matters, and he showed great interest in our discussions. He wanted to see theology function in the service of the church's mission. He also had a deep appreciation of theology as something valuable in itself, apart from any use that might be made of it for an ulterior end. Very early in the three years of his archiepiscopal ministry he explained to me that, while of course the church was engaged in a pastoral reaction to the persecution and martyrdom it was undergoing, a theological reflection would be necessary as well. He asked me to write about this, and I did. My research turned up very little existing theology on persecution and martyrdom of the kind that were occurring in El Salvador, and I had to begin to build my theological argumentation from a point of departure in reality. Archbishop Romero also asked me to reflect on the church and its mission, and on evangelization, especially as the latter is presented in Paul VI's *Evangelii Nuntiandi,* on which I based a three-day workshop for priests. A number of us Salvadoran theologians, social analysts, and pastoral ministers now began to address the urgent problems of our land—the popular organizations, the violence all around, and the mission of the church in the presence of these concrete realities. I remember the many long meetings we held with Archbishop Romero—the discussions, the explanations he asked for, the drafting and redrafting of what we proposed to publish, and his final decision. Before he went to Puebla he called me to see him three times, to talk over the most important theological points to be taken up by the bishops there. I recall particularly well that he wondered why some liberation theologians criticized the social teaching of the church. I explained this to him, identifying the various theoretical problems posed by the social teaching of the church and its pastoral application. But what struck me is how calmly he asked about this—simply from a need to understand, without feeling obliged as an archbishop to defend every detail of the social teaching of the church as a matter of faith, and yet without the slightest concern merely to keep up with the latest fashion in theology. He spoke completely naturally about these problems.

We talked a great deal about theology, then. What Archbishop Romero never knew, or what in his humility never occurred to him, was that, with his questions, his theological problems, and above all with his word and his life, he helped me a great deal in my own practice of theology. It may be that we helped him to conceptualize theological problems (and it seems to me that, as far as conceptualization is concerned, Archbishop Romero never got much beyond the theological level of Vatican II, although the theological content of his words and actions was biblical and historical as well, and perfectly adequate to the intentions of the theology of liberation). But he helped us, too, and more radically than we helped him. His theological assistance to us was not on the level of technical conceptualization, but on a much more important one: that of inspiration and light to see and better deal with the fundamental theological realities—God as seen from this world, and this world as seen from the standpoint of God. As Gustavo Gutiérrez puts it, the basic problem of liberation theology is how to tell the poor of this world that God loves them. And this is the problem on which Archbishop Romero was able to shed so much light.

The reason I have devoted so much space to detailing the impact that Archbishop Romero had on all of us, especially on me, is not that I am in any way concerned about biographical data for their own sake, but that I want to lay to rest for good and all the tired old allegation that Archbishop Romero was "manipulated" by us. I must sincerely say that if there was any manipulation, Archbishop Romero manipulated us more than we manipulated him. Archbishop Romero gave us more than we gave him. That is my conviction, and my hope.

VII

Between the day we met at Aguilares and the day he died, I spoke with Archbishop Romero time and again, at the chancery, in the little hospital, or in the house where we Jesuits live. He paid us fairly frequent visits. We could see that he was at ease at our house. I remember how, before taking his leave, he always stopped into the kitchen to thank our cook, which gave her a great deal of pleasure.

I shall not attempt to detail all of the things that impressed me in the remaining nearly three years of Archbishop Romero's ministry. Many of them are familiar to all: his Sunday homilies at the cathedral, his constant visits to the base communities, his pastoral letters, his openness to dialogue with one and all, even persons belonging to the oligarchy and the armed forces, who would sometimes go to see him under cover of night, like Nicodemus in St. John's Gospel, to ask his help with some personal problem. His national and international prestige grew by leaps and bounds. So did the hostility of the oligarchy, the army, the government, and his fellow bishops, until the alarm sounded in the offices of the North American government itself.

Were I to attempt to sum up in a single word the many, many aspects of Archbishop Romero's activity during these years, I should have to say that what impressed me most was his thoroughgoing *consistency* in following his chosen path—his *fidelity* to that path. The basic principle of this consistency was his option for the poor. For Archbishop Romero this was a theological principle in the strictest sense, since he had made God the prototype of all his activity. It was an ecclesiological principle, as well, since he had erected this option into the criterion of all of the activity of his church. And it was a prudential principle for him, since he had to see to it that the option for the poor assumed various concretions in function of the changing historical situation of our country. The heart and soul of this principle was the correlation between God and the poor, between the church and the poor.

It is not difficult to parrot the principle that the church exists for the sake of the Reign of God, that it should make an option for the poor—even that the poor are our evangelizers, and so on. But how difficult it is to practice this basic principle of hope and ecclesiology! And Archbishop Romero practiced it to the end. There cannot be the slightest doubt that he proclaimed the good news to the poor and defended them to the end. But since this is such a rare phenomenon—since he did so in such an exceptional, radical way—one is also struck by the clear-sightedness with which he expounded the option for the poor, the way he theorized it, and how he erected it to a criterion of action. It became the practical principle of all his activity, whatever the latter might happen to be. To use one of his own crisp, finely chiseled phrases: "The natural partner for the church's dialogue is the people, not the government." With these words—and their implementation in practice—he reduced centuries of Christendom, along with the ever-recurrent intentions of a neo-Christendom, to dust. The much desired, long sought after goal of harmony between the church and the powers of this world—the state, the armed forces, economic powers, political powers—simply did not figure among Archbishop Romero's goals. In practice this ideal could not have been attained in any case, of course, since these powers were constantly and viciously on the attack against the church. But this is not the point. Archbishop Romero opposed this ideal on principle. He opposed it simply because the world of power is not the world of the church. What was really to be desired and striven for was the church's harmony with, and compenetration with, the poor. Or in another lapidary expression of his: "The church will judge a given political project on the basis of whether or not it does the people any good." Here again was the novelty of Archbishop Romero. He was unwilling to judge political projects a priori, on the criterion of an ideology, as the church usually does, with its weakness for Christian Democratic ideologies and its mistrust of anything like socialism; and least of all was he willing to judge them according to whether they favor, flatter, or privilege the institutional church. His criterion was the good of the people, period—the impoverished masses. That criterion was no more and no less than the concrete application in El Salvador of the first and last scriptural criterion of the activity of God, of Jesus, and of the human being parexcellence: mercy.

If we see a suffering people, a people lying in the ditch by the side of the road, what must we do—with absolute urgency, over and above all other considerations? Must we not lift those people from their prostration, heal their wounds, and stay by their side until they are completely well? Next, Archbishop Romero emphasized, since the victim in the ditch is a whole people, the remedy, the healing, must be structural. Thus his pastoral letters analyzed the structural roots of our ills, and studied the possible paths to justice, the roads leading to liberation from those ills. Archbishop Romero was a visionary here.

Such was Archbishop Romero's compassion for the poor. All of his activity was steeped in this compassion, this mercy. In fact, his relationship with the poor went far beyond works of mercy. He fairly rushed to the poor, in order to receive from them, to learn from them, and to enable them to impart to him the good news. I recall how surprised I was when I learned that, in the course of his work on the document he intended to present to the Puebla Conference, a document on the condition of the archdiocese, he sent out a questionnaire to the parishes and base communities—some of whose members probably could neither read nor write—asking them what they thought of the country and the church, what they thought was the greatest sin, who Jesus Christ was for them, and what they thought of the bishops' conference, the apostolic nuncio, and the archbishop himself. I was surprised (sadly enough, since this ought to be a bishop's normal *modus operandi*) that Archbishop Romero would ask the people of God their opinion. But I was even more surprised when he took their answers seriously. I was part of the team that compiled and analyzed them, and I remember this very well. This meant that Archbishop Romero was really open to others— open to being helped and taught by the poor. He followed the same procedure in composing his pastoral letters.

Archbishop Romero believed in his people. You could see how proud he was of them. Here was the church of the poor. "You! A church so filled with life! A church so filled with the Holy Spirit!" he would tell them. He could not conceal the joy he had in this church composed of the poor, the *campesinos,* the outcasts. At the peak of their repression and persecution, he uttered the following words, which show what he thought of his church of the poor:

> If they ever take our radio [which had already been jammed and bombed], suspend our newspaper, silence us, put to death all of us priests, bishop included, and you are left alone—a people without priests—then each of you will have to be God's microphone. Each of you will have to be a messenger, a prophet. The church will always exist as long as even one baptized person is left alive!

The impact of words like these on the people was like a jolt of electric current. Archbishop Romero trusted his people. He was proud of them. He loved them. And he let himself be loved by them—something seemingly so easy, but actually very difficult. "I just love it when the people in those little villages, with their kids and all, run up and crowd around." Some of these poor once came to the archiepiscopal chancery with chicks for Archbishop Romero. I was told—and I suppose it really happened—that they once brought him a cow, causing no little consternation and commotion at the curia. They wrote him unpretentious, informal letters about their personal problems, and Archbishop Romero answered them. They sent him alms, out of their poverty: a peso, a few centavos. When his friends were murdered his innards wrenched with pain. He would say, "I love their names—Felipe de Jesús Chacón, Polín [as we called Apolinario]. . . . I just broke down and cried when I heard." His people filled his heart. He let himself be loved, and this is the most radical way to span distances and burst boundaries, which always exist between those of high and low estate.

He judged political and social forces from the viewpoint of the poor. He saw that the forces of the right (the government, the oligarchy, the army and the security forces, the judiciary, most of the media, and the U.S. Embassy) oppressed the poor, and he denounced them all, exposed them, and called for their radical conversion. All this is well known, and I need not belabor it. But I do want to recall Archbishop Romero's attitude toward the left, which is much less well understood. He defended, supported, and rejoiced in the rise of the popular organizations, which he went so far as to call "signs of the times" in the sense in which Jesus used the expression (Matt. 16:3). He surely saw far more representative popular reality in them than in their adversaries. "I don't call them the forces of the left," he declared; "I call them the forces of the people." Since he was responsible for pastoral ministry in his diocese, he insisted on a ministry of accompaniment, lest these organizations remain merely popular, and not imbued with the spirit of the gospel.

But he criticized them, as well, and certainly more forcefully and analytically than the church has done since then. He criticized them, however, not because they were of the left—the sole, simplistic objection of the other bishops, as if being on the left were the worst imaginable evil—but precisely because (if I may be permitted an expression that they would certainly find offensive) some of their attitudes were actually antipopular. He criticized their internal divisions, their eagerness for hegemony over other leftist organizations, and their chauvinism, as if only a popular organization could ever render service to the people. And of course he condemned certain terrorist activities and certain tendencies to manipulate popular piety in the interests of the organization. Archbishop Romero saw that none of this favored the poor. Archbishop Romero has been called uncritical and naive when it came to the people's organizations. Nothing could be further from the truth. Not only was he critical of them, he actually warned them of the danger of transforming themselves into an idol—the most serious warning that a religion can conceivably issue—just as he forthrightly denounced the idolatry of capitalism and the national security doctrine. In fact, under the first junta (October 15, 1979, to January 2, 1980) he was actually accused by some of our communities and priests of having given his blessing to the new rightist government! I recall a heated discussion between Rogelio Ponseele, a priest now serving in Morazán, and Archbishop Romero on this point in a clergy meeting. The discussion was a heated one, as I say, but Archbishop Romero stood his ground. Afterwards, Rogelio wept when Archbishop Romero was murdered, and wrote of him: "He was a unique occurrence in the history of the church. He is a miracle."

My point is that, contrary to the notions entertained by certain misinformed persons and groups, Archbishop Romero criticized the people's organizations. He did so, of course, only because their errors were harmful to the people. And the purpose of his criticism was to get the popular organizations back on track, back serving the people. Whether he was supporting the people's organizations or criticizing them, his operative criterion was that of the good of the poor, the Reign of God. It was this criterion that made him want to become more familiar with the organizations, and this was at the basis of his invitations to them to attend our clergy meetings and present their views—something the other bishops could not imagine doing, since their approach was simply to condemn the organizations out of hand for being on the left. Archbishop Romero wanted to inspire them to unite, to join forces. When he learned that the popular organizations had adopted a common platform, great was his joy. He saw this as an important step in terms of the good of the poor.

Today Archbishop Rivera tells of a conversation he had with Joaquín Villalobos—one of the five *comandantes* of the FMLN, the Farabundo Marti National Liberation Front—years after Archbishop Romero's death. Villalobos had mentioned Archbishop Romero's name several times in the course of the discussion, and finally told Archbishop Rivera: "If Romero were alive today he would really 'let us have it.' But he would also understand us." Personally I think Villalobos was correct. I think Archbishop Romero would denounce many of the things the FMLN does. He certainly would condemn its murder of civilians. But I think he would understand them—not as a politico-military movement, but as an expression (tragic or hopeful, depending on where your sympathies lie) of the desire to do away with the sufferings of the poor, the ongoing injustice, and institutionalized lying of which the poor are the victims. He would ask them to keep up these ideals, and he would criticize their errors. And most of all he would ask them—as he always asked everyone—to keep their eyes fixed on the good of the whole people.

Archbishop Romero's behavior was guided by his option for the poor, then. This had many consequences. Now the church was credible, religion was accepted or at least respected, and Salvadorans, especially the poor, were given heart and hope. But the effect I want to emphasize is that, with Archbishop Romero, the church—and the faith—became Salvadoran and Christian. The more the faith is lived in El Salvador in a Christian way, the more Salvadoran it becomes. And the more our Salvadoran reality is lived to the hilt, the more Christian our faith becomes. Faith and our Salvadoran reality, church and country, are no longer mutually diluting quantities. Now they reinforce each other.

Archbishop Romero expressed this convergence in his life as in his death. And he also spoke these most perceptive words, which sent chills up people's spines when they were pronounced, and sends chills up their spines today:

> I rejoice, brothers and sisters, that our church is persecuted precisely for its preferential option for the poor, and for seeking to become incarnate in the interests of the poor. . . . How sad it would be, in a country where such horrible murders are being committed, if there were no priests among the victims! A murdered priest is a testimonial of a church incarnate in the problems of the people. . . . The church suffers the lot of the poor—persecution. It is the glory of our church to have

mixed its blood—the blood of its priests, catechists, and communities—
with the massacres of the people, and ever to have borne the mark of
persecution. . . . A church that suffers no persecution, but enjoys the
privileges and support of the powers of this world—that church has
good reason to be afraid! But that church is not the true church of Jesus
Christ.

The goal for which Archbishop Romero strove was a Christian Salvadoran, or Salvadoran Christian, church. And he reached that goal. The price
the church had to pay was great: enrollment in the ranks of the victims of
the Salvadoran blood-letting. But the church was also richly rewarded:
now the Salvadoran poor have the knowledge and experience that they
are truly the church of Jesus Christ. After a talk I once gave on this subject
at a theological congress, an African priest commented to me that the
thing Archbishop Romero's words just cited made him think most about
was that no priests in his country had "been killed so far." His remark
made me shiver, but I think he was saying something very important. I
think he was saying that the Christian church will not become African in
his country until it shares the concrete sufferings and hopes of his people.

What Archbishop Romero achieved by practicing what he preached was
a Salvadoran church, and therefore a church of the people. If he were alive
today, I think it would give him a great deal of pain to hear the expression
"popular church" used—by those outside that church—in the sense of a
bad church, a suspect church. Archbishop Romero would continue to criticize the shortcomings of the poor in the church. But, he would wonder,
how can a genuinely Salvadoran church of Jesus be anything but a church
of the people?

VIII

The last time I saw Archbishop Romero alive was on my return from a
meeting of bishops, theologians, and pastoral ministers in São Paulo, Brazil,
in February 1980. I seem to recall he had been invited to the meeting himself, but had preferred not to leave the country in the current circumstances,
which were growing more alarming by the day. Then, some two weeks before his assassination, he came to the Jesuit house, and I conveyed to him
the greetings that had been sent him by a number of parties in Brazil, especially an expression of support from Bishop Pedro Casaldáliga, whom I had
met there for the first time. Dom Pedro also wrote Archbishop Romero a
letter, and it arrived in time for him to read it. His response would bear the
date of March 24, and would be found among his effects: it had been typed,
but not signed. Archbishop Romero must have dictated it only a few hours
before his death. A month later Archbishop Rivera had the thoughtfulness
to send it to Dom Pedro, who prizes it as a genuine relic. As it is one of

Archbishop Romero's last letters—the last one, in fact, that he ever wrote—
I shall reproduce it here verbatim.

San Salvador, March 24, 1980

His Excellency
Bishop Pedro Casaldáliga
São Félix, Brazil

Dear Brother in the Episcopate:

It is with deep affection that I thank you for your brotherly message of
regret over the destruction of our radio station. Your warm support is
a great inspiration to us as we strive to keep on with our mission of
expressing the hopes and the anguish of the poor, in a spirit of joy at
being accorded the privilege of running the same risks as they, as Jesus
did by identifying with the causes of the dispossessed.
In the light of faith, and in intimate union of affection, prayer, and
the triumph of the resurrection,

I remain,
Oscar A. Romero
Archbishop

"Joy at being accorded the privilege of running the same risks as they, as
Jesus did by identifying with the causes of the dispossessed." This is a perfect description of what Archbishop Romero did, and quite consciously, during the last months of his life. I have cited the consistency of his behavior.
Now let me speak of his fidelity in the face of so many attacks and threats
on his person and his life. Verbal assaults began very early. "Monseñor
Romero Sells His Soul to Satan," ran the headline of a little paper published
by the ultra-right, a paper which did not last very long after that. Physical
threats on his life came later. A few weeks before his death, dozens of sticks
of unexploded dynamite were found in a church in which he had celebrated
Mass.
    Archbishop Romero was aware that his life was in danger, but he re-
mained faithful to his convictions. He refused to run away, he made no
deals, and far from softening his denunciations, he redoubled them. In fact,
he refused the secret service protection offered him by the president of the
republic, his public response, in a homily, being: "I hereby inform the president that, rather than my own security, what I should like to have is security and tranquility for 108 families and their 'disappeared.' . . . A shepherd
seeks no security as long as the flock is threatened."
    It was not long before Archbishop Romero realized that he was threat-
ened with a violent death. Death was coming out of the woodwork in

El Salvador; why should the victims' leader be spared? In the last retreat he ever made, the one we have already mentioned, he jotted down what he had said to his director, Father Azcue, and what the latter had replied:

> My other fear is for my life. It is not easy to accept a violent death, which is very possible in these circumstances, and the apostolic nuncio to Costa Rica warned me of imminent danger just this week. You have encouraged me, reminding me that my attitude should be to hand my life over to God regardless of the end to which that life might come; that unknown circumstances can be faced with God's grace; that God assisted the martyrs, and that if it comes to this I shall feel God very close as I draw my last breath; but that more valiant than surrender in death is the surrender of one's whole life—a life lived for God.

Personally I never heard Archbishop Romero speak of these things. In any event, he kept moving ahead in the last month remaining to him, and preached valiantly. Afterwards, we learned that in mid-March he had told a journalist from Venezuela that he had often received death threats. In the situation in our country, with repression on the wax, with six priests already dead, it did occur to us that Archbishop Romero himself might be killed. But I think we tried not to believe it, such was our affection for him and the magnitude of the prospective atrocity. At any rate we never spoke of it. On March 23 we heard his last Sunday homily and his last public words:

> In the name of God, then, and in the name of this suffering people, whose screams and cries mount to heaven, and daily grow louder, I beg you, I entreat you, I order you in the name of God: Stop the repression!

I do not know whether these words were his death sentence or not. I suppose it takes more than a few days to work out a professional assassination, and Archbishop Romero had only a few days to live when he said these words. But these words certainly consummated the process of truth-telling and denunciation of atrocities that objectively led to Archbishop Romero's martyrdom. I was personally moved by his words, and most concerned.

On the evening of March 24 the telephone at the Jesuit residence rang. Someone wanted to talk to one of the Fathers. I was the only one there at the time, so I took the call. It was a sister from the hospital where Archbishop Romero lived. She was beside herself, and was screaming almost hysterically. "Monseñor has been shot! He's covered with blood!" That was the only thing she said that I could understand. She was obviously in no condition to explain anything. I was not even able to learn whether Monseñor was alive or dead.

I left the house at once and hurried over to the provincial's office, practically next door. I told Father Provincial César Jerez about the phone call, and we turned on the radio. And we heard: "Monseñor Romero is dead." César Jerez and I sat in silence for a good little while. Then I went to Central American University. I shall never forget the scene. Some twenty persons— stalwart persons, persons accustomed to being attacked, persons used to bad news—were standing motionless, their faces a study in helplessness and despair. They did not speak. Yes, Archbishop Romero was dead. (Days later I learned that I was the first priest to learn the news. The nuns at the hospital had tried to call Monseñor Ricardo Urioste, a vicar general, but they had not been able to locate him. Then they called the Jesuit residence. I say this in parentheses, but it was something of a little personal consolation to me to realize that the nuns he stayed with regarded us as close to him.)

The first hours after the murder would have reminded you of the behavior of the apostles after the death of Jesus. Despair, grief, and confusion reigned. But very quickly, in fact in a much shorter time than the ten days St. Luke says the apostles sat trembling in the Upper Room, the Spirit breathed, and mightily. A huge mobilization was suddenly under way. There were Masses for Archbishop Romero, meetings, communiqués, notes, and letters. Telephone calls began coming in from all over the world. Journalists requested interviews. Delegations arrived, conveying the support of some group that loved or admired him. Like Jesus—who was also murdered and martyred—Archbishop Romero began to generate life even after his own death, in El Salvador as elsewhere, among Christians and nonbelievers alike. I can recall nothing of the kind in my experience since the death of John XXIII. By way of one anecdote out of a thousand: a labor union in Czechoslovakia sent us a message of solidarity.

"If they kill me, I shall rise again in the Salvadoran people. I am not boasting; I say it with the greatest humility," Archbishop Romero had declared only a few days before. How quickly his words came true. His funeral on March 30 was, more than anything else, a formidable expression of that resurrection, one of the greatest I have ever seen. But it was also the largest popular demonstration in the history of El Salvador. And of course it was the most heartfelt, most sorrowful, and most affectionate demonstration El Salvador had ever seen. We all wept, and from the depths of us. Yes, there were a few Salvadorans who toasted Archbishop Romero's death with champagne. A few. But the masses of the poor wept for him as one weeps only for a mother or a father.

And as we know, on that March 30 there were new blood and new tears, at the most incredible funeral in modern history. The evening before, we had reflected that something could happen at the funeral, since the memory of the massacre at a popular demonstration on January 22 that same year was still fresh in everyone's mind. We did not speak a great deal of this, and we tried to persuade ourselves that nothing like that would actually happen. But it did. Several persons died of suffocation or gunshot wounds. Almost all of the bishops and priests stayed in the cathedral, to be with the thousands who tried to reach safety inside. We hoped we might be able to offer these defenseless persons some protection. Only Cardinal Corripio, Archbishop of Mexico City, who was the papal legate at the funeral, left, hurrying for the airport. Archbishop Romero's death had caused sorrow and confusion. His funeral caused indignation and incredulity. An Italian journalist wept. Another journalist, from a South American country, I believe, told me while we were there barricaded inside the cathedral: "I thought I'd seen everything. I was in Vietnam. But I've never seen anything like this." And as Archbishop Romero's body was buried in great haste in the cathedral, his spirit began to fly across the entire world.

Those days were days of great agitation for us, and a great deal of work, as well. I began to write my first reflections on Archbishop Romero's life and death. I had not even had the time to go to his wake in the cathedral. It was not difficult for me to describe the events of his life and the details of his death. But I quickly realized that it was going to be very difficult indeed to describe Archbishop Romero himself. Who was he? Who is he? This is a question that goes far beyond the details of his life and death. It is the question of the totality of Archbishop Romero. It is the question that arises with the death of John XXIII or Martin Luther King. I think that it is also the question—in due proportion, of course—that arose in the minds of the first Christians: Who was this Jesus of Nazareth, after all? Who was this person who had been murdered and then raised from the dead? I soon became convinced that Archbishop Romero was a "gospel"—good news from God.

We shall have to write his biography in detail one day. We shall have to analyze, interpret, and explain his actions and his thinking. That goes without saying. But I have become convinced that the reality of Archbishop Romero cannot be communicated through analysis alone. One must have allowed oneself to be affected by the totality of his person. We see the same thing in what the gospels say of Jesus. After Archbishop Romero's funeral I began to write a long article about him. I finished it on April 10. In it I sought to analyze his person as a believer, an archbishop, and a Salvadoran. And I generated a great deal of paper. But behind the analysis was the overall impact Archbishop Romero had on me. In those days I formulated it in this way: "Archbishop Romero believed in God." It was with that faith of his that he accomplished his infinitude of good. In that faith I discovered the root of everything else. And that faith, for me, was good news—a gospel.

I have personally verified this conviction of mine that it is impossible to communicate who Archbishop Romero is without allowing oneself to be affected by him, without comprehending him as the gospel that he so often was, especially to poor, simple people. Within days, within hours, handbills and posters carrying his picture had been printed and distributed. In no time at all, the people had composed songs and verses about him. Suddenly the people were explicitly referring to him as a shepherd, a prophet, and a martyr. But there was something that went even deeper. A number of times

I have asked simple people, in so many words, who Archbishop Romero was. And the answer has come back: "Archbishop Romero told the truth, and defended us because we are poor, so they shot him." There is perceptivity in these words, and admiration. But more than anything else, there is love. In Archbishop Romero people saw someone who really loved them. And this is a piece of good news, a gospel.

During these same days I received a letter from Dom Pedro Casaldáliga, bishop of São Félix, Brazil. I had written him on my return from São Paulo, asking him to write to Archbishop Romero to encourage him in his painful situation in the church itself. In his reply, Casaldáliga wished me Easter joy—as was his wont—and sent me the poem that has become a classic on our continent, "Saint Romero of the Americas." How many times I have read it in El Salvador, and how deeply it has moved my hearers and myself! I have become convinced that Dom Pedro Casaldáliga truly understood Archbishop Romero. He wrote about him in a way that showed that he had been affected by him: he wrote about him with truth and love.

Years later, in 1985, Dom Pedro came to El Salvador and visited Archbishop Romero's tomb. In the evening, in a little ceremony we had in the Archbishop Romero Chapel at Central American University, Dom Pedro spoke to us of many things. Finally he stood as if to leave. But a nun stood up and said: "Bishop Casaldáliga, we've read your poem about Archbishop Romero so many times. Now we'd like to ask you to read it." We all rose, and Dom Pedro Casaldáliga recited his poem. The silence, the devotion, and the joy with which every one of us listened convinced me all over again that Archbishop Romero was still good news. "I started to pray again tonight," a friend told me after the service.

IX

Dom Pedro's poem ends:

> Saint Romero of the Americas,
> our shepherd and our martyr,
> no one shall ever silence
> your last homily.

Is this true? Archbishop Romero has surely become a universal figure. He is obviously not the only Christian, or only bishop, ever to have been murdered. But in virtue of the quality of his life and work, in virtue of the historical circumstances of his martyrdom, by virtue of his incredible funeral, he has become a universal figure. We should have to go back to Thomas à Becket, archbishop of Canterbury—in the twelfth century—to find a bishop who was murdered at the altar. And even so there is a key difference. Thomas à Becket was assassinated for defending the rights and liberties of the church. Archbishop Romero was assassinated for defending the poor of the Reign of God. José María Valverde, professor of esthetics at the University of Barcelona, has said it this way, in verses of his own:

> Dark centuries ago,
> it is told, a bishop died
> by order of a king,
> spattering the chalice with his blood
> to defend the freedom of the church
> from the secular might.
> Well enough, surely. But
> since when has it been told
> that a bishop fell at the altar
> not for the freedom of the church,
> but simply because
> he took sides with the poor—
> because he was the mouth of their thirst for justice
> crying to heaven?
> When has such a thing been told?
> Perhaps not since the beginning,
> when Someone died
> the death of a subversive
> and a slave.

And indeed the martyrdom of Archbishop Romero and so many Latin American Christians bears a greater resemblance to the death of Jesus than do other martyrdoms. For a time, some disputed whether so many Christians murdered in El Salvador ought to be called martyrs. Archbishop Romero himself put the question to rest while he was still alive:

For me they are actual martyrs, in the popular sense. I don't mean "martyr" in the canonical sense, of course, when a martyr has been proclaimed as such to the church universal by the highest authority in that church. I respect this law, and would never refer to our murdered priests as canonized martyrs. But they are martyrs in the basic sense of the word. They have preached precisely immersion in poverty. They are genuine human beings, who have gone to the limit of danger, where the UGB [the White Warriors, a death squad] lurks, where someone can "finger" you for death and you die. This is how Christ died.

Inevitably, Archbishop Romero's death has raised the question of martyrdom in El Salvador and Latin America today. If Archbishop Romero is not a Christian martyr, who in the world is? The poor have no doubt that he is. Canonists may still have doubt. But Archbishop Romero died to defend the faith; he knew that what he was doing could cause his death, and so forth.

Then how can there be any doubt? Karl Rahner, in a theological reflection on martyrdom he wrote just before his own death, called for a broadening of the traditional notion of martyrdom. "Why would not Monseñor Romero, for example, be a martyr?" he wrote. "After all, he fell in the struggle for justice in society, fell in a struggle he waged from his deepest Christian convictions." I like to interpret these words of Rahner as the grateful encomium of a great theologian on a great bishop.

The figure of Archbishop Romero as a martyr has loomed larger with the passing years. There has also been the attempt to destroy this image. But it is easy to understand why such an image should prevail. The popular songs, the books about Archbishop Romero, the handbills with his picture on them, are countless. People make pilgrimages to his tomb to pray to him, to ask him for favors, to thank him. And in all of this, a heartfelt love of the poor is expressed, and a heartfelt love of all who would continue his work. People at base community meetings constantly quote his words, and this with the evident conviction that they are speaking of someone ultimate, someone sacred. We even find a linguistic phenomenon reminiscent of the sudden New Testament reservation of the title, "Lord," to Jesus Christ alone, so that there was no need to specify "Lord Jesus": in El Salvador, "Monseñor" (literally, "My Lord," or "My Lord Bishop") simply means Archbishop Romero. The people have already made him a saint.

Throughout Latin America, then, as in so many other parts of the world, Archbishop Romero is admired and loved. Persons who never saw him find in him great strength for their faith as believers, and the strength to live their dignity as human beings. Countless solidarity committees, and so many pastoral publications, bear his name. Innumerable books and articles cite him. Plays have been written about him, as well as a little opera, and even a commercial film has been made about him. March 24 is observed as a holy day in many places. El Salvador is known today for two things, the world over: the war that is tearing it limb from limb, and Archbishop Romero. A passenger on a plane was asked, "Where are you headed?" The answer was, "El Salvador." "Ah," said the questioner, "the land of Archbishop Romero." One could relate countless similar anecdotes.

I happened to be travelling frequently in Latin America, Europe, the United States, and Canada in those days. Wherever I went, I was asked to speak about Archbishop Romero. The only time I have ever been in Asia— where my intention had been to keep my eyes open and my mouth closed— I was also asked to speak about Archbishop Romero. In Tokyo, in New Delhi, and in so many other places, I have been struck by how much Archbishop Romero means to Christians, Marxists, Buddhists, and Hindus. "I have some bad news for you," a European told me one day (a Frenchman, as I recall). "Archbishop Romero does not belong just to Salvadorans any more. He belongs to the world now."

Archbishop Romero has touched something very profound in the hearts of human beings and believers. I think he offers all of us a pathway of humanization. He has helped all of us to know a little better what we are and what we ought to be. And to all of us he has offered the reality of Jesus, and God, that all may become believers and human beings. Dom Pedro Casaldáliga has summed it up so well: "The history of the church in Latin America is divided into two parts: before and after Archbishop Romero."

All of this is perfectly clear to me. But to my surprise and sorrow, a campaign has been mounted to belittle and silence this heroic figure. Archbishop Romero was surely a good man, we hear it said, but not a very prudent or intelligent one. He was actually a weak, impressionable person; and radical groups, among them the Jesuits, latched on to him and steered him along the path of their particular interests. I recall my stupor and indignation when I was told in Caracas in 1982 that the provincial of a certain religious order had heard in Rome that Archbishop Romero had become a product of manipulation by the Jesuits. I think the "manipulation theory" has been running out of steam. At least it is no longer officially propagated since Pope John Paul II's visit to El Salvador in 1983. Altogether unexpectedly, by completely personal choice, the pope interrupted his planned itinerary and went to the Cathedral of San Salvador. On his knees he prayed at Archbishop Romero's tomb, then praised him as a "zealous shepherd, inspired by the love of God and service to his brethren to offer up his very life, suffering a violent death while celebrating the sacrifice of forgiveness and reconciliation." I have heard that the holy father regards Archbishop Romero as a genuine martyr.

Still, it will not be superfluous to devote a few lines here to an analysis of what lurks behind the oft-repeated manipulation theory. To me it is clear that Archbishop Romero was subjected to many pressures. It could not have been otherwise. The government, the oligarchy, the Vatican, and the Salvadoran Bishops Conference all pressured him. The most alert elements among the clergy, and the popular organizations, also sought to influence him. In fact, among the ten points Archbishop Romero proposed to analyze about himself in the course of his last retreat was the following: "I am afraid of ideological and political pressure. I am very vulnerable when it comes to being influenced. I may very well be under people's influence."

That Archbishop Romero was under pressure, then, and vulnerable to that pressure, is one thing, and something he recognized himself. But that his life and work are to be explained purely in terms of outside manipulation is something else again—an unwarranted conclusion, and a matter of wishful thinking. The pressure from the right was stronger. First came the cajolery, then the threats. But Archbishop Romero did not yield to this pressure. There was also real pressure from the left at times, and I think the better-advised clergy did attempt to move Archbishop Romero more toward their line of thought and action—which, for that matter, would seem to be legitimate enough. Then why not accept the obvious explanation for Archbishop Romero's behavior—that he found one line so much more evangelical than the other? I think that, *through* the pressures of the left,

Archbishop Romero found the more evangelical line. But what moved him to implement this line rather than the other was not these pressures, but the intrinsic truth he was discovering, as I have tried to explain in discussing his conversion. Pressure from the left may have been one important *occasion*, among others, for his change. But they were not the *cause* of his conversion, or at the very least they were not the basic cause.

Further, I think that, whatever may have been the pressures from the left in the beginning, Archbishop Romero very quickly acquired and manifested an identity of his own. What he did June 19, 1977, at Aguilares can in no way, shape, or form be explained in terms of remote control on the part of others. It was he, Archbishop Romero, who did that. As I have said, from that day forward we felt that he was out ahead of us—that it was not he who was following in our footsteps, but we who were following in his.

This is not to deny that, over the course of three years, Archbishop Romero often felt pressure from both sides. So many things happened, so many decisions had to be made. It would be an illusion to think that Archbishop Romero acted as if he were living in some sort of isolation chamber. Nor does it seem strange to me that, from time to time, he should unburden himself and say he felt pressured. I suppose he did so privately sometimes, and it seems to me normal that he should. But he did so publicly, as well, for example in the discussion with Rogelio Ponseele that I have already mentioned: he protested that the left was pressuring him. That Archbishop Romero should live under pressure, then, seems to me altogether to be expected. That he actually thought of himself as impressionable by temperament is certainly a fact. But to wish to conclude from this that his life and work were the product of pressure seems to me to be both logically fallacious and factually untrue. Archbishop Romero acknowledged that he was impressionable, and he did so during a spiritual retreat, traditionally a time for an honest analysis of one's limitations and problems. But—although in his humility he did not admit this to himself—he was also by nature enterprising, intelligent, courageous, and altogether a determined follower of the will of God. The texture of everyone's life—even that of the saints—includes all of the data of one's character, and these data make their contribution to all of the immanent and transient activities through which one may come to be a human being and even a saint. But to seek to explain the whole of a person's life and work solely in function of one aspect of his or her personality—especially if the analysis of that personality is faulty—is disastrous. It is as if we were to say that St. Ignatius Loyola must not have experienced divine grace because he was of a voluntaristic, stubborn, and tenacious character; or as if we were to say that St. Teresa of Avila's experience of God was a delusion because she seems to have been somewhat emotionally unbalanced.

Whatever be the case with Archbishop Romero's character, then, the correct procedure will be to analyze how he reacted, with that concrete character, in the decisions he had to make in real life, and why he made these decisions. To my knowledge, whenever he had important decisions to make he asked for advice. It took him an infinitude of meetings, polls of the common people, rough drafts, and months of work to finalize his pastoral letters. Throughout the whole process, he constantly asked questions, made suggestions, and raised difficulties. This was how he proceeded. He would pray at length, then finally make his decision. In preparing his homilies, he would review the most important events of the week, and ask advice when he thought he simply had to take a prophetic, forthright, and therefore provocative position on anything. I have Sister Teresa's word for it how he would prepare his Sunday sermons. He would still be working on them on Saturday night. He would have his scripture commentaries and homiletic aids out on his desk, along with notes of his own and the newspapers of that week. He would stay up working until after midnight, sometimes until two or three in the morning. Sister Teresa would see him praying before retiring, and the next morning he would preach his homily. I think, then, that Archbishop Romero's final decision in all important matters was personal. I think that it often occurred to him personally what he ought to do, while at other times others made suggestions. Does not everyone have this experience? But the final decision was always his, and it was personal.

What really calls for analysis, it seems to me, is *why* Archbishop Romero made the decisions he made. And in order to be able to make this analysis, it seems to me appropriate to distinguish between, shall we say, the "major" and the "minor" pressures exerted on anyone. Minor pressures—the "categorical" ones, let us call them—are the thousand-and-one occurrences and contacts of daily life: conversations, discussions, possible annoyances, demands made by various persons. No one in the official church, from the pope to the simplest religion teacher, is exempt from these pressures. But the major pressures—the "transcendent" ones, let us say—are another matter. For Archbishop Romero, the transcendent pressures were the will of God and the suffering of the people. There is no doubt in my mind that, with the freedom he found bestowed upon him in his experience of God and his experience of the poor, Archbishop Romero was altogether willing to be "pressured" by these. If anything "manipulated" Archbishop Romero, it was the grace of God and the suffering of his people. It is these major, transcendent pressures that ultimately explain Archbishop Romero's life and work. The other pressures of life, the everyday, categorical ones, were part of his life as well, yes, but they were always secondary to the major pressures.

Why some persons would like to reduce Archbishop Romero to the product of manipulation is as obvious as it is tragic. Those who are unwilling to recognize his stature because he disturbs them or calls their lives into question look for a "reason why" Archbishop Romero was the way he was. Then they shall not be conscience-bound to imitate him. They look for excuses, but never logical or disinterested ones. Here again Archbishop Romero reminds me of Jesus. "He has lost his mind," some said of Jesus. "He is possessed by the devil," said others. "What do you expect? He's from Nazareth," jeered still others. They were dead set against following Jesus of Nazareth.

Archbishop Romero himself reflected on this kind of remark made about him, and we are fortunate to have his reflections on record. He expressed them publicly, in a homily on the fate of the prophets, July 8, 1979.

> This is the terrible thing about our society. It is a society that rejects the word of the gospel when that word does not suit its selfishness, when it does not suit its injustice. Suddenly a thousand questions arise. "Where does he get all these ideas? Who is manipulating him in this way? These can't be his own ideas!" And all of these foolish accusations, instead of becoming real questions ("Is he right or isn't he?"), remain purely rhetorical ones, and the victim is simply rejected.

It is sad to have to recall these things, and to have to observe that for some persons—even within the institutional church—Archbishop Romero was nothing but a product of manipulation in his lifetime, and nothing but an inflated myth in death. And it is sad not only because the appraisal is unjust, but because it is a sin against the light and therefore irremediable. If the good news comes and no response, no gratitude, no discipleship is forthcoming, but only tergiversation and rejection, then nothing will work a change. To me, Archbishop Romero is not an inflated myth or a product of manipulation. He had his limitations, as he himself noted in his retreat, but they were minor—very minor, from the spiritual viewpoint, and normal from the viewpoint of human psychology. But even with these limitations, Archbishop Romero was a Salvadoran, a believer, and an exceptional archbishop. So many persons, including important persons, who knew him, so many millions of persons who remember him today and who love him, cannot be mistaken on this point. As I have stated, if there was any manipulation, I believe and hope that Archbishop Romero manipulated us far more than we him.

All this talk of manipulation has pretty much died out—although Bishop Revelo of Santa Ana has brought it up again, and one Fredy Delgado, a priest of the diocese of San Vicente, has just published a pamphlet full of falsehoods in which this one is included. But something even sadder is now occurring in El Salvador. An attempt is under way to silence Archbishop Romero. Archbishop Romero is presumed to have been a great prophet, a martyr, even a saint—if the rumors are true that his cause is to be introduced—but of the *past*. Sad and unbelievable as it may seem, the Salvadoran Bishops Conference never makes any mention of him in its messages, never quotes his words of encouragement that they may inspire the Christians of today. Here Archbishop Romero is indeed dead and buried.

The reason given for this attempt to silence him is, once more, his alleged manipulation by the "left." While there is no longer so much insistence on his having been the product of manipulation by the left during his lifetime, it is now asserted that the left seeks to manipulate him for its own ends now that he is dead. And to prevent this, Archbishop Romero is subjected to the cruelest species of manipulation: silence. And the perpetrators of this deed even add: "Archbishop Romero is ours."

The question, "Who is Archbishop Romero?" can be answered only by way of honest analysis. Archbishop Romero was an archbishop, and so belongs to the hierarchical church. He was a Christian, and so belongs to all Christians. He was a Salvadoran, and so belongs to all Salvadorans. He was these three things in an outstanding way, and so can be taken as an example to follow by all three—and would that this should come to pass!—hierarchs, Christians, and Salvadorans. But to take Archbishop Romero as an example does not mean regarding him as private property—least of all in the sense of the talent in the parable that was buried to keep it from being lost. To take Archbishop Romero as an example means precisely to cease to keep him for ourselves and to put him to work, again like the talents of the gospel parable.

How many persons and groups here in El Salvador remember, love, and claim Archbishop Romero—base communities, groups of priests and nuns, union members, even the guerrillas of the FMLN (who celebrate March 24 in their camps)! Others are not pleased that things should be this way, but this is the way things are, and we must ask ourselves if it is objectively good or bad that they should be this way. In my judgment, as Archbishop Romero is both of God and of this world, an illustrious believer and an illustrious Salvadoran, all of those who have a genuine experience both of faith and of the reality of this world have a right to appeal to him, recall him, and celebrate him as theirs. Nor is this manipulation, as long as recalling either the sacred or secular dimension of Archbishop Romero does not mean rejecting the other. It is another matter who has the greatest right and greatest need to lay claim to him. These are those who invoke him as a Christian *and* as a Salvadoran: those Salvadorans who are poor and Christian, who find in him a light and hope that they find nowhere else, and who really love Archbishop Romero because he really loved them.

Manipulation of Archbishop Romero occurs when only one of these two dimensions of his is seized upon to the exclusion of the other. But the most despicable manipulation is that of his silencing, as if he no longer had anything to say, anything to offer his country and the church. Every now and then it is announced that there will be an investigation of his assassination. But this is to return only to his corpse, and not to his life. Of course, even more hypocritical than the triumphant proclamation that the government has solved this crime, when it makes no effort to solve the other sixty thousand murders of Salvadorans who held Archbishop Romero's principles; even worse than the attempted manipulation of publishing the results of these "investigations" during a political campaign (the party making the accusations seeking to place the blame on the other party)—the worst thing of all is that all of these self-servers are simply gathered around Archbishop Romero's dead body, waving their arms and shouting, while the living, enlightening, inspiring Archbishop Romero himself is gagged and silenced. Does Archbishop Romero have nothing to say today about the life and death of Salvadorans, about war and peace, about justice and reconciliation? Not one word of his is ever cited by the government, the Assembly, politicians, the armed forces, or the U.S. Embassy. Does Archbishop Romero have nothing to say about faith, hope, and Christian commitment, about priestly and parish life, about prophecy and mercy? Archbishop Rivera, the only bishop who was loyal to him in life, does occasionally quote him. Archbishop Rivera's work of dialogue and negotiation, his cooperation in attempts to humanize our conflict and alleviate its consequences, the support he shows for the Archdiocesan Legal Advocacy Office, do reflect something of Archbishop Romero's inspiration. But the bishops conference ignores him. Diocesan pastoral plans ignore him (where they exist). This is the saddest of all of Archbishop Romero's funerals.

Still Archbishop Romero lives. He lives in the person of those who go to the cathedral to pray to him: he lives in the depths of their hearts. He lives in shelters, relocation camps, the remote regions of the country, the bowels of city slums. He lives in some religious, some professionals, and some intellectuals. At the University of Central America, posters everywhere bear his likeness. For me there is no doubt that Archbishop Romero lives in the poor, for whom life—and life in the basic, literal sense of sheer survival—continues to be the fundamental task. He lives in all of those who make a decision to serve the life of these peoples, and who rely on their memory of him for the courage to face the risks they must take. And he lives in all of those who, now groping, now exulting, seek God in the sincerity of their hearts. Archbishop Romero continues to be the light by which they contemplate the mystery of this God, such a dark mystery in the crucifixion of the poor, and such a luminous one in their hope of resurrection, to which they commit themselves with all their heart and soul.

X

These are some of my recollections of Archbishop Romero. I have mentioned only a few—the ones most important to me, the ones that have most enlightened and encouraged me. Other persons may have similar recollections. Still others will cherish different, perhaps more significant ones. Surely the basic recollection is the one stored up in the hearts of the poor—which, when all is said and done, I cannot penetrate. And were we to attempt to gather together, one by one, all of the recollections anyone has of Archbishop Romero, then surely, in the words of St. John at the end of his gospel, "the whole world could not contain the books that would have to be written" to record them.

I should like to add that I do not offer these recollections in the spirit of a panegyric. A papal nuncio once told me that I "overdid" my praise of Archbishop Romero when I wrote of him. I think that this is untrue even objectively. It is certainly untrue in my intent. But I cannot deny the profound impact that Archbishop Romero had on me.

I should also like to add that not all of my exceptional recollections from those exceptional years in El Salvador are of Archbishop Romero. I recall Rutilio Grande, as well, along with many other priests, sisters, *campesinos*, union members, and university students who were also put to death for justice' sake. Some of them died more painfully than did Archbishop Romero—tortured to death. Recalling Archbishop Romero, then, does not mean isolating him from the other martyrs of our country, or exalting him in such a way as to leave the others in the shade. No, to recall Archbishop Romero is precisely to recall so many others as well—so many prophets and martyrs, so many *campesinos* and Delegates of the Word, all of them preachers, by their deeds, of the living word of God. And above all, to recall Archbishop Romero means recalling thousands of innocent, defenseless, and nameless martyrs: it means recalling an entire crucified people, whose names will never be publicly known, but who now are one with Archbishop Romero forever. He who in life was the voice of the voiceless, in death is the name of the nameless. God grant that one day we may see the canonization of "Archbishop Romero and the Salvadoran Martyrs," or "Archbishop Romero and the Latin American Martyrs."

In conclusion, then, I should like to insist that my recollections of Archbishop Romero surely have meaning only within the one great recollection of the whole Archbishop Romero. The recollections that I have offered are not intended as material for a biography of the life of this illustrious personage, this excellent human being. They are not like the pieces of a puzzle that only make a picture when you put enough of them together. On the contrary, to me the picture has always been perfectly clear, and alone gives meaning to the pieces. I may have gathered up the several pieces of the picture more or less adequately (although, in all honesty, I have made no attempt to do so). Or others may now come by with entirely different pieces, and thereby clarify (or dispute) the meaning of the pieces I have presented. I willingly accept either eventuality.

Might I be permitted to attempt to sum up in a single word the whole of Archbishop Romero? Could there ever be a one-word answer to the question, "Who was Archbishop Romero?" In the New Testament, after Jesus' death and resurrection, the various evangelists answered the question, "Who was Jesus?" in different ways. Some of them called him Messiah, others Son of God, others Word of God. And of course they were all correct. For my part, I have called Archbishop Romero a shepherd, a prophet, a martyr, a great believer, and a great Salvadoran. But if I had to sum up in a single word and concept the truth expressed by all of these titles together, I should have to say: Archbishop Romero was a gospel. Archbishop Romero was a piece of good news from God to the poor of this world, and then, from this starting point in the poor, to all men and women. To put it another way—an even more radical way, theologically speaking—I should like to close this introductory chapter with the words Father Ignacio Ellacuría used to describe Archbishop Romero in his homily at the Mass we concelebrated at Central American University only a few days after his martyrdom. They are engraved on my heart. "With Archbishop Romero, God has visited El Salvador."

—Translated by Robert R. Barr

Chapter 2

Maura, Ita, Dorothy, and Jean

I have stood by the bodies of Maura Clarke, Ita Ford, Dorothy Kazel, and Jean Donovan. Once more I felt what I have felt so often since the murder of Rutilio Grande, in 1977. Then, the martyrs had been a Jesuit priest—my friend and comrade—and two Aguilares campesinos. This time the martyrs were four American women missionaries: two Maryknoll sisters, an Ursuline sister, and a social worker from the diocese of Cleveland, Ohio. Between those two dates—March 12, 1977, and December 2, 1980—there has been martyrdom upon martyrdom—an endless procession of priests, seminarians, students, campesinos, teachers, workers, professionals, and intellectuals murdered for the faith in El Salvador.

Death has come to be the inseparable, dismal companion of our people. And yet, each time we gather to bid our martyrs farewell, the same feelings well up inside, surge to the surface again. First we are filled with indignation and grief, and we cry with the psalmist: "How long, O Lord? How long?" Then comes that feeling of determination and high resolve, and we pray with the psalmist: "Rejoice, Jerusalem. Your deliverance is at hand!"

This time, however, things are different. No one can conceal the new sensation we have. Not since the murder of Archbishop Romero (March 24, 1980) has there been a commotion like the one occasioned by this latest martyrdom. Neither within the country nor abroad has there been such a universal repudiation, such a feeling that God's patience must be exhausted and that this martyrdom is telling us that liberation is in the offing.

There were three hundred of us priests and sisters gathered in the chancery to hear Archbishop Rivera. His voice had a new and different ring, as he denounced the Security Forces of the Christian Democratic Junta. He tore the masks from their faces. He pointed the finger of shame and guilt. Once again the truth was crystal clear. And with the truth came courage, and the Christian resolve to keep on, shoulder to shoulder with a massacred people, even if it meant that the church must march once more to the cross.

First published in *Estudios Centroamericanos* (Jan–Feb. 1981), 51–53. The English translation appeared in Jon Sobrino, *Spirituality of Liberation* (© 1988 by Orbis Books), 153–156. The four American missionaries were raped and murdered on Dec. 2, 1980.

It was the first Christian Easter all over again. The horror, the abandonment, the solitude of Jesus' cross had driven the disciples to their refuge in the upper room. But Jesus' spirit was mightier than death, and it flung the doors wide apart. The disciples emerged stronger than before, determined to preach resurrection and life, determined to proclaim the good news of the reign of the poor. The archbishop's residence had been transformed into a latter-day upper room. The God of life was there. And that God was stronger than death, stronger than oppression and repression, stronger than ourselves and our fears and terrors. There, in the presence of four corpses, the Christian paradox came to life. Yes, where sin and crime had abounded, life and grace abounded even more.

This past Easter was a special celebration indeed. With this last murder the reservoirs of iniquity have overspilled their limits. The dams of evil have burst. We have seen everything in El Salvador. No barbarity would surprise us, we thought. But this time we were overwhelmed. Once more we witnessed the murder of the just, the innocent. But this time the murdered Christ was present in the person of four women, four missionaries, four Americans. This time the thick clouds of crime were pierced by a brand-new light.

The murdered Christ is here in the person of four *women*. In the drama of the world, and the drama of the church, all the actors are human beings. We are all of us equal, as well as different, in God's eyes. And yet, the two together—equality and difference—are hard to come by in our history. Then suddenly, with these four dead bodies, we see something of it. Men and women are oppressed and repressed in El Salvador. Men and women have raised their lamentation to God and begged God to hear the cries wrung from them by their exploiters. Men and women have thrown in their lot with the struggle for liberation. And men and women have fallen in that struggle. Here is the most profound equality of all: equality in suffering and in hope.

By making themselves one with the archetypical Salvadoran woman, these four sisters made themselves one with the whole Salvadoran people. Woman is the procreator of humankind. But she is the creator of humanity—of humanness and humaneness—as well, in a specific manner all her own: in the delicacy of her service, her limitless self-donation, her affective and effective contact with the people, and that compassion of hers that simply will not rationalize the suffering of the poor. Woman is the creator of a courage that will never abandon the suffering, as these four sisters did not abandon their people when they saw the danger. Woman is more defenseless physically. This fact points up the singular barbarity of their murder. It shows that barbarity for what it is. And it demonstrates the simplicity and gratuity of these women's self-sacrifice.

The murdered Christ is present here in the person of four *religious*. We hear a great deal about the renewal of the religious life today, in El Salvador as elsewhere. We hear a great deal about charisms and vows. And now these four dead bodies show us what a life of consecration to God today is all about. They make no fuss. They hold no grandiloquent harangues. They show us, simply, the basic element of all religious charism: service. Religious women today have been moving out more and more, reaching the most abandoned places, places where others cannot or will not go. They have drawn close to the poor, in genuineness and in truth, the poor of the slums, the poor of the working-class neighborhoods, and especially the poor campesinos. Consecration to God today means service and dedication to the poor.

Just as quietly, women religious have exercised their prophetic charism, which is part and parcel of the religious life. By their presence, by their activity, they have denounced the petrification of other echelons of the church. They have denounced the alienation of the hierarchy from Christian peoples. Above all, they have denounced the death-dealing sin that decimates the Salvadoran population. Therefore they have suffered the fate of the prophets, and shared the people's own lot: martyrdom. And so religious women, too, have their representatives among the martyrs of all social classes. They too have made an option for the poor, and therefore they too had to die.

The dead Christ is present among us in the person of four *Americans*. The United States is everywhere in El Salvador. We have U.S. businessmen and military experts. We have a U.S. embassy here to decide the fate of Salvadorans without consulting them. We have U.S. arms, we have U.S. helicopters to pursue and bombard the civilian population. But we have something else from the United States, too. We have American Christians, priests, and nuns. These have given us the best the United States has to offer: faith in Jesus instead of faith in the almighty dollar; love for persons instead of love for an imperialist plan; a thirst for justice instead of a lust for exploitation. With these four Americans, Christ, although he came from a far-off land, was no stranger in El Salvador. He was a Salvadoran, through and through.

In these four religious women, the churches of El Salvador and of the United States have become sister churches. After all, Christian action is helping others for their own sake, not blackmailing them with economic aid or babying them with paternalism. El Salvador gave these four sisters new eyes, and they beheld the crucified body of Christ in our people. El Salvador gave these four sisters new hands, and they healed Christ's wounds in the people of our land. The United States of America gave us four women who left their native land to give. And they gave all, in utter simplicity. They gave their very lives.

What has brought these two churches together? What has enabled the churches of El Salvador and the United States to contribute so much to the upbuilding of the world church? The poor. Service to the poor. How moved I was to hear from Peggy Healy, the Maryknoll sister who was a friend of the murdered sisters, that the high-ranking officials sent here by President Carter were to investigate not only the death of four American citizens, but the genocide of ten thousand Salvadorans.

Today as yesterday, there is no other Christian formula for building the church or unifying the various churches throughout the world: we must emerge from ourselves, we must devote ourselves to others—to the very poorest, to the oppressed, to the tortured, to the "disappeared," to the murdered. If this is the attitude with which Christians of the church of the United States come to their fellow Christians of the church of El Salvador, then the church of El Salvador can only say: "Welcome." And if that attitude leads Christians of the church of the United States down the path of martyrdom, we can only say: "Thank you, from the bottom of our hearts."

Christ lies dead here among us. He is Maura, Ita, Dorothy, and Jean. But he is risen, too, in these same four women, and he keeps the hope of liberation alive. The world is moved, and indignant, and so are we Christians. But to us Christians, this murder tells us something about God as well. We believe that salvation comes to us from Jesus. And perhaps this is the moment to take seriously something that theology has been telling us in its too spiritualistic and too academic way: salvation comes by way of a woman— Mary, the virgin of the cross and of the Magnificat. Salvation comes to us through all women and men who love truth more than lies, who are more eager to give than to receive, and whose love is that supreme love that gives life rather than keeping it for oneself. God is here today. Yes, their dead bodies fill us with sorrow and indignation. And yet, our last word must be: Thank you. In Maura, Ita, Dorothy, and Jean, God has visited El Salvador.

—Translated by Robert R. Barr

Chapter 3

Companions of Jesus

I have often been asked to write something immediately after some tragedy happened in El Salvador: the murder of Rutilio Grande, of Archbishop Romero, of the four North American sisters, to name only the most prominent cases. All these were occasions for both sorrow and indignation. But in some way or another, we who survived managed to transform these feelings quite quickly into hope and service. In my case, this took the form, as we say, of analyzing the events theologically. This time it was different. In order to write you need a clear head and courage in your heart, but in this case, for days my head was just empty and my heart frozen.

Now, some time later, as I am gradually feeling calmer, I am setting out to write these reflections. I do it in grateful homage—a small unnecessary homage perhaps—to my six martyred brothers. I am also doing it to try to bring some light and cheer to those of us who are still in this world, a cruel world that murders the poor and those who cast their lot with them, a world that also tries to paralyze those who are alive by killing their hope.

I am writing personally, because at the moment, with my memory of my murdered brothers still fresh in my mind, I cannot do it any other way. Later on will be the time to interpret what happened in a more considered and analytical way, but now I could not do it. And I prefer to do it this way because perhaps writing like this, under the impact of sorrow and my sense of loss, I may be able to communicate a little of what hundreds of thousands of Salvadorans have also felt. Between seventy thousand and seventy-five thousand people have died in El Salvador, but now that it has hit home to me, I have felt something of the sorrow and indignation that so many Salvadorans must have felt, peasants, workers, students, and especially mothers, wives, daughters, when their loved ones were killed.

First, I am going to relate simply what I felt when I heard the news and during those first days, in a very personal way. This experience is not important in itself, because it is only a drop in the ocean of tears that is El Salvador,

This essay was first published in English by the Catholic Institute for International Relations (© 1990 by CIIR) and in the United States by Orbis Books (© 1990).

but perhaps it may help to convey the pain of the Salvadoran people. After that I shall offer some general reflections on my friends and various important matters that their martyrdom raises. I shall speak of them as a group, especially the five who worked in the Central American University, the UCA, whom I knew best. I shall say a bit more about Ignacio Ellacuría, because I lived with him for longer and it was he who most often put into words what these Jesuits accepted as fundamental in their lives and work.

"Something Terrible Has Happened"

From November 13 I was in Hua Hin, about two hundred kilometers from Bangkok in Thailand, giving a short course on christology. I was following on the radio the tragic events taking place in El Salvador and I had managed to speak to the Jesuits by telephone. They told me they were all well, and Ellacuría had just come back from Europe and entered the country with no problems. That same Monday 13 the army had searched our house, room by room, and the Archbishop Romero Center in the UCA, without further consequences.

Very late on the night of November 16—it would have been eleven o'clock in the morning in San Salvador—an Irish priest woke me up. While half asleep, he had heard news on the BBC saying that something serious had happened to the UCA Jesuits in El Salvador. To reassure himself, he had phoned London and then he woke me up. "Something terrible has happened," he told me. "It is not very clear, but it seems they have murdered a Jesuit from the UCA; I don't know whether it is the Rector. London will give you more information."

On the way to the telephone, I thought, although I did not want to believe it, that they had murdered Ignacio Ellacuría. Ellacuría, a brave and stubborn man, was not a demagogue but a genuine prophet in his writings, and even more publicly on television. A little while ago an ordinary Salvadoran woman had said to me after seeing him on television: "Not since they murdered Archbishop Romero has anyone spoken out so plainly in this country." All these thoughts were going through my head on my short walk to the phone.

At the other end of the telephone, in London, was a great friend of mine and of all the Jesuits in El Salvador, a man who has shown great solidarity with our country and our church. He began with these words: "Something terrible has happened." "I know," I replied, "Ellacuría." But I did not know. He asked me if I was sitting down and had something to write with. I said I had and then he told me what had happened. "They have murdered Ignacio Ellacuría." I remained silent and did not write anything, because I had already been afraid of this. But my friend went on: "They have murdered Segundo Montes, Ignacio Martín-Baró, Amando López, Juan Ramón Moreno, and Joaquin López y López." My friend read the names slowly and each of them reverberated like a hammer blow that I received in total helplessness. I was writing them down, hoping that the list would end after each name. But after each name came another, on to the end. The whole community, my whole community, had been murdered. In addition, two women had been murdered with them. They were living in a little house at the entrance to the university and because they were afraid of the situation they asked the fathers if they could spend the night in our house because they felt safer there. They were also mercilessly killed. Their names are Julia Elba, who had been the Jesuits' cook for years, and her fifteen-year-old daughter Celina. As in the case of Rutilio Grande, when two peasants were murdered with him, this time two ordinary Salvadoran women died with the Jesuits.

Then my friend in London started giving me the details that were coming through in international telegrams. The killers were about thirty men dressed in military uniform. He told me they had taken three of the Jesuits out into the garden and tortured and machine-gunned them there. The other three and the two women they had machine-gunned in their beds. My friend could hardly go on speaking. Like many others during those days, he had no words to express what had happened. He managed to give me a few words of comfort and solidarity, and finally he wondered what strange providence had seen to it that I was not in our house at the time.

I spent several hours, or rather several days, unable to react. As I said at the beginning, on other tragic occasions we recovered our courage fairly quickly and were fired with a sense of service, which made us active, in some way alleviating our sorrow by pushing the scenes of terror out of our heads. The Masses we celebrated for the martyrs even filled us with joy. But this time, for me, it was different. The distance made me feel helpless and alone. And the six murdered Jesuits were my community, they were really my family. We had lived, worked, suffered, and enjoyed ourselves together for many years. Now they were dead.

I do not think I have ever felt anything like it. I told the Irish priest who was with me that night that it was the most important thing that had happened to me in my whole life. I do not think that is an exaggeration. My long years in El Salvador, my work, including risks and conflicts, the difficult situations I had been through, even my religious life as a priest, seemed much less important things than the death of my brothers. They did not seem very real in comparison with these deaths. I felt a real breakdown in my life and an emptiness that nothing could fill. During those moments I remembered the biblical passage about the mothers of the murdered children who wept and could not be comforted. When I thought about things in my normal life, writing, talks, and classes, the things I had been doing for the last sixteen years in El Salvador and might be doing in the future, it all seemed unreal to me, with nothing to do with the reality. The most real reality—as I have often written from El Salvador—is the life and death of the poor. From thousands of miles away, and although I was still alive, the death of my brothers was a reality, compared to which everything else seemed little or nothing. Or rather, a reality that forced me to look at everything else from its standpoint. The church, the Society of Jesus were not for me in those moments realities in terms of which—as it were, from a distance—I could understand or interpret their deaths, but the reverse. As a result of these deaths all those realities became questions for me and, very slowly—and I say this with gratitude—answers too to what is most fundamental in our lives: God, Jesus, vocation, the people of El Salvador.

I kept asking myself too why I was alive, and the Irish priest who was with me asked me the same question. I wanted to answer with the traditional words: "I am not worthy." But really there was no answer to that "why?" and I did not dwell on the question. Instead I began to have a feeling of irreparable loss. The UCA will never be the same, and I shall never be the same. After living and working with these brothers for so many years, it had become second nature to me to rely on them for my own life and work. Whatever idea, whatever plan, came into my head, always ended the same way: but they are not there any more. Ellacuría is not there any more, to finish the book we were editing together. Juan Ramón is no longer there to finish the next issue of the *Revista Latinoamericana de Teología*. Nacho [Martín-Baró] is no longer there to give the psychology of religion course I had asked him to give for the master's in theology. Montes is no longer there to understand the problems of the refugees and human rights. Lolo— that's what we called Fr. Joaquin López y López—is no longer there: he was usually silent, but had a great feel for the thoughts and hopes of the poor persons he worked with in the Fe y Alegria education program. The examples I have given are not important in themselves, of course, but I give them to show that I had lost the direct links that connected me to real life. And I remembered from my years studying philosophy that a writer (I do not remember who) defined—I am not sure if it was death or hell—as the total absence of relationships.

This was my experience in the first hours and days. It was my strongest sensation, beyond any doubt, but it was not the only one. The next morning the people in the course came up to me and embraced me in silence, many of them in tears. One of them told me that the death of my brothers was the best explanation and confirmation of the class we had held the previous day about Jesus, Yahweh's suffering servant, and the crucified people. The comment cheered me a little, not because it referred approvingly to my theology, of course, but because it linked my Jesuit brothers with Jesus and the oppressed. That same morning we had a Mass in Hua Hin with an altar decked with flowers in the beautiful Asian style, with the name of El Salvador written on it and eight candles, which people from different Asian and African countries—who were acquainted with sorrow and death—lit in turn while I spoke the names of the eight victims. That night in another city five hours away by car, I had another Mass with various Jesuits and many lay co-workers working with refugees from Vietnam,

Burma, Cambodia, the Philippines, Korea. . . . They also knew about suffering and could understand what had happened in El Salvador. On Saturday and Sunday back in Bangkok, I gave two talks—as I had been asked to give beforehand—on Jesus and the poor. Personally I did not feel much like speaking, but I thought I owed it to my brothers and talking about them was the best possible way of presenting the life and death of Jesus of Nazareth and his commitment to the poor today. Of course in Thailand, a country with a tiny number of Christians, someone asked me ingenuously and incredulously: "Are there really Catholics who murder priests in El Salvador?"

So it was not all darkness and being alone. I began to hear the reactions in many places, the solidarity of many Jesuits all over the world, the clear words of Archbishop Rivera, the promise by Fr. Kolvenbach, our Father General, to come to El Salvador for Christmas, the immediate offer by various Jesuits from other countries to come to El Salvador and continue the work of those who had been murdered, the Mass in the Gesu, the Jesuit church in Rome, with about six hundred priests at the altar, another Mass in Munich with more than six thousand students, Masses in the USA, Spain, England, Ireland, and many more all over the world. I also received cards and telephone calls, full of tears and sorrow, but also full of love and gratitude to the six Jesuits. When they told me about the funeral Mass in the Archbishop Romero chapel, with Jesuits determined to carry on the work of the UCA, little by little I came out of the dark and got my courage back. From what I can tell, the human and Christian reaction to these murders has been unique, only comparable perhaps to the reaction to Archbishop Romero's murder. Politically there is no doubt that these murders has had the most repercussions since Archbishop Romero's. In several countries, they tell me, nothing has so galvanized the Jesuits as these martyrs. If this has been so, we can say without triumphalism that this martyrdom has already begun to produce good, and this is what keeps up our hope now, even though our sorrow and sense of loss has not diminished.

I have described this experience because I want to say that now I understand a little better what this world's victims mean. The figures—seventy thousand in El Salvador—are horrifying, but when these victims have particular names and are persons who have been very close to you, the sorrow is terrible. I have told this story because I also wanted to say simply that I loved my murdered and martyred brothers very much. I am very grateful to them for what they gave me in their lives and for what they have given me in their death. Finally I have told the story so that what I am going on to say can be more easily understood. I am not going to say anything extraordinary, but things that are well known. I do so honestly and sincerely, not as a matter of course but with the conviction aroused by this tragic event. First I am going to say a few words about who these Jesuits were and then I will reflect a little about important matters that their deaths have thrown light on.

Who Were They?

Who were they? Many things could be said about them. When their biographies are written, some of them, like that of Ellacuría, the rector of the university, will fill several volumes, because his life of fifty-nine years was prodigiously creative intellectually, in church and religious matters and in politico-social analysis. Others, like Fr. Lolo's, may be shorter, not because in his long life of seventy years he did not do many good things in the San José day school, his early years at the UCA and his last twenty years of direct service to the poor in Fe y Alegria, but because his humble and simple talents made him always want to be unnoticed. There will be such a lot to say about the others too. Segundo Montes was fifty-six, a sociologist; he spent many years in the Colegio and the UCA; he investigated the human problems, especially refugees, he was the director of the UCA Institute of Human Rights. Nacho Martín-Baró was forty-seven, academic vice-rector, a social psychologist who assiduously studied the problems of the poor, the psycho-social consequences of poverty and violence, religion as a force for liberation. Juan Ramón Moreno was fifty-six, master of novices, professor of theology, vice-director of the Archbishop Romero Center, which was of course partially destroyed on the same day as the murders. Amando López was fifty-three, rector of the diocesan seminary of San Salvador, rector of the Colegio and of the University of Managua during the Sandinista revolution, and professor of theology in the UCA. And as well as all these "titles" we will have to mention all their devotion in their daily work of looking after the ordinary people who came to them with their problems, their Sunday pastoral work in parishes and poor suburban and rural communities, Santa Tecla, Jayaque, Quezaltepeque, Tierra Virgen, their struggles to build things in these poor places, a little clinic, a nursery, or put a tin roof over a few poles to create a church. We shall also need to write the biographies of Julia Elba and Celina, perhaps in just a few pages but telling the story of their lives as Salvadorans and Christians, their poverty and suffering, their daily struggle to survive, their hopes for justice and peace, their love for Archbishop Romero and their faith in the God of the poor.

I cannot write their biographies here, but I should like to say a few words about what impressed me most in these Jesuits as a group—although of course there were differences among them. I want to suggest what is their most important legacy to us.

Before all else, they were human beings, Salvadorans, who tried to live honorably and responsibly amid the tragedy and hope of El Salvador. This may not seem adequate praise for glorious martyrs, but it is where I want to start, because living amid the situation of El Salvador, as in that of any part of the Third World, is before all else a matter of humanity, a demand on all to respond with honesty to a dehumanizing situation, which cries out for life and is inherently an inescapable challenge to our own humanity.

These Jesuits, then, were human in a very Salvadoran way, solid, not like reeds to be moved by any wind. They worked from dawn to dusk, and now will have presented themselves before God with their calloused hands, maybe not from physical work, but certainly from work of all sorts: classes, writing, the important if monotonous work of administration, Masses, retreats, talks, interviews, journeys, and lectures abroad. Sometimes they gave brilliant performances, as participants in international congresses or appearing on television, in discussion with well-known personalities, diplomats, and ambassadors, bishops, political and trade union leaders, intellectuals, and recipients of international awards. On November 1 Segundo Montes received a prize in the United States for his investigations into refugees, and Ellacuría, a few days before he returned to El Salvador, received from the mayor of Barcelona an important prize awarded to the UCA. They worked sometimes in the parishes, in the communities and in their offices, talking to simple people, to peasants and refugees, to mothers of the disappeared, trying to solve the everyday problems of the poor. Sometimes—most of their time—they followed the dull routine of the calendar—even though in El Salvador no day is like another—working at everyday tasks, meeting the demands of that structure of reality called "time." Through this everyday work they accumulated a great knowledge of the country and the credibility that came from being always at their posts; this gave them great prestige and massively reinforced their work and influence.

They were men of spirit, although outwardly they were not "spiritual" in the conventional sense. From Ellacuría I learned the expression "poor with spirit," to express adequately the relationship between poverty and spirituality. Above all I want to call these Jesuits "men with spirit." And this spirit showed itself, as St. Ignatius recommends in the meditation to attain love, "more in works than in words."

Above all, a spirit of service. If anything emerges clearly from this community, it is their work, to the point where they were called fanatics. But it was work that was really service. In this they were certainly outstanding disciples of St. Ignatius. They did not think of work as a way of pursuing a career. Some of them could easily have been world figures in their professions and some indeed were, although they never directly sought to be. It was not that they did not enjoy peace and quiet. But given the needs of the country and Ellacuría's creativity in always proposing new plans and never letting us rest on our laurels, work is what dominated the community. This had its disadvantages but above all it was the witness of lives dedicated to serving others. They nearly all did pastoral work in poor parishes and communities on Sundays after an exhausting week, and on many Saturday and Sunday afternoons they could be seen working in their offices. I remember, for example, that at times we discussed finishing the week's work in the UCA on Friday afternoons, and not at noon on Saturday, as was our practice, but the discussion always ended with these words: "That's for the First World. In a poor country like ours, we have to work harder, not less hard."

In fact even the notion of holidays, never mind a sabbatical year, disappeared from our lives. And although this really excessive workload also had its dehumanizing aspect and effects on health, these men lived this way because they were trying to respond to the countless urgent needs of the situation in El Salvador. I remember when Fr. Kolvenbach visited us El Salvador Jesuits in 1988—a very encouraging visit for which we are sincerely grateful—he recommended, as it was his responsibility to do, that we should not work to excess and that we should take care of our health and strength. And I remember that someone in the community replied that in situations like ours it is necessary to be indifferent to health or sickness, a short life or long, as St. Ignatius says in the Principle and Foundation. It was not that we did not understand or were not grateful for what Fr. Kolvenbach was telling us, but we wanted to stress that the situation in El Salvador—not just ascetic or mystical inclinations—required that we should be indifferent and available to give our lives and health. Whether or not this was exaggerated, these men saw their work as a way of serving and responding to the situation in El Salvador.

However, this work had a very particular aim: to serve the poor. When we used religious language, we spoke of the poor, those to whom God gives priority. When we used the language of Salvadoran history, we spoke of the mass of ordinary people. Really these are the same. We wanted to serve the millions of men and women who live lives unfit for human beings, and sons and daughters of God. The deepest thing in these Jesuits' lives was this service and they really did have a spirit of compassion and pity. If they worked like fanatics and ran very conscious risks, it was because they had a gut reaction—like the good Samaritan, Jesus and the heavenly Father—when they saw a whole suffering people on the road. They never passed by on the other side like the priest and the Levite in the parable, so as to avoid meeting and being affected by the people's suffering. They never said no to anything people asked them if it was possible for them to oblige. They never sought refuge in academic work to avoid the needs of the people, as if university knowledge was not also subject to the primary ethical and practical requirement to respond to the cry of the masses. So the inspiration of all their work and service was this compassion and pity, which they truly put first and last. The language they used as university men was of "justice," "transformation of structures," "liberation," including, of course, "revolution," but this was not a cold academic language, of ideology or politics. Behind it lay the real language of love for the Salvadoran people, the language of pity. With this people and for this people they lived many years. And they all made this people their own, although all of them except Father Lolo had been born in Spain. "Your people shall be my people," as scripture says.

Their spirit was one of courage. They had energy and endurance for everything, for the constant hard work, for dealing with the thousand and one problems that arose every day in the university, strictly university problems and problems that arose day after day in the country and reached the university. So they had to combine classes with giving urgent help to some refugee or someone who had disappeared; they endlessly had to interrupt their writing to deal with calls and visits. There was not much external peace for working and sometimes it seemed that their shoulders were not broad enough to bear everything loaded on to them. But they did not withdraw from problems or let people down.

They had courage to keep going amid conflicts and persecutions. In the last fifteen years they received many threats from phone calls or anonymous letters, and especially in the newspapers, with fantastic accusations in editorials and advertisements—sometimes paid for by the army—which suggested in one way or another, or plainly demanded, the expulsion or annihilation of these Jesuits. In recent months clear threats appeared in the press and on television, especially against Ellacuría and Segundo Montes. The final threats were on the radio, when from November 12 onward all the transmitters were in government hands and issuing threats against the Jesuits and the archbishop.

And as well as verbal threats, they suffered physical attacks. From January 6, 1976—I remember the date very well—when they placed the first bomb in our university, there have been fifteen occasions when bombs have been planted, in the print room, the computer center, the library, the administration building. The last one exploded on July 22 this year, partially destroying the printing press. The police came to our own house four times and on the last occasion they stayed for eleven hours. In February 1980 the house was heavily machine-gunned at night, and in October of the same year it was dynamited twice: on the 24th and three days later, on the 27th. In 1983 a new bomb exploded in our house; this time because we had defended dialogue as the most human and Christian solution for the country. A tragic irony, but in those days the very word "dialogue" was synonymous with betrayal.

So their service to the mass of the people was very aware of the risks. They accepted the risk perfectly naturally without any fuss, and not even through any special spiritual discernment, because one only discerns what is not clear and for these men it was absolutely clear that they had to go on with their work in the country. That is why they remained in El Salvador and I never heard them saying they should leave, whatever the threats and dangers. Perhaps the very fact of their remaining in the country was a great service to many who might have left if they had abandoned the country. In 1977, after Rutilio Grande was murdered, we all received death threats. The names of various UCA Jesuits were always on the lists of dangerous persons. And remember that in El Salvador leaflets were even thrown in the street saying "Be a patriot, kill a priest." Sometimes we spent nights in nuns' houses or with friendly families, but the next day we all returned to work at the UCA.

Only once, in November 1980, did Ellacuría leave the country under the protection of the Spanish embassy, because his name was top on a secret list of persons who were going to be killed. And remember that that year the threats were very real; it was the year when Archbishop Romero was murdered, as were four priests, four North American sisters, a seminarian, the rector of the National University, the five principal leaders of the Democratic Revolutionary Front (FDR) and, as always, hundreds of peasants, workers, trade unionists, students, teachers, doctors, journalists. . . . Ellacuría later returned to the country with no guarantee, fully aware that he was taking on all these risks again. There is no doubt that they were brave men, of a piece with the Salvadoran people who molded them and who have given an example to the world of how to bear endless misfortunes, how to survive and how to struggle for life with a creativity that astonishes all those who know them. So these men were true Salvadorans, and I should like to add that the courage and honesty and service with which they lived were returned in full measure by this people. The people's sufferings transformed and purified them, by their hope they lived, and their love won their hearts forever.

These men were also believers, Christians. I do not mention this here as something obvious or to be taken for granted, but as something central in their lives, something that really ruled all their lives. They were not conventionally "pious" types, repeating "Lord, Lord" in the temple, but they were people who went out into the street to do God's will. So when we spoke about matters of faith in the community, our words were sparing but really meant. We spoke about God's kingdom and the God of the kingdom, of Christian life as a following of Jesus, the historical Jesus, Jesus of Nazareth, because there is no other. In the university—in teaching and theological writings, of course—but also in solemn moments and public acts we recalled our Christian inspiration as something central, as what gave life, direction, force, and meaning to all our work, and explained the risks the university very consciously incurred. There was plain speaking about God's kingdom and the option for the poor, sin and the following of Jesus. This Christian inspiration of the university was never just rhetoric when these Jesuits talked about it, and people understood that this was really the university's inspiration. Even some who would have been reluctant to call themselves believers realized and were grateful because this Christian faith lived in this way made the university more Salvadoran.

It is difficult or impossible to see to the bottom of these men's hearts, their faith, but for me there is no doubt that they were great believers and that their lives alone had meaning as followers of Jesus. What was their faith like? Thinking of each one of them singly, with their different life stories and characters, I feel fascinated and grateful above all for the fact that they did have great faith, because in countries like El Salvador faith is not something obvious, amid so much injustice and so much silence from God, and I never fail to be impressed by the very fact that there is faith.

I think they believed in a God of life, who favored the poor, a beneficent utopia amid our history, a God who gives meaning and salvation to our lives and hence a radical hope. I think they found God hidden in the suffering face of the poor and they found God crucified in the crucified people.

And they also found God in those acts of resurrection, great and small, by the poor. And in this God of the lowly—God ever littler—they found the God who is ever greater, the true inexhaustible mystery, which impelled them along untrodden ways and to ask what had to be done. I should like to say of them what I have written elsewhere about Jesus of Nazareth. For them God was a good father, history's beneficent utopia, that attracted them and made them give more and more of themselves. In God they could rest and find the ultimate meaning of their lives. But for them the Father went on being God, the mystery beyond our control, and therefore God did not let them rest and drove them to keep seeking new things to do to respond to the new and sovereign divine will.

I have already said that our community was not very prone to put things into words, preferring to say them with our lives. Now my brothers have said them with their blood. But I want to mention someone they often did talk about: Archbishop Romero. And when they did, they spoke the language of faith. Loving and admiring Archbishop Romero is not at all difficult, except for those who deny the light and have hearts of stone. But trying to follow him and accept all of Archbishop Romero is a matter of faith. I believe that for them, for me and so many others, Archbishop Romero was a Christ for our time and, like Christ, a sacrament of God. To come into contact with Archbishop Romero was like coming into contact with God. Meeting Archbishop Romero in person was like meeting God. Trying to follow Archbishop Romero was like following Jesus today in El Salvador. This is what my brothers wanted to do. I do not think that either the Lord Jesus or the heavenly Father are jealous of my speaking like this about Archbishop Romero. After all, Romero was God's most precious gift to us all in these times. And when you feel strongly attracted by a witness like Archbishop Romero, whom we have seen, heard, and touched, I believe that it can truly be said that you are being attracted by Jesus and his gospel, the Jesus we have only read about and not seen definitively.

In any case if it is true that we all feel our faith supported by the faith of others, I have no doubt that our community was supported by the faith of others, by our brother Rutilio Grande, so many Salvadoran believers who proved their faith by shedding their blood, and by the faith of Archbishop Romero. I do not know whether I am projecting on to others what faith in God means for me, but I believe and hope that it is not just a projection. If I have learned anything in El Salvador, it is that faith is on the one hand something that cannot be delegated, like Abraham's when he stood alone before God, but on the other hand something supported by others. The two things combine in El Salvador, reinforcing each other. Thus amid so much darkness it continues to be possible, I believe, to have the light of faith. As the prophet Micah says, in a passage I have often quoted, it remains very clear that God requires us human beings to "do justice and to love loyalty." And it is also clear—now in the bright darkness of mystery—that thus we "walk humbly with God in history."

The first thing, the absolute requirement of justice, is what clearly revealed to these Jesuits the real situation of the poor and—in their doing justice—what made them relate to God. And the second, the difficult task of walking with God in this history of darkness—where can we get the strength to do it? I think what made it possible for them was the memory of Jesus, of his witnesses today and the faith of the poor themselves. These brothers joined the current of hope and love that is still running through history in spite of everything, that historical current driven ultimately by the poor. They worked to make this utopian hope constantly increase and gain more body, but this hope also sustained them in their hope and faith. I believe they saw the poor from God's point of view and walked with them toward God. This, I believe, was what my brothers' faith was like.

These men, these believers, were lastly Jesuits. I believe they were profoundly "Ignatian," although they sometimes did not appear very "Jesuitical," if I make myself clear, to those who are always waiting for the latest word from Rome or those who think that the Society of Jesus is the most important thing that exists on the face of the earth. Nevertheless they were sincerely proud of being Jesuits. It is not that they were outstanding in everything Ignatian, but they were outstanding in the essentials of the Spiritual Exercises. I remember that in 1974 Ellacuría and I gave a course on the exercises from the Latin American viewpoint. And in 1983 in our Provincial Congregation we wrote a joint paper based on the structure of the Exercises to be presented to the General Congregation of that year. Normally it was left to us two and Juan Ramón Moreno to put into words what was Ignatian in our lives and work, but I believe the rest of them accepted and heartily shared this vision.

From St. Ignatius we used to recall the great moments in the Exercises. The contemplation of the incarnation, to enable us to see the real world with God's own eyes—that is, a world of perdition—and to react with God's own compassion, that is, "to make redemption." And it is important to remember this because, as for many other Salvadorans, it was not anger—which was sometimes completely justified—or revenge, much less hatred that was the motive force in their lives, but love: "making redemption," as St. Ignatius called it. We also used to stress Jesus' mission in the service of God's kingdom and translate this into our own historical situation; the meditation on the two flags with the inevitable alternative of wealth and poverty, with the Ignatian intuition that poverty, assumed in a Christian way, leads to all good, whereas riches, by its very nature, leads to all evil; taking on the sin of the world and the concealment of Christ's divinity in the passion, as St. Ignatius says.

Something that was very original and extremely relevant to our situation was Ignacio Ellacuría's interpretation of the meditation on our sins in the presence of the crucified Christ. He related it to our Third World, and asked what have we done to cause all these people to be crucified, what are we doing about their crosses and what are we going to do to bring them down from the cross. From him too I learned to apply the expression "crucified people" to our people. We should not only speak of Moltmann's "crucified God," Ellacuría used to say, although this is necessary. He compared these people with Yahweh's suffering servant, as Archbishop Romero also intuitively did: the suffering servant is Jesus and the suffering servant is the crucified people. Our reply to these questions is expressed with utter seriousness in the conversion demanded by St. Ignatius.

We also reinterpreted St. Ignatius's ideal of "contemplatives in action" as "contemplatives in action for justice." I do not know how much contemplation there was in their lives, in the conventional sense, but I have no doubt that their way of contemplating God's face in the world was in their action to change God's face hidden and disfigured in the poor and oppressed into the face of the living God who gives life and raises from the dead.

These were the Ignatian ideals that moved this group. They put them into practice, with limitations of course, but I have no doubt it was these ideals that inspired them and they bore outstanding witness to them. And this spirit of St. Ignatius is what gives us the clue to understanding how they saw themselves as Jesuits in the world today. They and Jesuits like them are the ones who are bringing about the changes that have taken place in the Society's mission to the world, a change comparable to Vatican II or Medellín, and therefore a real miracle and gift of God. The Society's present mission was formulated as "service of faith and promotion of justice" (32nd General Congregation, 1975), taking the form of an "option for the poor" (33rd General Congregation, 1983). This change has been very radical. For the Society it has entailed conversion, abandoning many things and many ways of behaving, losing friendships with the powerful and their benefits, and gaining the affection of the poor. It has meant above all returning to Jesus' gospel, to the Jesus of the gospel and to the poor whom Jesus preached for and was gospel—that is, good news for. But it has also been a very important change and very beneficial, especially for Third World countries. It has meant that the Society has become truly Christian and truly Central American. It has meant keeping the Society's identity in a way that makes it relevant to our world and giving it a relevance that helps it to rediscover its Ignatian identity. This is no small benefit to the Society, and was produced very largely by Jesuits like the six who were murdered.

Jesuits like them have proved the truth of something else our 33rd General Congregation said: "We cannot carry out our mission of service to the faith and the promotion of justice without paying a price." In the last fourteen years since these words were said, many Jesuits have been threatened, persecuted, and imprisoned in the Third World. I believe the number of Jesuits murdered is about twenty, seven of them in El Salvador—Fr. Rutilio Grande and now the six from the UCA. Although it is tragic, it needs repeating: these crosses are what show that the choice made by the Society was correct, Christian and relevant to the needs of today. These crosses also show above all that this choice has been put into practice. And again this is no small benefit their martyrdom has given the Society of Jesus.

I believe, therefore, that they were Ignatians and Jesuits of the sort the Society wants today. Without fuss, sugary words, or triumphalism, they felt themselves to be Jesuits, again more in deed than word. Certainly it was they who asked Ignatius's two great questions: "Where am I going and what for?" They tried to answer these questions honestly, without dressing them up in florid devotional language or disguising them in diplomatic worldly caution. They did not even cover them with discerning insights that can sometimes be paralyzing, because, as I said before, the obvious is not an object of discernment. They were persons who sought the greater glory of God and remembered Ignatius's saying: "Whatever good, more universal, more divine." This is how they saw their work, especially their university work, which was directed toward the transformation of the structures of their country, so that salvation could reach more people. They were in the vanguard, in the trenches, fighting for solutions to the gravest problems of our time. They were the ones closest to the noise of battle. If they fell in the battle, it is because they were in it.

This is how I remember them, as human beings who were honest about reality, as believers in God and followers of Jesus, and as leading late twentieth-century Jesuits in a Third World country. Of course they had limitations and defects, both singly and as a group. They were sometimes harsh and stubborn, even pigheaded, though not to defend what was theirs but in fighting for what they considered better for the country, the church and the Society of Jesus. But this did not prevent them from living and working in unity, bearing each other's burdens, and supported by each other's spirit. In this way they were companions of Jesus and they fulfilled the mission of the Society of Jesus, the Jesuits, in the world today.

Why Were They Killed?

Now I want to try to throw a little light on their murder and martyrdom. A murder is darkness, but *sub specie contrarii* it throws light on many things. A martyrdom has its own strong light, which says more than a thousand words about life and faith. So I am offering these reflections in search of light for us who are still alive to clarify the reality in which we live and give us courage to transform it.

The answer to the question continues to be extremely important, because understanding who these Jesuits were and what they did depends on it. But not just this. The answer also enables us to understand what is going on in El Salvador and understand our faith, which, let us not forget, begins at the feet of a crucified figure who was executed by the powerful of this world. "They kill those who get in their way," Archbishop Romero used to say. And really these Jesuits did get in the way. There is no other explanation for all the verbal and physical attacks I mentioned earlier.

And whom did they get in the way of? Whom did they annoy? Their enemies and murderers used to accuse them of many things. They accused them of being communists and Marxists; sometimes they said they were antipatriotic; sometimes they even called them atheists. They even attacked them for being "liberationists." What an ironical and tragic distortion, to use a term that is central to the gospel—liberation—to denigrate a believer. In fact they did not mean anything particular by these accusations, they were merely expressing their total repulsion and fervent wish to see them silenced, expelled from the country, disappeared or dead. And remember that in this country even Paul VI was accused of being a "communist" when he published *Populorum Progressio*.

Others made more specific accusations: they supported the FMLN, they were its ideological "front," they were responsible for the violence and war, and so forth. This assumes, of course, that the FMLN is the worst of evils in the country and anyone who supports them is automatically a murderer. Of course for the extreme right, anyone is an FMLN "front" who defends the poor and tells the truth about the violation of human rights: from trade unionists who are fighting for their rights and the committees of mothers of the murdered and disappeared, to the excellent *internacionalistas,* men and women who have left behind the peace and comfort of their own countries to serve the poor in El Salvador—even to Archbishop Rivera and Bishop Rosa Chávez and the Archdiocesan Legal Aid Office.

The first accusation is simply false. These Jesuits were honest human beings and Christian believers, convinced that Jesus brought a demand for liberation and the way to achieve it, total utopian liberation. Of course they were familiar with Marxism, its useful contribution to the analysis of oppression in the Third World, and its serious limitations. But Marxism was in no way their principal source of academic inspiration—Ellacuría was an eminent and creative disciple of the Spanish philosopher Zubiri. Neither was it their ultimate ideology for transforming society, nor what inspired their personal lives. That was the gospel of Jesus, and from its standpoint they sought the best available scientific knowledge with which to scrutinize various ideologies and use them in the service of the poor.

The second accusation is not true either. This needs explaining in some detail so that the truth may be known about what happened. This is also to prevent the public from saying—or whispering, because hardly anyone dares at the moment to say it aloud—that even though it was tragic, they did seek their own death. (Things like this have been said in the past few years, even by prelates, when a priest has been killed.) However simple it may sound, what these Jesuits firmly supported and were really committed to was the mass of ordinary people, and nothing else. They repeated endlessly that it was not their role to support a political party or a particular government or even a particular popular movement. Their task was to judge them and support anything in them that helped bring justice to the people. In this too they were faithful to the words and spirit of Archbishop

Romero: "Political processes must be judged according to whether they are or are not for the good of the people." Therefore they analyzed and supported what was positive and just in the popular movements, including the FMLN, but they criticized what they thought was politically mistaken, especially purely militarist tendencies abandoning the social and popular dimension, and what was morally reprehensible, especially a few acts of terrorism and murders of civilians by the FMLN. No one who has read the UCA publications can be in any doubt about this.

Regarding the conflict and the war, I remember well that even in February 1981, after the FMLN's first major offensive, which failed, Ellacuría said then that the solution for the country lay in negotiation, words that the right regarded as treacherous and were not very agreeable to the left either. That same year, in May, the journal ECA devoted a whole issue to dialogue and negotiation. Although they were not absolute pacifists, any more than Archbishop Romero was, although they understood and analyzed the causes of the war, its tragic inevitability and possible legitimacy at the end of the 1970s, they were not advocates of war: they regarded war as a terrible evil that ought to disappear. They were fully aware of the good things the FMLN had brought to the country and scandalized the extreme right by acknowledging them. They were fully aware of the creativity, heroism, and love of many FMLN combatants. But this did not blind them to the evils of war, and they were never carried away in theory—or of course in practice—by what Archbishop Romero condemned as the mysticism of violence. With great human and ethical compassion, Ellacuría said plainly: "The way of war has now given all it had to give; now we must seek the way of peace."

Therefore they strongly supported dialogue and negotiation, especially in recent months. The university did everything it could to enable dialogue to take place by itself speaking to both sides. President Cristiani knows this perfectly well. Some of the Jesuits spoke to him several times in private and the UCA invited him to be present on September 19, 1989, when it conferred an honorary doctorate on the president of Costa Rica, Oscar Arias, for his work for peace. In order to make dialogue easier, they spoke to FMLN leaders, with some members of the government, and all kinds of politicians and diplomats, including some military officers, but they did all this with the single purpose of supporting a more human and more Christian negotiated solution to the conflict. So they had knowledge, contacts, support for the positive, and criticism of negative things, in the FMLN. There were also talks with some government forces, including support for anything that offered a little light in the cul-de-sac El Salvador is in, whether this came from the government, political parties, or the North American embassy, although obviously they remained firm in their denunciation of the abuses and violations of human rights committed by the army and the death squads, in stating the government's responsibility for these and denouncing unpunished crimes and the useless state of the administration of justice. They continued to unmask the dependency on the USA. So they were not a "front" for the FMLN, or of any other group or political project, although they analyzed them all and promoted the good, whether it was much or little, that they found in them. If they were a "front" for anyone, these Jesuits were a "front" for the mass of ordinary persons, the poor and oppressed in the country. And—this is the tragedy—it was for this that they were finally killed.

These things are well known in El Salvador. I have recalled them here in order to stress that none of the things they were accused of was the reason for their deaths. As in the case of Archbishop Romero, many other martyrs, and Jesus of Nazareth, the simpler and deeper reason lay elsewhere. I mean that those who killed them gave false reasons, if it is possible to speak of "reasons" for such an abominable crime. And of course these "reasons" had no ethical justification. But fundamentally they did not make a mistake, just as, in spite of what Bultmann says, the execution of Jesus of Nazareth was not a mistake. There were no just reasons for eliminating them, but there was a necessity to eliminate them. And this necessity—tragically—is structural and does not derive from the cruelty of this or that person or group. It is the necessary reaction of the idols of death toward anyone who dares to touch them.

There is a deep conviction in Latin America that idols exist in this world. Puebla spoke of them and also Archbishop Romero in his last pastoral letter of 1979, certainly written with the help of Ellacuría. Liberation theology has done what is not done elsewhere, and developed a theory of idols. As has been said so many times, but needs repeating because it continues to be a horrific reality, idols are historical realities, which really exist, which pass for divinities, and reveal themselves with the characteristics of divinity. They claim to be ultimate reality, self-justifying, untouchable, offering salvation to their worshipers even though they dehumanize them. Above all, they require victims in order to maintain their power. These idols of death were identified in El Salvador by Archbishop Romero as the idol of wealth, making capital an absolute—the first and most serious of idols and the originator of all the others—and the doctrine of national security. Then he added a serious warning to the popular organizations, that they should not become idols themselves and never adopt a mystique of violence, even when violence became legitimate. So idols exist, and as Archbishop Romero chillingly said, you cannot touch them without being punished. "Woe to anyone who touches wealth. It is like a high tension cable that burns you." This is what happened to the six Jesuits and so many others.

The UCA Jesuits interfered with the idols *by telling the truth about the situation,* analyzing its causes, and proposing better solutions. They told the truth about the country in their publications and public declarations. This seems such a good and beneficial thing to do and should be praised and supported by all. They said that the most serious matter is the massive, cruel, and unjust poverty of the majority. When, with every right and justice, these majorities organize simply in order to survive, they are repressed. All this continues to be true in the country, although both government and U.S. politicians refuse to recognize it. Their policies do not address this fundamental reality or seek a solution for it.

As well as making this fundamental prophetic declaration, they analyzed the situation and its causes in a way appropriate to a university. In 1971 the UCA published a book on a famous teachers' strike, which supported the teachers' cause. This cost them their government grant. They began to demand agrarian reform as the most radical and necessary solution to the country's ills. From then onward their enemies realized that they were interfering with the idol. In 1972 the UCA published another important book revealing, denouncing, and analyzing the electoral fraud in the presidential elections. This fraud made Salvadorans begin to lose faith permanently in a solution to the injustice coming from elections alone. In 1976, another important moment, when President Molina went back on incipient (and minimal) agrarian reform, Ignacio Ellacuría published an editorial in the ECA journal entitled "My Capital at Your Service." From then on he continued to tell the truth and objectively analyze the Salvadoran situation. He told the truth about poverty, unemployment, the terrible homelessness, lack of education and health, the truth about repression and violation of human rights, the truth about the progress of the war, about dependence on the U.S.A., and also the truth about the FMLN and the popular movements, their correct and mistaken actions and strategies. . . . And so many other truths. As another expression of this desire for the truth, two years ago the UCA opened an institute of public opinion, directed by Fr. Martín-Baró, which very soon became the most objective source of information about what Salvadorans were thinking.

The truth, expressed in a university way, is what these Jesuits tried to tell and analyze as objectively as possible. This was acknowledged by countless international institutions, many politicians, ambassadors, analysts, and journalists, who poured through the UCA to hear the truth about El Salvador from these men's own mouths. These visitors did not always agree with all their analyses, but everybody, with the exception of the extreme right, recognized their desire for the truth. So they were not spokesmen of any group or institution, they were spokesmen for the reality itself. If they had or recognized any bias, it was that they saw reality from the viewpoint of the poor. And if they told the truth so decidedly, it was because they were convinced that truth at least is on the side of the poor, and sometimes that is all they have on their side.

Telling the truth, communicating it in a way appropriate to a university, as these Jesuits did, or in a pastoral way, as Archbishop Romero did, has always been dangerous because the idols seek to hide their true face of death and necessarily generate lies in order to conceal themselves. Sin always seeks to hide itself, scandal to cover itself up. So telling the truth becomes an unmasking of lies, and that is not forgiven. The sin of the world, the structural injustice that brings death, is not only unjust but also tries to hide its evil nature, even pretending to be good. It may dress up as something desirable; it disguises reality by using euphemisms: "freedom of expression," "democracy," "elections," "defense of the democratic and Christian Western world." And the world of injustice and power, which brings death to the poor, creates a gigantic cover-up to conceal the scandal of the victims it produces, a cover-up compared with which Watergate or Irangate are small faults or venial sins.

So telling the truth does not just mean dissipating ignorance but fighting lies. This is essential work for a university and central to our faith. If I have learned anything during these years in El Salvador, it is that the world in which we live is simultaneously a world of death and a world of lies. And I discovered this in scripture. As Paul says, the world imprisons the truth with injustice. These Jesuits wanted to free the truth from the slavery imposed on it by oppressors, cast light on lies, bring justice in the midst of oppression, hope in the midst of discouragement, love in the midst of indifference, repression and hatred. That is why they were killed.

The truth they told was illumined by knowledge elaborated in the university, as rationally and objectively as possible. But it was also and essentially illumined by the poor. They accepted the prophet Isaiah's scandalous statement: the crucified people, disfigured and faceless, Yahweh's suffering servant, has been placed by God as a light to the nations. This is, for those who seek the truth, the option for the poor. This option is not just a professional option, required by the church and the Society of Jesus only of those who do pastoral work. It is a total option that affects every believer and all of us in what we know, hope, do, and celebrate. It is a total option for the church and for the university. This was the option these Jesuits made, in their academic work as in everything else. They believed—and experience confirmed it—that more can be seen from below than above, that reality can be known better from the standpoint of suffering and powerlessness of the poor than from that of the powerful. So their truth was made possible by the poor.

However, the option also means returning to the poor the truth that is theirs, and so they returned to the poor the truth the university generated, to defend, enlighten, and encourage them. The UCA made an option for the poor and put it into practice in various ways. In teaching they tried above all to communicate what the real national situation is—this is the major teaching material, the compulsory part of all courses. This is so that the reality of the lives of the vast majority of ordinary people—the true national reality and not the exceptions and anecdotes about it that are sometimes taught in universities—with its suffering and also with its hope and creativity has a voice.

The question that dominated any research was to discover the reality of oppression and its causes in depth, and actively to offer the best solutions. This was a great ideal, difficult to attain, but one to which these Jesuits devoted immense effort. They tried to offer models, with real possibilities, of an economy, a policy, a technology for housing, education, health, an educational, artistic, and cultural creativity, a Christian and liberating piety, which would make life possible for ten million human beings at the end of this century in this small, poor country of El Salvador. This was the goal of their research.

In its outreach the UCA opened itself directly and immediately to the mass of the people, through its publications, the numerous, brave, and public stands it took, through the Institute of Human Rights, directed by Fr. Montes, through the Information Center and through the Archbishop Romero Center in theological, pastoral, and religious matters. They wanted to help generate a collective awareness in the country, which would be both critical and constructive, and to help the poor. Toward the popular movements these Jesuits were very open and they strongly supported them insofar as they were the people, although not for their particular organizational line. Theoretically and practically they sought to explain the necessity, justice, identity, and purpose of the popular movements. And this was strikingly visible on the university campus itself, which never closed its doors to trade unionists, the marginalized, the mothers of the disappeared, human rights groups, popular pastoral workers, and others.

Where the truth is told, analyzed, and presented in a university and Christian way, this is a kind of university that the idols will not tolerate. They murdered these Jesuit academics because they made the university an effective instrument in defense of the mass of the people, because they had become the critical conscience in a society of sin and the creative awareness of a future society that would be different, the utopia of God's kingdom for the poor. They were killed for trying to create a truly Christian university. They were killed because they believed in the God of the poor and tried to produce this faith through the university.

Who Killed Them?

Who killed them? This question always arises when there are notorious murders. Archbishop Rivera has stated that there is a strong presumption that it was the armed forces or the death squads related to them. The report by the Archdiocesan Legal Aid Office (Tutela Legal) on November 28 concludes after thirty-eight pages of analysis that "All the evidence, taken together, establishes that those responsible for the murder of the six Jesuit priests and the two women domestic workers were elements belonging to the armed forces." It is difficult to explain, in fact, how in an area totally controlled and guarded by soldiers—who had already searched the house two days before and asked which Jesuits lived there—at 2:30 in the morning, in a state of siege and martial law, a large number of persons, about thirty, could freely enter the house, remain there for a long time, murder eight persons and destroy part of the building's installations, using lights, making a lot of noise and causing a visible fire, without being interrupted by soldiers in the immediate vicinity, and leave afterward unchallenged. Furthermore witnesses present have testified that they saw these thirty men dressed in military uniform. Indeed—ironically and tragically—the Jesuits stayed in the house to sleep—despite their fear, reasonable in the light of their experience, that a bomb might be planted—precisely because the area was surrounded by many soldiers and they thought it would be impossible in these circumstances that anyone would dare to make a physical attack on the house. So the conclusion as to who committed the murders is obvious.

But what I want to stress here is not so much who actually did the killing, but who the real murderers are, those who promote the antikingdom and do not want God's kingdom of justice, fellowship, peace, truth, and dignity to become a reality in El Salvador. It is a whole world of sin that has once more inflicted death on innocent people, people who worked for the poor. When they asked Archbishop Rivera who committed the murders, his reply was very straightforward: "It was those who murdered Archbishop Romero and who are not satisfied with seventy thousand dead."

This is the deepest and most challenging truth. It was the idols, the powers of this world, those who do not want anything important really to change in the country, even though they are forced to accept small cosmetic changes because the situation has forced them to. These murders prove that the idols are continuing to commit hideously barbaric acts and get away with them completely. It shows that there may have been a few changes in the country in recent years, but these changes come to a stop when they touch the idols. They tolerate elections, and in seven years there have been five elections, two for president and three for the assembly. They tolerate a few reform laws, which are gradually watered down, they tolerate pressures from the U.S.A. to control the death squads, they tolerate the millions of dollars that the U.S.A. has given to improve the administration of justice— that is, so that it can begin to function at all—they tolerate that the huge military and economic aid be made conditional, so they say, upon their improving human rights. . . . But it has all been in vain. The idols continue active and recalcitrant, committing ever more wicked crimes. Therefore we need to understand well who really put these Jesuits and so many thousands of others to death. We must not confuse the physical authors of this horrendous deed with the actively idolatrous reality in El Salvador. These Jesuits, like Archbishop Romero, have forgiven those who actually did the deed because "they know not what they do." But they never forgave the idols, but lived and fought to destroy them.

I stress this point for several important reasons. The first fundamental one is that real responsibility for these murders does not lie with the thirty men dressed in military uniforms who perpetrated the crime and destroyed part of the Archbishop Romero Center. There is an "analogy" in responsibility, and even though this is well known, we may recall it here. Of course those who thought up and carried out the crime are responsible. But many others are also responsible, to a greater or lesser extent, through their actions or omissions. Those who cause repression in El Salvador so that justice does not come to the country, share the responsibility for the crime. In the U.S.A. countless persons today rightly accuse their own government of favoring a policy that is incapable of stopping the repression. But it is not enough just to say these things.

What about all the governments in Europe and the rest of the world, claiming to be so democratic? What have they done effectively to stop the barbarities that have been going on in El Salvador for the last fifteen years? What effective words have been uttered by religious leaders, episcopal conferences, universities in democratic and Christian countries? What have the Western media done during these years, when day after day human beings are dying of poverty and repression? Through action and above all through omission, many human beings have ignored, hushed up, or distorted the tragedy of El Salvador. I can understand that for citizens of the First World it may be difficult to grasp the scope of this tragedy, because for those who take life and liberty for granted, it is difficult to understand what poverty and repression mean in Third World countries. Therefore they tend to ignore, fail to understand, and keep quiet. But perhaps they also keep quiet through an unconscious feeling of guilt. It is not possible to keep on living in abundance, having practically everything and wanting more and more, when many millions of human beings are dying of hunger every day. This whole set of actions and omissions is what causes the death of the poor and those who defend them. Therefore the question who murdered them is a question addressed to us all.

I am very much aware, and grateful from my heart, that many persons, communities, and groups throughout the world have shown solidarity with El Salvador, and among them are priests, nuns, some bishops, some journalists, politicians, and academics, many human rights institutions and many Christian or just honest men and women, who have given the best of themselves, their talents, their time, their possessions, even their lives for the poor of El Salvador. Now once more many of them have been expelled or forced to leave the country. As a symbol of them all, I should like to recall the four North American women missionaries who gave their lives in 1980, the United States' most precious gift to El Salvador. They have the eternal gratitude of the Salvadoran people. But for the others, those who are not interested in the poor of this world, but only think about their own interests, "national interests"—as rulers say—or simply want "a better standard of living," without being horrified at the increasing abyss between the rich and poor countries, the causal relationship that exists between the superabundance of some and the dire poverty of others, the freedom of some and the repression of others, for them these murders are a challenge, a call for conversion. For Christians, it is the inescapable demand required to place ourselves before this crucifix composed of the crucified peoples and ask ourselves what we have done and what we are going to do for Christ.

A second reflection is that these murders of priests and Jesuits occurred in the democratic and Christian Western world, as it likes to call itself, which invokes God. Indeed it says it invokes the true God and thereby defends God from Marxists and atheists. We should not forget that Latin America, a Western and Christian continent, is the continent where there have been the most Christian martyrs since Vatican II. More than a thousand bishops, priests, and nuns have been threatened in one way or another, imprisoned, expelled, tortured, and murdered. And tens of thousands of Christians have been murdered for preaching the true word of God, for possessing a Bible or the Medellín documents and putting them into practice. Given this, we cannot fail to ask ourselves what the Western Christian world's reaction would have been if these things had happened in Hungary or Poland, what an outcry there would have been in the U.S. Congress or the British Parliament, what might have been said in bishops' conferences and in the Vatican. But the reactions of the "official" Western world have been very slight compared to the size of the tragedy. It is because it refuses to recognize that the world cannot simply be split into good and bad humans, Christians and democrats on the one hand and communists and atheists on the other. It refuses to recognize that the dividing line in humanity is idolatry, which is present everywhere, among so-called communists and so-called democrats, so-called unbelievers and so-called believers.

At the very least, the murder of these six Jesuits must make the Western Christian world honestly ask itself whether it is as good and holy as it says it is, whether it is as human and free as it claims. The murder should strip off the mantle of hypocrisy with which it tries to envelop democracy and freedom for the few at the expense of repression and poverty for many. It should lead to the suspicion at least that wealth, national security, individual freedom for the few necessarily generate idols who produce many victims in other places, even though these may be thousands of miles away. The murdered Jesuits insisted on this to the end of their days, and I remember that a very short time ago we were remarking with Ellacuría on the absolute truth of the simple scriptural words: "The desire for money is the root of all evil." All those who seek to accumulate wealth and only think about living better and better, should look at themselves in the mirror of the victims of this world and see plainly the evils they are causing.

Thirdly I want to reflect on the investigation that is demanded when notorious murders take place. It is natural that those close to the victims should demand one and understandable that, in some cases, those for whom the political cost of these murders is very high should also demand an investigation, the government of El Salvador and the U.S.A., in this case. But we need to be clear about what demanding and pursuing an exhaustive investigation means in El Salvador. There have been seventy thousand murders and the only ones that have been solved—even then superficially and not in depth—are the murders of the four North American sisters and perhaps one other person. The case of Rutilio Grande, in spite of the promises of the president of the day, Molina, still has not been solved. The case of the five leaders of the Democratic Revolutionary Front (FDR), who were hauled out of the Jesuit school and killed in broad daylight, still has not been solved. The case of Archbishop Romero, although it has been investigated so much, is still notoriously unsolved. And if this happens in famous cases, it is easy to imagine what happens when unknown campesinos are murdered, thousands of them, sometime in great massacres, as in El Mozote and Sumpul. . . . And this despite the fact that many human rights institutions have given important leads on the culprits. Various human rights organizations in El Salvador do this. Among them, with admirable objectivity, are the Archdiocesan Legal Aid Office (Tutela Legal) and the UCA Institute of Human Rights. International institutions also provide information, Amnesty International in London, Americas' Watch in New York, CODE-HUCA in San José, Costa Rica. For several years the UN special envoy, Pastor Ridruejo, has also been doing so, and in his recent report a few days ago he noted a worsening of human rights and an increase in torture in El Salvador. In special cases, when the murder victims are foreigners, as in the case of the murder of the Swiss Jurg Weiss and the French doctor Madeleine, there have been thorough investigations by representatives from the victims' own countries, which have given more than sufficient information to find the culprits.

Nevertheless, in spite of all this information, with so many important clues and leads, the administration of justice in El Salvador has done very little serious investigating indeed. Moreover, when the first government junta in 1979 appointed a special investigatory commission, it resigned as a body a few weeks later, when the second military junta of military and Christian Democrats came to power, because as a commission they were unable to do anything serious and they had a well-founded suspicion that those responsible for the crimes would never be brought to justice. Certainly some members of the commission had to leave the country. And on other occasions lawyers or judges conducting important cases were also threatened and had to abandon them.

So what is the point of the investigation into the murder of the Jesuits? Hitherto investigations have achieved very little. Let us hope that this case will be investigated and the other seventy thousand too, of course. Let us also hope that those who are now promising an investigation in order to convey a sense of normality and democracy, first investigate why there have not been and could not have been any serious investigations in El Salvador. And let us hope they investigate why the vast majority of victims of notorious crimes—and also of course of the less well-known crimes—happen to be persons devoted to defending the poor.

Personally I have begun to be fed up with the very word "investigation." In our community when successive governments announced that they were conducting "an exhaustive investigation" into a notorious crime, we used to comment ironically that a simple, normal, rapid investigation would do because the "exhaustive" investigations never come to an end. Let us hope that promises of investigation do not become an elegant excuse not to stop the repression. And let us hope the investigation of this case, if it is carried through to the end and those responsible are brought to justice, does not become a cover-up to distract attention from the seventy thousand cases also needing investigation, and does not become that most bitter of ironies, an excuse for saying that things are getting better in El Salvador.

The word "investigation" has gone the way of other noble words like "democracy" and "elections." They say little or nothing, and are often used for the opposite of what they mean. Personally I sometimes think it is better that there should not be an investigation, and that it goes down in history that the murderer of Archbishop Romero and thousands of Christians was the sin of the world, the antikingdom, the idols. Because it is much more important to repeat and proclaim this great truth than to find out one day the name of the actual killer. And it is important not to let the idols and those who support them ease their consciences because, after all now, it is known who pulled the trigger.

My fourth reflection is necessary. If it is possible to kill with impunity these well-known and respected Jesuits, some of them with international reputations, even when it was easy to foresee the world reaction that is now taking place, the high political cost, international pressures, if none of this could hinder the barbarity of murdering six priests, it is not difficult to imagine what defense peasants hidden away in little villages and country districts might have. Practically none. Even though it is obvious, it needs repeating. Who in the world is really working to stop this from happening and demanding an investigation of the El Mozote and Sumpul massacres, or the most recent one, on October 31, 1989, when ten trade unionists were murdered in broad daylight? This time the names of the two ordinary women who were killed are known, Julia Elba and Celina; their deaths are being investigated together with the Jesuits'. But countless others remain anonymous and their deaths are not investigated. As the Lord Jesus said, if they do these things with green wood, what will they do with dry wood?

My last reflection is something that has often come to my mind in thinking about Archbishop Romero. Of course it is important for the country to solve his case if this shows a desire for the truth and acts as some check on future possible murders. But I often have the feeling that investigating his case, and now that of the Jesuits, is like walking around corpses without any interest at all in what these murder victims were in their lives or bequeathed to us. The El Salvador and U.S. governments are talking now about investigating the case of the six Jesuits. Let us hope they do it. But is it not much more important for the country to remember what they did in their lives and to keep their spirit present?

The poor of El Salvador weep for their dead but what they want above all is that what they gave their lives for should remain alive. Is it not more important to keep these martyrs alive than to investigate their corpses? Is it not much more important for the country to hold on to the truth, mercy, justice, and dignity for which they lived than to discover the names of their murderers? The latter is not at all easy, as we know, but the former is much more difficult and more necessary. Let us hope—dream—that one day the Salvadoran government, the U.S. government and congress act on what these men were in their lives, seriously study the solution they proposed for the country, recognize the truth as they analyzed it, acknowledge that without justice and without respect for human rights there can be no solution—with or without elections. These martyrs do not seek revenge, they are not even concerned with obtaining justice for themselves. What they want is that peace and justice should come to El Salvador, and that in order for this to happen we should follow the best ways they showed us.

These are the reflections that come to my mind in connection with the murder of my six brother Jesuits. It is important to know who killed them, but more important to know why it is possible to murder them with such impunity, before, during, and after the event. It is important to investigate the murders of the past, but much more important once and for all to stop murders happening in the future. It is important to solve notorious murders but more important to clear up the mass murder of peasants who die anonymously. It is important that justice should be done to my brother Jesuits in death, but it is much more important to keep them present by trying to keep what they were and did during their lives.

A New Idea of a Christian University

These dark and tragic murders reveal some very important things. There are idols in this world and they produce victims; there is sin and it produces death. But when as well as murder it is martyrdom—there have been thousands in El Salvador—it testifies to what is the most important thing in our lives. With death we tell the truth about our lives and by their death these Jesuits told the truth about what they were and did. And because they died a martyr's death, this also confirms that what they were and did was true. So now, although it may seem a digression, I should like to mention three important things their martyrdom throws light on. What is a Christian university? What is the church of the poor and liberation theology? These subjects are important, topical, and disputed. They need illuminating and here these Jesuits bequeathed us an important legacy.

What kind of university did they leave us? Above all, they left us a new idea of a Christian university for our time, comparable in importance to that of John Henry Newman a century ago—and also many models of this new Christian university. When I was speaking about why they were killed, I said a little about what the UCA meant to them—ideally, of course, but also in many of its actual doings. In a word, what they left us was the belief that academic and Christian knowledge must be and can be at the service of the poor.

They wrote a great deal about this idea of a new Christian university in the service of the poor. And although I have avoided long quotations, allow me one exception, a quotation from Ignacio Ellacuría's speech when he received an honorary doctorate from Santa Clara University, California, in 1982.

> The starting point of our conception of what a university should be consists of two considerations. The first and most obvious is that the university has to do with culture, knowledge, a particular exercise of intellectual reason. The second consideration, which is not so obvious and commonplace, is that the university is a social reality and a social force, historically marked by what society is like in which it lives. As a social force, it should enlighten and transform that reality in which it lives and for which it should live. . . .
>
> Our intellectual analysis finds that our historical reality, the reality of El Salvador, the reality of the Third World—that is, the reality of most of this world, the most universal historical reality—is fundamentally characterized by the effective predominance of falsehood over truth, injustice over justice, oppression over freedom, poverty over abundance—in sum, of evil over good. . . .
>
> This is the reality with which we live and have to cope, and we ask ourselves what to do about it in a university way. We answer, first, from an ethical standpoint: we must transform it, do all we can to ensure that good predominates over evil, freedom over oppression, justice over injustice, truth over falsehood, and love over hatred. If a university does not decide to make this commitment, we do not understand the validity it has as a university, much less as Christian-inspired university. . . .
>
> A Christian-inspired university focuses all its academic activity according to what it means to make a Christian preferential option for the poor. . . . The university should become incarnate among the poor, it should become science for those who have no science, the clear voice of those who have no voice, the intellectual support of those whose very reality makes them true and right and reasonable, even though this sometimes takes the form of having nothing, but who cannot cite academic reasons to justify themselves.
>
> Our university has modestly tried to adopt this difficult and conflictive course. It has obtained some results through its investigations, publications, denunciations; particularly through certain persons who have abandoned other more brilliant, worldly, and lucrative alternatives to devote themselves to making a university contribution to the liberation of the Salvadoran people; sometimes through students and staff who have paid very painfully with their own lives, exile, ostracism, for their dedication to the university's service of the oppressed majorities. . . .

For this work we have been severely persecuted. . . . If our university had suffered nothing during these years of passion and death for the Salvadoran people, it would mean it had not fulfilled its mission as a university, never mind displaying its Christian inspiration. In a world where falsehood, injustice, and oppression reign, a university that fights for truth, justice and freedom cannot fail to be persecuted.

There in few and lucid words is what these men thought about what a Christian university in the Third World should be. They arrived at this conclusion not just through theoretical reflection but also through historical experience of what a university in the Third World is. Therefore they were very much aware of the possibilities and also the danger of a university aimed at extending God's kingdom. Perhaps it sounds odd, but they were very aware that a university is also threatened by sinfulness, that it can serve the antikingdom, or more particularly, it can reinforce through the professionals it produces and through its social position the unjust structures in a society. Not only can a university do this, but it frequently does so and introduces sin into society. Therefore these Jesuits were not at all naive about the possibilities of a university, but critical. They believed that, like any other human body, the university and its specific instrument, rational knowledge, is also threatened with sinfulness, and therefore that a Christian-inspired university must above all be a converted university. Conversion means putting all its social weight through its specific instrument, rational knowledge, at the service of the oppressed majorities. This is what these men wanted to do and did: in a university and Christian way, they made an option for the poor.

So the final lesson remains—and perhaps it may be useful now when a document is being drawn up in the Vatican on Catholic universities—that a Christian university is possible in the Third World, a university that is not isolated as an ivory tower and stone-hearted toward the suffering of the poor, but a university sharing bodily in their suffering and hopes, a university with a heart of flesh. Another unforgettable lesson is that any Christian activity, including academic activity, is done in the presence of the antikingdom, which is opposed to it and fights against it. In the case of a university, this may take the form of lies. The lesson remains that—as always happens, from the prophets onward, from Jesus onward—stating and analyzing the truth means defending the poor and therefore confronting oppressors. The lesson remains, the most important lesson that was these men's life, that a university can be the voice of the poor; it can keep up their hope and help them on their way to liberation.

And we are left with the supreme lesson, that of the greatest love. Tragically, throughout history those who proclaim God's kingdom have to confront the antikingdom. It does not matter whether they do it as peasants, workers, nuns, priests, bishops, professionals, or academics; they are all persecuted. These university Jesuits were also killed for defending the poor. And if the magnitude of the attack is in proportion to their defense of the poor, then we can say that the UCA defense of the poor has been firm indeed.

Their Church

What kind of a church did they leave us? It is a difficult and even polemical matter to speak of the church today. The reader will understand that it is not at all my intention and neither is this the moment to enter into polemic or defend interests. It is a moment for sincerity before God and ourselves. Therefore in the presence of their corpses, I want to consider calmly the perennial and fundamental problem, raised again by Vatican II and Medellín, of what is the true church of Jesus and what followers of Jesus, who are members of his body in history, should be like in our world today.

At the funeral Mass in the presence of the six corpses, the papal nuncio called them true sons and members of the church. And he gave them the name reserved by the church for her finest children: martyrs. He is completely right, because they really were ecclesial. I have often said, sincerely and without irony, that although as is well known there have been many tensions between Jesuits and some members of the hierarchy, we Central American Jesuits have become more ecclesial in these recent years. The reason for this is that now we are more integrated within the people of God, we share more of their real life, we feel ourselves to be less elitist and triumphalist, more supported by the faith, hope, and love of others, especially of the poor, the people of God. We are able to follow Christ better, and make him present in history, as we are his body making him present in the world as a sacrament of salvation. This is the church given to us by Vatican II, to which we try to be faithful. Medellín stated very clearly that the poor offer the church the greatest challenge. The church cannot refuse to listen to them, it must live and die for their total liberation. In a word, the church must be converted and become the church of the poor. To that church too we want to be faithful.

This is the church the six Jesuits belonged to, which they also officially represented in their strictly priestly work. This, above all, is the church they wanted to build. In this church they lived and enjoyed themselves but also suffered. The church hurt them when it did not measure up to circumstances, when it looked more to its own interest as an institution than to the suffering of the people, when some of its officials lacked understanding and were indifferent to the suffering of the people, rejecting their best aspirations, when—incomprehensibly—they silenced Archbishop Romero. On the whole the Jesuits thought the church is turning in on itself, that little by little it has tried to silence Vatican II, Medellín, Archbishop Romero, the ecclesial base communities, religious life in Latin America. And how they suffered because of this! That is also why they were critical within the church, of course in a free and mature way, and they thought that prophetic denunciation within the church was a great and indispensable service to it, whereas adulation and servility—which are always rewarded—were grave wrongs done to the church. In a word, they knew they belonged to the church, they wanted the best for the church and, above all, they wanted and worked to build the best possible church for the Salvadoran people.

If I recall these things, it is because their martyrdom helps us all to clarify and solve a serious church problem, which is growing rather than diminishing. For some years now, particularly in Latin America, an old problem has resurfaced: What is the true church? We are not talking about it now in dogmatic terms, of course, but in operational terms. It is not very clear by what actual name the true church is officially called today. It tends to be along the lines of "communion" effectively understood as submission from below upward. Its "mystery" is rightly stressed. But the term "People of God" is discredited and suspect. This way of talking enables the church to detach itself from the historically lowly, the poor. Thus it withdraws from seeking inspiration from the poor, from the spirit of the beatitudes, the light that shines from Yahweh's suffering servant. Although such a church does some good to the poor, it does not make them central within it, or see service to them as its central mission.

On the other hand, in Latin America we have the expression "church of the poor," the church that makes the poor of this world central to its mission and shape. This church of the poor is treated with suspicion when it is called the "popular church," meaning a dangerous and mistaken way to be a church, in order to discredit or condemn it. We all know this and many suffer for it. We suffer because this church is often condemned by those who do not know it and are unwilling to converse with it. Above all, we suffer because it is not recognized or gratefully accepted that this church of the poor, with all its limitations and mistakes, is producing a great deal of faith, much hope, much love, and much martyrdom.

I say all this now without bitterness and with the hope that these six new martyrs, together with so many others, may make us all reflect. These murdered Jesuits enjoyed the friendship and respect of some—very few—brother bishops. Certainly they were intimate friends and close collaborators with Archbishop Romero and they often collaborated fraternally with Archbishop Rivera. Bishops like Pedro Casaldáliga have been in our house and felt at home there. Catholic bishops and bishops from Protestant sister churches visited us in the UCA and we conversed in a friendly and Christian way as members of the people of God and the church of Jesus, each with his own function and specific charism. But in some way these Jesuits were also seen as members and representatives of a supposedly dangerous church, one that was disobedient, suspect, perhaps even unorthodox. In their pastoral work as priests they were accepted in the archdiocese and some of them were invited, exceptionally, to give talks and retreats to other priests. But as a whole they were not very well regarded by many bishops in El Salvador and in Central America. Their ideas, their theology, their commitment were suspect. None of them, not Ignacio Ellacuría, nor Amando López, nor Juan Ramón Moreno—to name the three who were professional theologians—were normally invited to offer their theological ideas, useful though they were for the country's grave problems and those of the Central American region as a whole. One Salvadoran bishop, now retired, publicly accused us UCA Jesuits of being the cause of all the evils, including the violence, in the country. Through caution in some cases, through positive rejection or disagreement with them in others, these men who had much to offer the church were ignored and sometimes even attacked from within. They came under suspicion of belonging to the "popular church" or of exercising a so-called parallel magisterium.

Again, without any harshness or bitterness, I should like these martyrs, together with so many other Christians, to help us reflect on this burning Latin American issue: What is the true church of Jesus? In order to decide, we can and should use various criteria: communion with the hierarchy, orthodox formulation of the faith, and so on. But it would be dangerous and fundamentally absurd if other more fundamental and primary criteria were not also used to judge what the essence of the church is. Does not the true church exist when—as well as communion from below with the hierarchy—there is also communion from above with the people of God, the poor of this world, those really preferred by God? Does not the true church exist where, as well as traditional sacramental and apostolic practices, there is a determined effort to preach the gospel to the poor, to communicate and put into practice God's good news for them, solidarity and commitment to them, to the point of sharing their cross? Does the true church not exist when—as well as obedience and faithfulness to what has been handed down by tradition—persons are obedient and faithful primarily to God's will for today, even to the point of giving their lives?

I have formulated all this as a rhetorical question because the answer is obvious. We do not have to choose between the things I have mentioned, but it is important to stress what has priority. To serve the church and the hierarchical church is important for a Christian and a Jesuit of course, and these men always did any work they were asked to do. But we should not forget something even more obvious and fundamental: that the church is the sacrament of something greater than itself, a sacrament of the kingdom of God and the God of the kingdom. Our final loyalty cannot be to the church, but in the church to God and the poor, because God is greater than the church. Telling the poor the good news is the reason why the church exists at all, as Paul VI beautifully put it in his exhortation *Evangelii Nuntiandi.*

This produces tensions, as we all know, which we must endure honestly and fully with charity and hope. However, that should not make us lose clarity. We truly love and serve the church when, within it, we decenter it in favor of the kingdom of God, when we make the church a sacrament of something greater than itself, when it becomes a sign of God's kingdom and wholly devoted to the poor of this world, for whom the kingdom of God exists. This is what these Jesuits' life in the church was about, and the lives of so many others. This, although many will not accept it, is their greatest contribution to the church. This is what makes them awkward, of course, but their shake-up of the church is not to destroy it, as some indeed claimed, or to weaken or attack it. On the contrary, it is to help it become more the church of Jesus.

This church, as I have said, is commonly called the church of the poor, and pejoratively, the popular church or parallel church. I do not wish to deny that there are exaggerations or mistakes in this way of being the church, sometimes an excessive politicization or dependence on popular political movements. This occurs more in some of its leaders than among the ordinary Christians who make up the base communities. In fact, this problem has been discussed in some of the UCA publications with criticism of what appeared to need criticizing.

But this being said, even admitting the limitations and mistakes of the church of the poor, there is something that cannot be ignored and it would be dangerous and wrong to do so, for us and for the institutional church itself. This church of the poor is the most active and creative church, it is the most involved in the people's just causes, it is the church that does the most in the community to overcome the endemic evil of individualism, including religious individualism. It is the church that arouses the most hope to overcome resignation, that does most to unite what is Salvadoran and what is Christian, and certainly the church that generates the most mercy, justice, commitment, and love for the suffering people. If we are seeking criteria and want to know how the church behaves, we cannot ignore these realities.

Another thing that cannot be ignored is that this church has been ferociously persecuted; it has generously shed its blood and produced innumerable martyrs, who are the proof of the greatest love. And if the end of life is what expresses the deepest truth about life itself, it cannot be denied that in this way of being a church there has been much that is Christian. If so many have died like Jesus, it is because so many lived like Jesus. This is what is illustrated in the life and death of Archbishop Romero, the murdered priests and nuns, so many ordinary Christians, catechists, preachers of the word, members of base communities, and now these six Jesuits.

It would be tragic for the building of the kingdom of God and the building of the real church to take as a criterion of truth what is important but secondary, and to spurn what is primary and essential. We all know this but need to remind ourselves of it. El Salvador and all Latin America have given proofs of incredible faith and incredible love. There are countless martyrs in our countries, and if this greatest love is not a criterion of what makes a true church, we may well ask what is. Let us recall that not all members of the church have been persecuted; many have been favored and flattered by oppressors. The ones most like Jesus were the ones who were persecuted, those who, like Jesus, truly opted for the poor. And that is why the persecution takes no account of denominations: Catholics, Lutherans, Episcopalians, Baptists, Mennonites—all have suffered persecution when they served the poor.

Let us say in conclusion that these murdered Jesuits felt a deep affection for the church. Is this not the moment, in the presence of this new bloodshed, together with the blood of so many priests and nuns in Latin America, and above all in the presence of the blood shed by so many Christians in the communities in Latin America, to reaffirm the church of the poor? It is urgent and necessary for the good of the poor, and the church itself, to point out once more with serenity, truth, and justice the anomalous situation in which a church that is more committed and producing so many martyrs is suspect, whereas the church groups with little commitment are not persecuted at all and not suspect at all either. It is urgent and necessary that there should be dialogue within the church, a calm, friendly dialogue in which all are prepared honestly to admit their own failings, and in which all are open to the love of those who shed their blood. We owe it to them and on them we will be able to build a church that is a true communion and a true church of the poor.

Their Theology

What theology did they leave us? Let us say a little about liberation theology too. Clearly this is not the moment for a stubborn defense of one's own interest, but a moment to reflect deeply on the truth of things and theology. Let us not forget that one of the murdered men, Ignacio Ellacuría, was a well-known theologian, and so too were Amando López and Juan Ramón Moreno. They all tried to do liberation theology. In order to grasp what light their martyrdom can throw on theology, let us recall the type of objections commonly made to it, again not in a polemical spirit but a spirit of calm reflection.

As is well known, this theology has long been criticized and, fortunately, the first to criticize it were the powerful of this world. With great perspicacity—from their point of view—it was severely criticized and attacked in influential U.S. analyses, from the Rockefeller report to the two Santa Fe reports written by advisers of Reagan. It was also criticized later by CELAM and the Vatican in its first instruction, though it softened its criticism in its second instruction. All this is well known and I will not go into it here, because there have already been many replies, and Ignacio Ellacuría wrote an excellent, long article in response to the first instruction.

I would rather discuss here other charges against liberation theology, some well-intentioned, some ill-informed, and some based on total misunderstanding, more a reaction of self-defense against the questions raised by this theology. I think that this is a good way to get to the essence of liberation theology.

Some say that liberation theology is not scientific enough, that of course it is inspired by faith but it is uncritical and even naive. Others, on the contrary, say that liberation theology is basically elitist, an academic pursuit that does not reach the great majority. Many say, or imply, that liberation theology has now given all it had to offer and has gone out of fashion. I think that there is some or much truth in these criticisms, depending on the particular case, but they do not reveal the whole truth or even the most important truth about liberation theology. Certainly, they do not reveal the truth of liberation theology as practiced by these Jesuits.

The truth is that liberation theology must advance in all kinds of knowledge, in intellectual self-criticism and in its capacity for systematization. Ignacio Ellacuría frequently stressed this, and he was a thinker of genius who could never be accused of undervaluing the intellectual component of theology. In fact in the UCA we sometimes asked theologians from other countries to help us with the immense capital of theological knowledge they possess, the libraries and time, all of which we lack here. And remember a poignant symbol: the theological library of the Archbishop Romero Center was partially destroyed after the murders. We are very grateful to the theologians who have assisted us in all this, especially Jesuit and non-Jesuit theologians who have come from Spain to bring us things we lacked, including some of their positive and friendly criticisms, and who also came—as they kept telling us—to learn to do theology in El Salvador.

Having said this, we still need to ask which theology, among the academic and scientific varieties, has captured the essence of scripture and the gospel, God's word today for this moment of history, if we believe that God is still speaking today to creatures? We still have to ask which theology has given a response to humanity's greatest current problem, which is the spoiling of God's own creation through poverty, oppression, and death. We need to ask which theology has made it its business to combine faith and justice, theory and practice, which theology has united theology and spirituality—in the option for the poor. We are fully aware of our limitations and any help or criticism is cordially welcome. But it would be impoverishing and mistaken for academic critics of liberation theology to ignore its novelty and strictly intellectual contribution, its capacity to rediscover absolutely fundamental things about God's revelation, which have slept the sleep of the just for centuries in academic and scientific theologies, its rethinking of the nature of theological knowledge, its reformulation of the concept of verification of theological truths, and the like. Ignacio Ellacuría made an outstanding contribution to this work, insisting that theology should take seriously the signs of the times, so that theology should be the raising of social reality to the status of a theological concept, that theology should be understood as the theory of a historical and ecclesial praxis. (Personally I have reformulated this by saying that theology is *intellectus amoris, misericordiae, iustitiae*.)

There can be honest discussion about whether liberation theology covers many branches of the subject, and it can certainly be asked to systematize these branches better. But I am convinced that it offers us all fundamental knowledge about God and this world, which is really true, serious, reasoned, and well argued, and if you like, scientific. In any case, at least for brother

Jesuits who want to do theology, the theology of these Jesuits, liberation theology, shows that it is the most Ignatian theology in the world today, because it is guided by the search for God's will in order to put it into practice and by its following of Jesus today, the Jesus who was poor and lowly.

It is also true, as others say, that liberation theology, as a technically formulated theology, does not reach the majority of ordinary persons, who generally do not even know the name of this theology or of any other. If you like, liberation theology is done by "professionals." But none of this means that it is elitist, pursued by members of an elite in their studies and read by others in their studies too.

Liberation theology is not—directly—a theology for the masses, for the people, any more than any other conventional theology, but it is related very specifically to the lives of the mass of the people because it deals with their real situation, certainly their poverty, their suffering, and hope. Not only that; it also draws on many of the reflections and popular theologies of the communities. Those who do theology about this situation may be few, an elite; but the situation they study is that of many, the poor. Ignacio Ellacuría kept on saying that theology might be done sitting in a study but its starting point was not the study but the poor. The theological truth that is discovered from their viewpoint is returned to them, even though the forms in which it reaches them are not academic, obviously, but little leaflets, sermons, biblical reflections in the communities, song books, and so on. If the mass of ordinary people today understand a little better that what they are suffering is the sin of the world, that God is a God of the poor, their God, that what Jesus proclaimed was a kingdom of life and justice for them, that it was for this that he suffered the fate of the poor and was murdered; if these poor people feel a little more encouraged to work and struggle generously and nobly for life to belong to all, then, even if they have not heard a word of liberation theology, it has still reached them.

Lastly, it is true that liberation theology cannot rest on its laurels. It must address new problems, as it is trying to do: popular religion, the indigenous religions, women, ecology. . . . But what takes my breath away is when people keep saying that liberation theology has gone out of fashion. Of course, it is possible or even probable that this or that book or writer on liberation theology may be going out of date, and as time goes by all of them may gradually become so. But none of this means that liberation theology as such is not—unfortunately—very topical and very urgent, in fact increasingly so. Dom Luciano Mendes de Almeida, the Brazilian Jesuit who is president of the Brazilian bishops' conference, once said, "Liberation theology has put its finger in Latin America's wound." This was true then and it is still true today. Oppression in the Third World is not a fashion, but something very present and increasing. Latin America's wound is not healing but growing bigger and more infected. As Ellacuría repeatedly said, God's creation has not turned out well and it is getting worse. Today there are more millions of poor in the world than yesterday, and fewer than there will be tomorrow.

So it is very important to remember and hold on to the fundamental point: liberation is correlative to oppression, and oppression and injustice are still with us and increasing. Poverty is increasing in the Third World, the gap between the rich and poor countries is widening, there are wars—more than a hundred since the last world war and all of them in the Third World. Cultures are being lost through the imposition of foreign commercial cultures. . . . Oppression is not a fashion. The cries of the oppressed keep rising to heaven and, as Puebla says, more and more loudly. God today goes on hearing these cries, condemning oppression and strengthening liberation. Anyone who does not grasp this has not understood a word of liberation theology. What I ask myself is what theology is going to do if it ignores this fundamental fact of God's creation as it is. How can a theology call itself "Christian" if it bypasses the crucifixion of whole peoples and their need for resurrection, even though its books have been talking about crucifixion and resurrection for twenty centuries? Therefore if those doing liberation theology are not doing it well, let others do it and do it better. But someone must keep on doing it. And for the love of God, let us not call it a fashion.

Let us hope that the day will come when oppression, demeaning and unjust poverty, cruel and massive repression cease to exist. On that day liberation theology will be obsolete, and this is the day that liberation theologians are working for, even though on that day they will be out of a job. But while oppression lasts—and all statistics show that Latin America is getting poorer—liberation theology is necessary and urgent. It is the only theology that defends the poor of this world—or at least the only one that does so seriously. And let us remember that it is a theology that has martyrs like Ignatius of Antioch and Justin in the early centuries, which, as always, shows that at least it has been a Christian theology.

I do not want what I have been saying to sound abrasive, much less a defense of personal interests, which have little place in my thoughts at the moment. But I do want this to be an appeal for seriousness in theology. The corpses of the Jesuits show that this theology is not elitist but of the people, because it has risen in defense of the people and shared the people's destiny. They show that this theology has said something serious, even scientifically and academically. For let us not forget that what was most feared in these men was their serious and reasoned word, their theological word. They show that oppression—taking the form here of brutal murder—goes on being a horrific reality to which theology must respond. If it does not, it is in vain that it calls itself Christian.

Their Legacy

So what remains? After these reflections, digressions almost, I should like to return, in conclusion, to the fact of the murder itself and ask myself what remains in Salvadoran history and deep in the hearts of us who are still alive. I said at the beginning that for me this murder and martyrdom has been different from all the many others. On other occasions, at the funeral Masses of martyrs, together with the sorrow there was a feeling of hope and even pride and joy in being Christian. This time things have been different and the question that remains has been forced on me in a different form. In this case my answer is very personal, but I hope it will go beyond the personal and say something for everyone.

Above all, the suffering people remain and they have lost some of their protectors. These murders happened in a week of war that left about a thousand dead, countless wounded, many poor houses destroyed and the poor forced to leave their homes and seek refuge elsewhere, as has happened so many times in El Salvador. Others will have the task of political and ethical analysis of the responsibility for what happened, the rightness or wrongness of the FMLN action in the city during these days. And they will have to analyze and judge the reaction of the armed forces. But as always, what is clear is that a people remains who during this week has been even more impoverished, terrorized, and whose hopes of peace have been dissipated yet again.

This is the context in which I see the ultimate malice of the murder of these Jesuits. They have murdered men who defended the poor, and the poor are even more unprotected. And if to these murders are added the persecution campaign during these days against all the churches—something Archbishop Romero condemned—the meaning is very clear: the people are now more helpless. During these days Catholic priests have been murdered, churches full of people seeking refuge have been attacked, Archbishop Rivera and Bishop Rosa Chávez have been threatened and the Salvadoran government even asked John Paul II to remove them from the country. Many members of the Lutheran Church, the Episcopalian Church, and of the Baptist and Mennonite communities have been attacked and captured. Many priests, other Christians, and social workers were threatened with death, in earnest. Bishop Medardo Gomez of the Lutheran Church had to leave the country under diplomatic protection. And of course they have tried to intimidate and muzzle the UCA, the Christian university.

There has been, in other words, an attempt to dismantle the church of the poor, to take from the poor the support and defense these churches offered. Salvadorans know all too well what this means. During the years 1977 to 1980 they tried to dismantle the church in the first big wave of persecution, and we all know what an irreparable loss was suffered in the murder of Archbishop Romero, priests, nuns, catechists, members of base communities. . . . Little by little they have been recovering and now again they are trying to dismantle the church and its defense of the poor. This is the nub of the question and the ultimate malice of these murders: the church is left decimated and the poor even more unprotected. The murder of the six Jesuits has been first and foremost a great loss for the poor. And as has been said in the past, before the church made an option for the poor, the poor had already made an option for the church, seeking support and hope in it that they could not find anywhere else.

The pain, the doubt, the darkness remain too, and we must not trivialize it. We should not be surprised or ashamed if during these days we feel Job's desolation at God's silence and Jesus' cry on the cross: "My God, my God, why have you forsaken me?" It is not easy to find light and courage in this situation of repression and death, in which the poor are ever more impoverished and weakened. At least for me it has not been easy this time to say from the beginning the true and scandalous words we said on other occasions: "Martyrs are the seed of life"; "Let us give thanks to God for our martyrs." I do not deny the truth of these words, but I did not find it possible to utter them at once, and certainly not as a matter of course.

So what really remains from the martyrdom of these six Jesuits? I believe and hope their spirit remains, that they rise again, like Archbishop Romero, in the Salvadoran people, that they continue to be a light in this dark tunnel, and hope in this country of endless misfortunes. All martyrs rise again in history, each in their own way. Archbishop Romero's is exceptional and unrepeatable, but Rutilio Grande is also present in many peasants, the North American sisters are still alive in Chalatenango and La Libertad, Octavio Ortiz in El Despertar, and the hundreds of martyred peasants in their communities.

The martyred Jesuits too will live on in the Salvadoran people. Fr. Lolo will live on in the Fe y Alegria schools and among the poor who loved him so much for many years. I do not know how the UCA martyrs will rise again. I would like it if the Salvadoran people remembered them as witnesses to the truth, so that they go on believing that the truth is possible in their country; that they remember them as witnesses to justice—structural justice, to put it coldly, or more expressively, love for the people—so that the Salvadoran people retain the courage to believe that it is possible to change the country. I hope they remember them as faithful witnesses to the God of life, so that Salvadorans go on seeing God as their defender; that they remember them as Jesuits who tried to undergo a difficult conversion and paid the price for defending faith and justice. This is what I hope these Jesuits leave the Salvadoran people and that in this legacy they go on being alive, an inspiration and encouragement.

I should like the church, and believers, to remember them as those witnesses to the faith spoken of in the Letter to the Hebrews, and above all, as followers of the witness to *antonomasia,* Jesus, whose life is summed up in Hebrews as compassion to the weak and faithfulness to God. Translated into Jesuit language, may they be remembered as men of justice—the present-day version of mercy—and as men of faith in the God of life in the presence of death—the present-day version of faithfulness. I hope my brothers will stay alive in this legacy.

I hope too that when peace and justice come to the country, succeeding generations remember that these Jesuits were among those who made it possible. I hope that future Christian generations remember their contribution to creating a Salvadoran faith and church, that they are grateful for their witness to the fact that faith and life in El Salvador are not contradictory but empower each other. I hope they recognize that in this way these martyrs guaranteed that faith in Jesus was handed on in El Salvador. I hope, then, that in the future Salvadoran Christians will be grateful to them that the country has attained justice and grown in faith.

The price to be paid for all this has been very high, but inevitable. Today, when so much is said about evangelizing cultures, we should remember a deeper form of evangelization: the evangelization of social life so that society itself becomes good news. And for this to happen it is necessary to become incarnate in that reality, as Archbishop Romero said in words that make us shiver to this day: "I am glad, brothers and sisters, that they have murdered priests in this country, because it would be very sad if in a country where they are murdering the people so horrifically, there were no priests among the victims. It is a sign that the church has become truly incarnate in the problems of the people."

These words, so brutal at first sight, are far-seeing. There can be neither faith nor gospel without incarnation. And with a crucified people, there can be no incarnation without the cross. Ignacio Ellacuría said many times that the specifically Christian task is to fight to eradicate sin by bearing its burden. This sin brings death, but taking it on, gives credibility. By sharing in the cross of Salvadorans, the church becomes Salvadoran and thus credible. And although in the short term this murder is a great loss, in the long term it is a great gain: we are building a church that is really Christian and really Salvadoran. Christians have shown truly that they are Salvadorans and thus that Salvadorans can really be Christians. This is no small fruit of so much bloodshed in El Salvador, Salvadoran and Christian blood: that faith and justice should walk hand in hand forever.

Finally they leave us a cry to the whole world that does not want to listen, that easily ignores the cries of anonymous peasants, but this cry at least it cannot ignore. This cry is an accusation and a call to conversion. "Blood is the most eloquent of words," said Archbishop Romero. World reaction—even though I do not know whether it will be strong enough to stop the tragedy—have made many think. I am told that even in the U.S. Congress, tough men wept.

They also leave us good news, a gospel. On this sinful and senseless earth it is possible to live like human beings and like Christians. We can share in that current of history that Paul calls life in the Spirit and life in love, in that current of honesty, hope, and commitment that is always being threatened with suffocation but that time and again bursts forth from the depths like a true miracle of God. Joining this current of history, which is that of the poor, has its price, but it encourages us to go on living, working, and believing, it offers meaning and salvation. This is what I believe these new martyrs bequeath us. With it we can go on walking through history, humbly, as the prophet Micah says, amid suffering and darkness, but with God.

In El Salvador today there is much more darkness than light, and the question of hope cannot be answered as a matter of course. In one of the letters I received from El Salvador a great Christian woman wrote to me:

> Suddenly it seems that everything has been like a dream and I see all our martyrs going about their daily business. I am not worried about the fathers because I know that they are enjoying our heavenly Father with their robes washed in the blood of martyrdom, but I think about their families and all of us who are still here.

It is not easy to know how to keep on hoping and we must all answer this question in our own way. It seems that everything is against hope, but for me at least, where I see there has been great love, I see hope being born again. This is not a rational conclusion and perhaps not even theological. It is simply true: love produces hope, and great love produces great hope. From Jesus of Nazareth, with many before him and many after him, whenever there has been true love, history has gone on, sinners have been forgiven and offered a future, which, it is hoped, they will accept. Many human beings and Christians have been given that hope. And together with the great love these martyrs had, there are the faces of the poor, in which God is hidden but nevertheless present, asking us to keep going, a request we cannot ignore. The history of sin and grace continues, the history of the poor goes on, and so does the history of God. To keep going amid such darkness is not at all easy, but it is something the poor and the martyrs help us to do so that it becomes possible. It is something we owe the poor and these martyrs.

My six brother Jesuits are at rest now in the Archbishop Romero chapel under a big picture of him. All of them and many others will have given each other a warm embrace and been filled with joy. Our fervent desire is that the heavenly Father send this peace and joy very soon to all Salvadorans. I have written these pages essentially in the hope that the memory of these new martyrs may contribute to peace, justice, dialogue, and reconciliation among all Salvadorans.

Rest in peace Ignacio Ellacuría, Segundo Montes, Ignacio Martín-Baró, Amando López, Juan Ramón Moreno, Joaquin López y López, members of the Society of Jesus, companions of Jesus. Rest in peace Elba and Celina, beloved daughters of God.

May their peace give hope to us who are still alive, and their memory not let us rest in peace.

November 29, 1989
—*Translated by Dinah Livingstone*

Part Two

THEOLOGICAL REFLECTION

Chapter 4

From a Theology of Liberation Alone to a Theology of Martyrdom

Liberation and martyrdom are fundamental realities for liberation theology, and they endow it with a specific direction and *pathos*. This is true because in our time the hope of liberation and the drama of martyrdom are very real in Latin America, and—when we relate them to the kingdom of God and the cross of Jesus—they help us to recover the essence of the gospels. The importance of this theme is obvious: It confronts us with something fundamental and central, on which all theology turns. But for the same reason it requires us to focus on a few points, since it would be impossible to discuss the theme in all its depth.

To begin with, our main thesis: Although it is right to evaluate the ways in which liberation theology has developed the theme of liberation and martyrdom, in Latin America there is no question about the need to hold them up as central realities, and to do so intentionally, in the presence of political and theological forces that would rather ignore them.

In this presentation we shall reflect on that need, but to begin, let us dwell briefly on two prior concerns: first about the standpoint from which we are reflecting, and second about the precise meaning of the title of this presentation.

Prior Reflections

Liberation and martyrdom are discussed in different ways, in different Latin American contexts. Here we are speaking from Central America, and more specifically, from El Salvador. I want to emphasize that this place is above all an historical reality, something very real, a substantive *quid* rather than a simple categorical *ubi*, a true *Sitz im Leben,* and—without exaggeration—also a true *Sitz im Tode.*

A talk delivered at the II Encuentro Fe Cristiana y Cambio Social, El Esconal, Madrid, 20–24 June, 1992. First published in *Revista Latinomericana de Teología* 28 (Jan–April 1993), 27–48.

As a concrete place, this one is limited, but as a real place it enables and requires our theological reflection to emerge from, and invest itself in, real things. The oppression and hope of the poor, the processes of liberation and the popular movements that have carried them out, their successes and failures: These are real things. So, on the other hand, are the countless martyrs and victims: active martyrs, eliminated because they fought for liberation, and passive martyrs—the nameless, massacred dead, eliminated in order to terrorize the survivors.

In other words, theology has to do not only with *concepts*—philosophical, political, theological, biblical, or systematic—but with *realities*. Theology deals with the concepts of liberation and martyrdom, but reality gives these concepts a specific weight. Theology cannot use a remote, secondhand concept of martyrdom, or one drawn from a few real-life cases, as well as it uses a concept of martyrdom derived from a massive, inexorable, unconcealable reality. This is what we mean by the "weight" of a concept.

To put it differently, the theology of liberation was never cultivated as a fashion in Central America, but it also was never just an imported article, although many ideas, good ones, have come from outside and been received with appreciation. Rather, the Central American reality has demanded it, and continues to demand it. And Central American theology has not responded out of naïveté, but responsibly and lucidly. It reflects on the achievements and successes of the struggles, but also on the faults and failures of the liberating processes; on international solidarity, but also on the changing geopolitical situation; on the glow of martyrdom, but also on its blackness.

Despite all this—accepting the serious difficulties that reality presents—in El Salvador people have insisted, and still insist, that theology must be a theology of liberation.[1] Allow me to put it forcefully: If such a theology didn't exist, we would have to invent it. Because despite the current efforts of the first world to deny it, crudely or subtly,[2] that is the unanimous demand of a world in which oppression is increasing.

᛫ This is not to deny that a reflection done in Central America has specific limitations.[3] But we hope it can be useful, because what has taken place there is so intense that it can serve, we think, as a universal reality—as a paradigm of the way theology deals with liberation and martyrdom, and the path between them.

The second consideration has to do with the title of this presentation, as it was given to me, which implies some sort of change or movement, *from liberation "alone" to martyrdom*. I want to take it seriously, because I believe it helps us to deepen our understanding of both liberation and martyrdom, and also of the theological task itself. So we must ask what that movement or change means: a distinct step from one thing to another, a theoretical step forward or backward, a self-criticism of past naïveté, or a proud recognition of newfound honor. Or if it simply makes a virtue of necessity: "Since there is no liberation, let us praise martyrdom."

There may be some truth in each of these interpretations, but it is necessary to mention them in order to describe the whole of reality, from a dynamic and structural standpoint. It is not a matter of abandoning liberation in favor of martyrdom, nor yet of simply juxtaposing them. It is rather about complementarity and mutual clarification, because liberation is weakened if it is separated from the reality of martyrdom, and the reverse is also true. More concretely—and as a matter of principle—martyrdom has to be understood in its essential relation to liberation, both as the negative consequence of a liberation praxis, and because it endows that praxis with the positive power of light and energy. Let us look at this a little more closely.

In my view Latin American theology in general, especially in its first ten or fifteen years of existence, focused its reflection much more on liberation than on martyrdom.[4] But in El Salvador the two themes emerged almost simultaneously. This happened because repression, persecution, and martyrdom[5] were unleashed soon after the beginning of action for liberation, and theological reflection quickly began to look at both aspects together. It happened that way, not by accident but for two reasons among others, which were well expressed in the thinking of Archbishop Romero and Ignacio Ellacuría.

The first reason is an emphasis—in El Salvador more than in other places, I believe—on the theological and Salvadoran importance of martyrdom itself, and, as I have said, on the essential relationship between martyrdom and liberation. The latter was demonstrated in two ways. On the one hand, martyrdom was understood early on as something that must be thought about *a priori* in the liberation processes, because according to the Christian faith, although it is true that historical sin can only be eradicated by means of a power outside the sin, it also has to be done by someone willing to bear the burdensome reality of that sin which destroys and sows death. On the other hand, martyrdom—like the death of the servant and of the crucified Christ—was also understood in the context of its salvific power.

From the beginning the need to relate martyrdom to liberation was clear, but so were the benefits of doing so. That is what Archbishop Romero did at the pastoral level, in proclaiming the need for martyrs in a sinful world and pointing to the fruits they might produce.[6] This means that for Archbishop Romero, we must speak not only of a Church of martyrs, but of a Church built on its martyrs, making the most of their gift. The first—to accept that there are martyrs—is difficult, but not uncommon; the second—to make them productive—is a rare exception. I. Ellacuría did so in his own life and in his theology, by reflecting on two dimensions of the suffering servant of Yahweh: bearing the burden of sin and being destroyed by it on the one hand, and being light and salvation on the other. Already in 1978 he published his well-known work, *El pueblo crucificado. Ensayo de soteriología histórica.*[7]

The second reason is that Archbishop Romero and I. Ellacuría, despite brutal persecution and the high value they placed on martyrdom, never used martyrdom as an excuse to avoid the main point of salvation—that is,

God's will: the liberation of the oppressed. This is not as obvious as it seems. The New Testament shows that soon after the first Easter, for all practical purposes the paschal Christ was absolutized while Jesus' proclamation of God's kingdom was ignored. In modern words, Christ's martyrdom was absolutized (placing the emphasis on salvation as redemption from sin), while the liberation implied in the kingdom of God was ignored.[8]

In El Salvador, even with its high respect for martyrdom, that was not the prevailing perspective. It is common knowledge that Archbishop Romero worked for liberation to the end of his days; that was the reason for his active intervention in national affairs.[9] The same is true of I. Ellacuría, as shown by his theoretical writings;[10] he always said that salvation would be found by moving down from the cross toward the crucified people.

To summarize this brief review: I believe that we have always discussed the relationship between liberation and martyrdom, not simplistically but in all its complexity. We have not simply moved from one to the other, but used each to deepen our understanding of the other, illuminating both. Liberation and martyrdom, kingdom and cross, work together for understanding in our reflections as they did in Jesus' life.

Now we shall look briefly at the theological consequences of taking liberation, martyrdom, and the relationship between them seriously, at four levels: methodology, systematic theology, basic theology, and spirituality.

Importance for the Theological Task

In language that goes back to the dawn of Western thought, this section will portray the task of theology in three dimensions: Aristotelian, Socratic, and pre-Socratic. We believe that liberation theology needs to draw deeply on the Aristotelian or analytical dimension, and for this it must be open to and learn from other sciences and theologies. But liberation theology has also incorporated the pre-Socratic and Socratic dimensions in its efforts; this new aspect, seldom seen in other theologies, is our focus here.

> First thesis: To do theology means, in part, to face reality and raise it to a theological concept. In this task, theology should be honest with the real. Here is where the pre-Socratic dimension of the theological task comes in.

Facing reality. From the outset the theology of liberation has proclaimed that "the irruption of the poor," the most striking and "real" expression of reality, is what makes reflection possible and necessary. Methodologically, this means that from the outset this theology was based on the signs of the times in a historical-pastoral sense: as the characteristic marks of an era (cf. *Gaudium et Spes* 4). Then in discussing martyrdom, liberation theology has followed the same formal method: it considers martyrdom a sign of the times because it is a mark of our era. (Persecution and martyrdom were oc-curring massively in the Southern Cone of South America two decades ago, and later in Central America.) I. Ellacuría used the term "signs of the times" in 1981, to describe a reality very similar to martyrdom. The crucified peo-ple are always "the" sign of the times, he said.

But this theology also considers liberation and martyrdom as a sign of the times in its historical-theological sense: as the way in which God or God's will is made present (cf. *Gaudium et Spes* 11). This is of decisive im-portance in understanding the theological task, and ultimately it shows that doing theology means raising reality to a theological concept. Theology, of course, has need of other kinds of knowledge and tools (which we have called the Aristotelian or analytical dimension of theology), but here we see that analytical knowledge alone is not enough to discern realities and iden-tify them as signs of the times. To identify these signs in both the historical-pastoral and historical-theological sense requires something new, which cannot be mechanically derived from any method.

It is true that the realities reflected upon by theology are never completely new, and it is also true that in reflecting on them, we always, necessarily, use our prior knowledge to interpret them: revelation, theological history, and other kinds of knowledge. But no amount of knowledge can substitute for a direct encounter with the newness, in order to discern whether God is pre-sent in it or not. And facing reality in this way, with a certain degree of help-lessness, is the first meaning of what we call the pre-Socratic dimension of theology: having to face reality directly, in a sort of intellectual loneliness, without being able to cite anyone as an absolute authority. That of course was true at the beginning of the Old and New Testament, when the theolo-gians had to look directly at oppression and liberation, at the life and des-tiny of Jesus, at the history of the early communities. Today also, in order to recognize liberation and martyrdom we must find it in history, without looking to an earlier theological tradition for a definitive identification.

The inability of prior conceptual categories to recognize new realities. This pre-Socratic attitude is necessary in order to discern liberation and martyrdom as signs of the times, but it is even more necessary when, after all the work and struggle for liberation, the old and scandalous injustices re-main and painful new ones surprise us. In spite of our theories and prac-tices, history is still full of the laments of Job, the suffering of the servant, the cross of Jesus, and also the beatitudes and the call to walk humbly with our God, etcetera.

In other words, reality becomes what it will, and does not change its course to fit dogmatic manuals of any stripe; not even to fit the most lucid, well-meaning predictions. This has been true in nearly every concrete process of liberation, and it shows us daily that prior knowledge—no mat-ter how venerable, even that of the theology of liberation—is not enough to give conceptual guidance. Honestly accepting and acknowledging this fact is also necessary, and it requires a new kind of pre-Socratic attitude: We cannot assume that we already have the necessary categories with which to analyze the changing reality.

Honesty with respect to reality. Here we must add another primary dimension of the theological task: honesty toward reality. To move beyond liberation "alone" to martyrdom does not mean leaving behind the original intuition of liberation, or falling into pure spiritualism, martyrism, or tragic existentialism; rather, it means understanding reality with an honest attitude. The shocking thing would be if theology did not take that step, because it would mean ignoring a dramatic reality characteristic of our time, a reality central to our Christian faith; or falling into a dogmatic voluntarism of liberation, or into a view of the martyrs merely as a necessary and foreseeable social cost, which can be budgeted for the sake of liberation. This is a simple answer to the question, why should we make martyrdom central to the theological task? We do it out of intellectual honesty toward reality.

> Second thesis: The movement from liberation to martyrdom has not occurred only in theological conceptualization, but in the personal reality of the theologian; this shows that the theological task has been carried out Socratically.

In recent years, some theologians have turned theory into a praxis of liberation; for this reason they have themselves been threatened, persecuted, and assassinated. The persecution has sometimes come from the ecclesiastical power, but much more often and more decisively, from the oppressive powers of this world. In other words, these theologians are reproducing in their own lives—sometimes to the end—the theological movement from liberation to martyrdom.

Beyond the respect and admiration that they generate—which is easily granted—we must ask what this means for theology. It means that theology can and must be carried out *Socratically,* that is, with the immediate purpose of transforming the *polis*—and therefore in direct confrontation with the powers of this world.

That is the meaning of the praxis and assassination-martyrdom of I. Ellacuría. He has been compared to Socrates: "The characteristic mark of Ignacio Ellacuría's intellectual labor is not so much that he put the historic praxis of liberation at the center of his theological reflection, as that he made theology a constitutive element of an existence dedicated to liberation."[11] In the well-known words of Ellacuría, the exercise of all intelligence, especially theological intelligence, consists of "getting a grip on reality" (a noetic, meaning-giving dimension), and also, just as importantly, of "taking responsibility for reality" (the praxic dimension), and "bearing the burden of reality" (the ethical dimension).

This intellectual way of proceeding is what we call the Socratic dimension of the theological task: that is, facing reality directly so as to transform it, and with all its powers so as to combat them. Like the martyrdom of

Socrates, Ellacuría's martyrdom shows that there is a way to exercise intelligence whose purpose is to affect reality directly, to transform things and structures really. Thus the change that is sought, liberation, is not only one possible consequence of theology; rather, liberation is the direct purpose that governs the theological task.

To summarize: The three dimensions we have mentioned are clearly present in I. Ellacuría's theology. The first, the *pre-Socratic,* is expressed in the directness with which he faced reality, especially the suffering reality of the crucified peoples, without assuming that he already had adequate conceptual categories with which to grasp the newness of that reality. The second, the *Aristotelian* or analytical dimension, is expressed in his diverse theoretical analyses: theological, philosophical, political, religious, with all the Rahnerian, Zubirian, and Marxian instrumentation he brought to them (superficial readers remember him mainly for the last of these). The third, the *Socratic,* is expressed in his will to transform reality, to bear its burden, without evading the consequences of direct confrontation with the powers of the world: like Socrates, to be accused and punished for atheism and the corruption of citizens.

These reflections could have occurred, theoretically, in any context, but it is the concrete Central American reality of liberation and martyrdom that has made them both necessary and meaningful.

Importance for Systematic Theology

To begin, we must remember that liberation and martyrdom correspond to central realities of the Christian faith. Liberation refers in effect to the kingdom of God, and martyrdom refers to the cross (and resurrection) of Jesus. Each sheds light on the other. Kingdom and cross have helped us to understand our reality as liberation and martyrdom; conversely, liberation and martyrdom have led to a rediscovery of the centrality of the kingdom of God and the cross of Jesus. In addition, the relationship between kingdom and cross, liberation and martyrdom—not a substitution or juxtaposition, but a complementary and mutually reinforcing relationship—has helped us to understand each of these realities; therein lies an important and decisive contribution of the theology of liberation.

> Third thesis: Liberation and martyrdom recover and maintain two essential and foundational realities of the New Testament, the kingdom of God and the cross of Jesus;[12] the relationship between them strengthens them both.

The kingdom of God and liberation illuminate each other. It is liberation that makes it both necessary and possible to reflect on the kingdom of God. To summarize the basics: From the standpoint of liberation and the synoptic gospels, and for our own time, the content of the kingdom has been defined as "life with justice and dignity for the poor, always open to the beyond." The historical, partial, exclusive, suffering, and ecumenical dimension of the kingdom has been emphasized. The poor are identified as the addressees of the kingdom, but in a very specific way: those who are (a) materially poor, (b) historically impoverished, (c) conscious of the causes of their poverty, (d) organized to combat it, (e) imbued with spirit, and (f) endowed with evangelizing potential. Its theological transcendence is described—it is *God's* kingdom—but there has always been an insistence on making it historical through its transcendence: the unfolding of life with justice and dignity at every possible level, personal, social, moral, religious, spiritual, etc.

The theology of liberation has made this kingdom of God its central purpose, and believes that from that standpoint it can reflect on all other theological contents. Moreover, it believes that in doing so it can more easily resolve the two fundamental problems of theology. The first, which touches on its *identity* (this indeed is the christological dogma of Chalcedon), consists of maintaining the unity between transcendence and history; in our case, this is made easier because from the outset the whole is considered as a dual unity, God and kingdom, without division and without confusion despite the perennial temptation to separate them. The second, which touches on its *relevance*, consists of presenting the kingdom ecumenically— that is, in a human way—as a fundamental way of being human and being in history, offering hope to the victims and working for that hope, marching toward utopia and toward God, etcetera. This is a human possibility that can be refused, of course, but it can also be shared with non-Christians and nonbelievers. And this fact should not be undervalued: the theology of liberation is probably the theology most accessible to any human being who is even minimally affected by humanity.

The cross of Jesus and martyrdom illuminate each other. With respect to *the cross of Jesus,* there can be no doubt that martyrdom today has greatly helped people to understand the most important question: why did they kill Jesus? For us—in contrast to most people in the first world—reality is a great hermeneutical aid.

In the first world, hermeneutical principles are developed in order to bridge the historical distance that separates us from centuries-old texts, and from the realities they describe. In other words, today's reality is more an obstacle than an aid to understanding the past. But in Central America, reality often serves as a positive aid to understanding the biblical texts. This is certainly true with respect to the death of Jesus. Any Salvadoran peasant, no matter how limited in social awareness and in the ability to read and write, knows perfectly well why they killed Jesus: They killed him for the same reason that they killed Archbishop Romero and many others.

We shall not dwell on this, for it is obvious, but we do want to stop and think about something more surprising and important. The present-day martyrdoms help us to understand the cross of Jesus, but that cross in turn illuminates an important aspect of the present-day martyrdoms: Like Jesus, today's martyrs are martyrs of the kingdom of God. This on the one hand de-ecclesializes the concept of martyrdom; on the other, it Christ-ologizes and theo-logizes it. Today's martyrs are martyrs *in* the Church, but not *of* the Church. They are martyrs *of* humanity, *of* the poor.[13] And this has led to a series of important reflections.

The first is that in relating martyrdom to the defense of the poor, we are led—and pushed—to an analogous understanding of martyrdom. This is fundamental in our world, where so many human beings are killed violently or slowly, and we often don't know what to call them. In my view we should speak of active martyrs, those who have struggled directly against oppression, and who have freely and consciously lost their lives because of it. And we should also speak—at least as a *quaestio disputata*—of the fallen ones, who were not defenseless but lost their lives for defending the people in accordance with their conscience. Finally and above all, we must speak of the anonymous martyrs, the immense majority of the poor, who died innocent, defenseless, unjustly, in their day-to-day poverty or in great massacres.

The second reflection is that the massive scope of martyrdom has also led to a theological rediscovery and revaluation of sainthood. It is ancient wisdom that the most excellent death, the quintessentially Christian death is martyrdom; those who suffer it share in the highest merit of the Christian life, that is, sainthood. Certainly those we have called active martyrs are saints; they are like Jesus, they live and die as Jesus did, and they are the prototype of the modern-day saint. They have shown the greatest love, according to the New Testament, and in that love—as St. Thomas said—is the formal reason for martyrdom. In more simple words, our martyrs—Rutilio Grande, Archbishop Romero, and so many others—are the saints of today and for today, which is the important thing.

The third reflection is what to do with the anonymous and passive martyrs: children, the elderly, women, those who are killed simply for being poor and to keep them from trying to be anything else. Killed in their total defenselessness, without weapons of war, without even the weapon of public speech; in their total innocence, having done nothing bad; in their lack of freedom, often lacking even the opportunity to escape death. As we said, these human beings push us to look again at the idea of martyrdom; they also push us to look again at the idea of sainthood. These poor do not even qualify to be declared martyrs, mainly because they never have a chance to accept martyrdom freely; but neither can they cultivate the so-called conventional heroic virtues required for sainthood, because of the socioeconomic conditions in which they live. Their heroism is evident, but it is of a different kind. For most of them it consists of work, the struggle to survive, and the hope that life is possible; in many cases it also means the incredible heroism and commitment that they have shown in recent years.

There is no adequate word to describe this reality, but we like to call it *primary sainthood.* These words may seem odd to us who take life for granted, but we need a name for such people: those who on the one hand are privileged by God, and on the other are so poor that they have neither the freedom nor the heroic virtues that would enable them to become martyrs and saints.

We need to take seriously the sainthood of the martyrs: those who have died for actively defending the oppressed, and those who are themselves oppressed, who die bit by daily bit, or in violent massacres. This is so crucial for the Christian faith, that if recovering the concept of martyrdom were the only accomplishment of Latin American theology, it would deserve deep gratitude.

Martyrs of the kingdom of God. Finally, let us look at the mutual relationship between kingdom and cross, symbolized in a phrase that we use often these days: martyrs of the kingdom.

Let us begin by remembering that not every kind of liberation—not the purely spiritual and inward form, for example—leads to martyrdom; if there truly is martyrdom, it stems from a particular kind of liberation. This is obvious, but it shows the importance of establishing the relationship between liberation and martyrdom in order to understand them both. It also helps us understand a fundamental Christian theme: Not every kingdom leads to the cross, and not every cross stems from the kingdom. But when cross and kingdom are inherently related, then we can better understand them both in all their importance. Above all, what we learn in the most fundamental and radical way from the reality of martyrdom is that the kingdom is not built from a *tabula rasa,* but in the presence of the anti-kingdom. That is, apart from the horizon of the kingdom there is the reality of the anti-kingdom. It was thus in Jesus' time, and it is thus in our time. And it seems very important to reflect on that now.

First, as macabre as it seems, an analysis of the anti-kingdom shows us what the kingdom should be. Certainly the fullness of the kingdom is more than the overcoming of the anti-kingdom; but the historical journey to the kingdom in its fullness begins with the overcoming of the anti-kingdom. This was Ellacuría's special way of posing the dialectic, which today is still very enlightening and revealing: To understand what the *common good* is, he began by analyzing the *common evil.* He drew a similar connection between utopia and prophecy: Utopia begins as the overcoming of what prophecy denounces, and prophecy is the driving force toward utopia.

To put it graphically and simply, let us say that the killers of the martyrs help us understand, *sub specie contrarii,* what kind of cross the anti-kingdom brings and from what kind of cross the kingdom must liberate. For instance, liberation is needed from the death and torture produced by the military powers and death squads; from the hunger produced by the economic powers and oligarchies; from the submissiveness and indignity produced by the political powers and rulers; from the lies produced by the powers of the communications media; from the ideological evasion and justification produced by the religious powers; from the infantilization produced by the powers of entertainment, etcetera.

Second, the reality of the martyrs makes it clear that the kingdom is not only beneficial but truly liberating. To benefit means to do good, and that's fine, but to liberate means to do something good in the face of an enslaving power that is determined to prevent it. Jesus acted in a liberating, not only beneficial way, when he healed the sick and cast out demons, and when he embraced sinners marginalized by social and religious conventions. This incidentally is the minimal requirement and the *sine qua non* for the mission of the Church. The church must not only look beyond itself, evangelize and build the kingdom—which is hard enough—but also confront, denounce and destroy the anti-kingdom, which is even harder. Without this double movement the Church cannot honestly call its mission a liberating one. Without it, the Church's mission can be at best a beneficial one, but it will not be like the mission of Jesus.

Third, because the kingdom is not built from scratch, from a *tabula rasa,* but in the midst of and against the anti-kingdom (in religious terms the Evil One, the demons; in historical terms, the powers of this world), it requires a decision. Here is the true option for the poor, not only a preferential option (as people like to say so sweetly), but an option in favor of the victims and against their killers—which is not, unfortunately, a merely rhetorical way of putting it.

From the viewpoint of martyrdom and its consequences, then, we see the rock-bottom partiality of Christian faith and existence. Choosing and doing-against are not optional but necessary and fundamental conditions. Because Christian existence is partial toward the oppressed, it is automatically exclusive and oppositional. That is also why hope is against all hope, love against injustice, celebration against mere entertainment, faith against idolatry. All these things, in their diverse modes of expression, show the struggling, risk-taking, wrestling character of Christian existence.

This, we believe, is the importance of drawing the connection between liberation and martyrdom and making them central to theology, as the theology of liberation has tried to do. Other theologies have made important contributions, but they do not easily establish and maintain the centrality and specificity of the kingdom of God, especially its partiality toward the victims. And it's not that there are no longer utopias or crosses in the north of the planet, which would make it unnecessary to speak of liberation and martyrdom; the existence of victims in the world, and also utopias, is unconcealable. In this sophisticated world, taught by the masters of suspicion, we should at least be made suspicious by the existence of victims, so close to the suffering servant of Yahweh and so anxious to live.

Let us end this reflection by saying that when the theology of liberation is accused of economic reductionism, when it is urged to reflect on other types of poverty and oppression—ecological destruction, or racial, sexual, cultural, and religious oppression—we believe that what we have said about the kingdom and the anti-kingdom is a more than adequate framework in which to raise and seek solutions for these new problems. There is no doubt in my mind that the theology of liberation needs to move forward on many things, and correct others, but I believe it is essential to raise these themes from the standpoint of the kingdom and the cross. Until now, at least, no broader and more fruitful framework has presented itself.

> Fourth thesis: The reality of liberation-martyrdom has been considered in many theological treatises, certainly those relating to christology and theo-logy.

Christ: messiah, servant, and lord. Liberation, martyrdom, and the movement between them make clear the fundamental structure of the mission of Jesus (the evangelizer and martyr), his option for the poor, and his prophetic denunciation. They also make clear the process of his life, two primary stages separated by the crisis in Galilee, and his destiny on the cross, and have led to other important reflections.

- Above all, liberation has led us to recover the original importance of Christ's identity as *the messiah,* which was already disappearing in the New Testament. Early in its development—L. Boff's book was written in the early 1970s—Latin American christology drew the connection between Jesus and liberation, with important consequences. He recovered the earliest meaning of the title "messiah," that is, as a response to the historical hope of the people; thus in modern terms, the title "liberator" would be the closest equivalent of "messiah," "anointed one," "christ." For our time, this shows the connection between Christ and the hopes of the people, and it draws on the christological significance[14] that the New Testament attributed to titles.
- Today's martyrdom has also helped to recover the christology of the *suffering servant,* who bears the burden of sin in order to eradicate it. According to servant christology, salvation is urgent and all possible means must be used to achieve it, but it cannot come entirely from outside; he had to be incarnated and bear the sin that he wanted to eradicate. As hard as they are, these words are central to Scripture and to the whole tradition of the Church: "There is no salvation without bloodshed." They show that salvation and liberation must become incarnated, become Latin American, become Salvadoran.

On the other hand we also recognize the liberating potential of martyrdom, which makes clear—although it is not as clear historically as the previous case—that there is salvation in the cross. The martyrs show us the light: the servant is "light of the nations"; Jesus on the cross is "the wisdom of God." As if in a glass, darkly, the oppressors can see themselves and confront their deepest truth in the crucified peoples.[15] And more than light, they bring the energy that makes conversion possible; that attracts people to communion, solidarity, utopia; that makes life possible.

- Liberation and martyrdom, together, have also helped to recover—and not in a magical way—Christ as the exalted *Lord*. Martyrdom is seen in two ways in Latin America: as murder, in all its blackness and sinfulness; and as martyrdom, bearing light and salvation. Thus the martyrs are present and taking shape in history. Without a trace of spurious sentimentalism, we can apply Archbishop Romero's *resurrectional* words to many other experiences: "If they kill me, I will rise again in the Salvadoran people." By analogy but very truly nonetheless, the martyrs' presence explains the resurrection and the presence of Jesus. And by analogy but very truly, in celebrating their own martyrs, the grateful poor recreate the original experience of the Christian liturgy.
- Finally, martyrdom and liberation have led to new pastoral and existential appreciation of a *christology of the body of Christ*. This has not happened as a purely conceptual exercise but out of an immediate experience and discernment, seeing Jesus in the poor of this world. Archbishop Romero, after his life-change and conversion, wrote a pastoral letter titled "The Church, body of Christ in history"; that phrase was later radicalized by I. Ellacuría, who affirmed that the poor of this world are the true body of Christ.

We know from other words of theirs that these words were neither perfunctory nor sentimentalized. Ellacuría spoke of the oppressed majorities as the "crucified people," thus connecting them with the suffering servant and with the crucified Christ. And Archbishop Romero said in a homily about the suffering servant that Jesus Christ was "so completely identified with the people, that biblical scholars are not sure whether the Servant of Yahweh proclaimed by Isaiah is the suffering people, or is Christ coming to redeem us." And in strong words he told the peasants of Aguilares, terrified after a month-long siege by the army which included many assassinations: "You are the suffering of God, that we heard about in the first reading."

This christology of the body of Christ, so vigorously expressed at moments of martyrdom, is also expressed in terms of liberation—of resurrection, if you will. As the Lord's body in history, we must let him be the Lord; we must make his lordship felt in history. That happens when we—his body—reshape history in line with his ideal of the kingdom, and when we show by our behavior the already visible signs of personal triumph in liberation and in the resurrection: hope, freedom, and joy.

The God of life and the idols of death. The meaning of liberation and martyrdom for theology in a narrow sense is also evident. Here we will focus on three points.

- What to call God is a perennial question; it is impossible to name the unnameable, but we humans always want to identify God with what is most important. Liberation theology introduced such names as the

God of the poor, God of the victims, God of life. Scripture speaks in the same way: "You are the Father of orphans," "the poor find protection and refuge in you." In El Salvador, Archbishop Romero brilliantly paraphrased the famous words of Irenaeus: "The living poor are the glory of God." He also said it another way: "We have to protect the minimum, which is the maximum gift of God, life."

- Liberation theology also began the process of reflection on the how and why of God's revelation. It is by now a theological given that God's self-manifestation does not happen so much in an epiphanic way, as through historical action. What liberation theology adds is that this action is more accurately a *re-action;* not just any reaction (for example, against those who forget God), but a reaction against the oppression of some human beings by others. Through that reaction, God is manifested as the just and liberating God.

Despite all the differences between the Old and New Testament, this thread unites the historical expressions of the fundamental biblical faith in God. In Egypt, God hears the cries that the overseers' cruelty forces from the people. For that reason alone God stoops to liberate them, and by doing so, reveals himself as their God. In Jesus' trial, God sees the injustice committed against the just and innocent; God reacts and raises him from the dead, and by doing so, reveals himself as the one who holds power over death.

This means, yes, that the reality of God is love as the New Testament says, but we have to keep sharply in mind the specific ways God shows that love, so as not to dilute or manipulate it as has happened throughout history. God's loving reaction occurs simply because someone is suffering (God's mercy), and it is directed especially, preferentially, to human beings who have been victimized by other human beings (God's justice). The God of life is the liberating God.

- Finally, martyrdom shows that alongside the God of life and the liberating God, there are idols of death. In Europe, J.L. Sicre has rightly called them "the forgotten gods"; here we call them "the hidden gods." The important thing is that the martyrs and victims emphatically reveal their existence and their essence.

Idols are existing historical realities; they offer (apparent) salvation, they demand worship and orthodoxy, but in reality they dehumanize those who worship them—and what is worse, they need human victims in order to survive. That is what the martyrs show us, and the reason is not primarily to be found in psychology but in historical necessity. Archbishop Romero said matter-of-factly, "they kill whoever gets in the way." And he dared to name very specifically the Salvadoran idols of his time: absolutized capitalism and the doctrine of national security, and also the popular organizations, which are very dangerous when they are absolutized.

By unmasking the idols we also discover the theologal structure of history. What is immediately clear is that the mediators are in combat (Jesus or Archbishop Romero on the one hand, the oligarchs and the death squads on the other), and the killers are claiming victims. Behind them is a more structural problem: the mediations are also in combat (on the one hand the kingdom of God, or a just, loving, peaceful society; on the other a capitalist, dictatorial, unjust society), and the anti-kingdom is prevailing over the kingdom. Finally, the divinities are in combat (the God of life and the idols of death); the struggle is between the gods, and the God of life appears as a crucified God. . . .

Importance for Basic Theology

Fifth thesis: Liberation makes faith relevant, and martyrdom makes it credible. The movement between liberation and martyrdom both challenges the reasonableness of faith, and makes it possible.

The task of basic theology has traditionally been understood in terms of the reasonableness of faith: that is, drawing a positive connection between reason and faith. The theology of liberation has given a new focus to basic theology, more in terms of the relevance of faith than of its reasonableness alone. It has not rejected the traditional focus, of course—it has also contributed at that level[16]—but its characteristic task has been to draw the connection between justice and faith.

This is well known, so we will mention it only briefly. Liberation has restored relevance to the Christian faith, because in a world of injustice and oppression "it has touched the Latin American reality where it hurts," as I. Ellacuría used to say. To paraphrase Kant, it has aroused people—no longer from their "dogmatic slumber," but from the "slumber of cruel inhumanity." The first of these is important; the second, even more so. Antonio Montesinos spoke of that slumber—or rather, that nightmare—in his sermon at La Española: "How could you fall into slumber so lethargic?"

And let us remember that from a positive viewpoint, liberation theology has rediscovered and reaffirmed the practical dimension of a scriptural understanding of God. "He judged the cause of the poor and needy. . . . Is not this to know me?" says the Lord (Jer. 22:16). In other words liberation is a contribution to basic theology, at both the practical and the theoretical level.

The contribution of martyrdom has been to restore credibility to the faith. The massiveness of martyrdom not only shows the subjective conviction and holiness of the martyrs; it also enables us to preach the gospel to the victims. We can engage in theoretical debate about whether and why that is so, but in practice it is clear that the poor of this world listen to and trust the people who risk their lives for them to the point of martyrdom.

With regard to the reasonableness of faith: on the one hand, the martyrdom that ensues from liberation poses the greatest possible challenge to the truth of faith, and more directly, of God, not only in the traditional sense of theodicy—every innocent death is a great question about God—but also in the specific sense that the liberating God, the God of life, the God of the victims, is central to the theology of liberation. In the face of martyrdom, such a God not only fails to liberate the victims; such a God is powerless even to avoid their deaths and that of their defenders. Thus God becomes a double enigma (or in the words of faith, a double mystery).

On the other hand, we believe that by holding liberation and martyrdom together, we can better show the truth of the Christian faith—not in a purely conceptual way, but mystagogically.

At a purely theoretical level, our theology does not approach the problem of truth through a concept of God that tries to explain everything, or to explain it better than other religions or ideologies (as does the theology of W. Pannenberg, to cite perhaps the leading exponent of that movement). Indeed, historical reality—martyrdom and the victims—seems to deny rather than confirm the theoretical truth of the God of the kingdom, the God of life.

But at the practical level, this theology shows the way to "something more," something that is always open to question, but that stays there in spite of everything. In this context, God is not directly the whole explanation, but it is God who keeps us going in search of a whole. To be more precise, it is not that faith leads us with absolute rational certainty toward the best utopia, but it is faith that keeps our utopian path absolutely utopian: a path toward every kind of fulfillment (justice, brotherhood, peace . . .) and all of them at the same time.

At the existential level, we might say that our theology—without excluding other formulations that God is the force which explains everything, or which transforms everything—affirms God as the force that keeps us on the journey toward the whole, in spite of everything. Then the other formulations also become valid, albeit at different levels of understanding.

This understanding of God, as the force that leads us toward utopia, can be directly and historically verified up to a point. The alternative understandings of God, as the reality that explains or transforms everything, cannot be verified quite so directly. What liberation theology has done is to invite—require—the latter verification, not in a purely conceptual context but in the midst of an historical journey. And we believe that the journey is most intense when it occurs in a process of liberation, shaken by a love so great that it is open to martyrdom.

Importance for Spirituality

Sixth thesis: to maintain theoretically the possibility of liberation and martyrdom, and to move historically from one to the other, is to understand and live the Christian faith as a journey toward God, which is the essence of spirituality.

The "journey"—not only the expectation of arrival—is essential to Christian faith, and it is radicalized by the connection between liberation and martyrdom. It is not just a matter of accepting that all human beings are travelers, nor even accepting the call to follow; more importantly, it means staying faithful to liberation "wherever it takes us," without counting the cost or resigning ourselves to its impossibility. This is what identifies openness to martyrdom, and shows the most radical meaning of Christian existence as a journey.

We call this spirituality because it is the most radical way to "live with spirit." Micah proclaimed it in the Old Testament: "He has told you, O mortal, what is good; and what does the Lord require of you but to do justice, and to love kindness, and to walk humbly with your God?" (Micah 6:8). In the New Testament, the Letter to the Hebrews shows the true meaning of human life as seen in Jesus, the quintessential witness, the elder brother, saying that he became human (not just "was" human; this too was a journey), the high priest in the exercise of faithfulness and mercy. And in the gospels, Jesus walks from Galilee to Jerusalem—a journey that is not only geographic, but anthropological and theologal; and he moves from proclaiming the kingdom of God (liberation) to accepting the cross (martyrdom). Thus the liberation-martyrdom connection is one way, the most effective way, to recognize the path in Christian existence—which is itself, more than anything else, a journey.

We can of course debate the merits of defining Christian existence in this way, but we believe it is justified even at the theoretical level. Indeed in formal terms Christian revelation and the faith it inspires show us the path: how to live in history, which in turn leads us to "metaphysicalize" the beginning and end of that history. Of course the essence of faith is accepting that God is in the beginning and in the end. But theoretically, as Rahner once said about the hermeneutics of eschatological affirmations, all we know of the content of eschatology is what we know of the present, but "in its fullness"; and all we know of the beginning is that it is the etiology that explains and justifies the present.

And this is much more true at the existential level. In faith, we accept that our origins and future, creation, and fulfillment are from God. But in what we understand by that—what we can understand of the love and grace that are in the origins and are therefore originating, of the love and grace that are in the future and are therefore pulling us toward fulfillment— we learn that and come to accept it on the journey, in the "more" that emerges on the journey, in what—in spite of everything—we find of love and grace along the way.

To follow, from an anthropological and theologal standpoint, means walking toward God and walking with God in history. It is to this journey that God invites and pulls us, and this journey is spirituality. In conclusion, although it may seem simplistic, we believe that "those who walk toward God are seeing God." And that walking toward God—if it is like Jesus' journey—follows the pattern of liberation-martyrdom, of kingdom-cross.

All this is involved, we believe, in the discourse of liberation theology about liberation and about martyrdom. There is room for debate about the limitations and flaws of that theology, and about the new challenges it faces. In my opinion, the greatest, or at least the newest, challenge is to address and try to understand "the other," and to receive from "the other"—those others who are not only poor, but are above all "other" to us: Indians, African-Americans, the urban poor. . . . May God help us to face this challenge with a pre-Socratic attitude, without assuming that we already have the categories we need to understand its newness to us.

But this does not detract from the continuing need for liberation theology and its unique contribution. Most of it is in danger of being taken for granted, or seen as outdated. By way of example, I remember that some fifteen years ago, Hans Küng proposed holding a Third Vatican Council to deal with the new problems emerging in history: the laity, the ordination of married men and of women, etcetera. Someone asked Rahner what he thought of Küng's proposal, and Rahner answered: "Vatican III? It will take the Church another hundred years to fully embrace Vatican II."

The theology of liberation has a long way to go in its analyses, in dealing with new issues, in reconsidering its positions, in discovering and accepting "the other." But I believe it is still useful, because for the most part its spirit and that of Medellín have not been co-opted. It is not presumptuous to say that no other theology has done better at touching the world where it hurts—and it really does hurt—at defending the poor and the victims; at generating hope; at eliciting a praxis and expressing a meaning that are not found anywhere else.

That *pathos*, we believe, needs to be kept alive.

—Translated by Margaret Wilde

Chapter 5

Jesuanic Martyrs in the Third World

In the past thirty years, more or less since Medellín, many Christians have been assassinated in Latin America. Without prejudging their status in the official Church (whether or not they are martyrs in the canonical sense), the people have spontaneously called them that. They are also called martyrs by some bishops, like Dom Pedro Casaldáliga who called Archbishop Romero "our pastor and martyr" shortly after Romero's assassination; and by theologians, like Karl Rahner, who wrote: "Why should Archbishop Romero, for example, who fell in a struggle for social justice, in a struggle inspired by his deepest Christian convictions, not be called a martyr?"[1]

Archbishop Romero himself saw it that way. He said of the assassinated priests: "In my view they are true martyrs in the popular sense. . . . They have preached just such an incardination in poverty. They have truly gone to dangerous limits, facing the threat of the Unión Guerrera Blanca, where people are targeted for death, just as Christ was."[2] And we are still living in that situation. On April 26 of last year (1998), Juan Gerardi, Bishop of Guatemala, was assassinated two days after he presented to the Guatemalan people a report on the truth of the recent repression. He is a martyr of a people's memory.[3]

From this we can derive two observations. The first and most important is that deaths of great Christian excellence are occurring. That seizes the attention of the Christian people (and all people of goodwill), and rightly so, whatever language we use to describe those deaths. The second observation is that many people have expressed the excellence of these deaths by calling these Christians "martyrs." We could add other descriptive terms, such as "prophet" or "saint."

Up to this point the matter is simple enough. There are magnificent Christian men and women who have lived and given up their lives for love,

The basic ideas in this article appeared in *Jesus the Liberator* (Orbis Books, 1993), and more recently in "Die Bedeutung der Märtyrer für die Theologie," in *Reflektierter Glaube. Festscrift für Erhard Kunz SJ zum 65. Geburtstag* (Egelsbach, Frankfurt a. M., Munich, 1999), 199–215. It has been reworked and systematized for this monograph, first published in *Revista Latinoamericana de Teología* 48 (Sept.–Dec., 1999), 237–255.

who bring salvation for others and for themselves, and who therefore remind us of Jesus. But if we call them "martyrs," there is a problem: whether or not the Church will accept them as such. To answer that question, the Church normally refers to earlier concepts of martyr (in the New Testament, in tradition, in canon law, etc.) and ascertains whether or not the murdered ones fulfill the requirements of those concepts. At that point it is no longer a question about the *reality* of the murdered ones, but of the correct *theoretical interpretation* of their death at each ecclesiastical level.

Let us say from the outset that the important thing is not what we call those Christians; their (lives and) deaths do not achieve Christian excellence because of what we call them. Whether or not Archbishop Romero is canonized, and whether he is canonized as a martyr or as a confessor, will not change our understanding of him and his great excellence as a Christian. Four days after his death, Ignacio Ellacuría said that "God passed through El Salvador with Archbishop Romero," and I doubt that any more eloquent words can be used to describe Archbishop Romero and the Christian excellence of his life.

But since the concept of "martyr" exists, and since the people are using it, it would be good for us to analyze it. In a pastoral sense, it helps deepen the people's devotion. It will also be helpful to faith and theology, because the analysis is not focused merely on the canonical requirements for being proclaimed a martyr; rather, it is about the martyr's relationship with other human beings, with Jesus, and with God. As always, to seriously analyze martyrdom is to rethink God.

So in order to understand the excellence of the violent deaths of Christians today, and to be able to declare them martyrs, we propose not only to *broaden* the concept of "martyr" (although that would be legitimate and necessary), but somehow to *change* the *analogatum princeps* of the concept. The point of this proposal is to identify as "martyrs," above all, those who die in the same way Jesus died and for the same reasons. They are the *Jesuanic martyrs*.

The Need to Historicize the Traditional Conception of Martyrdom

First proposition. The traditional meaning of martyr (witness)—one whose life is taken *in odium fidei*, who gives it up freely and without using violence—dates from the first centuries of the Church. That is an historical notion, which means that it can continue changing throughout history.

From the beginnings of the Church, violent death for the sake of the Christian faith was generally considered the quintessentially Christian form of death; that is why the list of people we now call "saints" included only martyrs at first. That death was excellent because it gave witness to the faith, to the gospel. A martyr is a witness,[4] which is more than just a linguistic tautology; around the middle of the second century it came to mean "giving testimony to the truth of faith with one's own life."[5]

Later persecutions led, naturally, to deeper reflection on concrete historical situations; here too it is history that inspires thought, rather than a timeless, predefined concept of what "martyrdom" might be. But it is important to note that from the outset martyrdom was not seen as something unexpected, but as historically necessary, a consequence of the specific, inherent conflictiveness of the Christian faith. In the first writing of the New Testament, we read: "Indeed, you yourselves know that this is what we are destined for. . . that we were to suffer persecution" (I Thessalonians 3:2–4). The New Testament also, in various ways, gives the theologal reason for that conflictiveness: "No one can serve two masters" (Matthew 6:24); "there are many gods and many lords—yet for us there is one God . . . and one Lord, Jesus Christ" (I Corinthians 8:6). The roots of martyrdom were already visible in the background of the dialectical and conflictive dimension of the faith.[6]

The excellence of martyrdom began to be formulated, gradually, in terms of the positive and insuperable relationship that the martyr achieves with God, with Christ, and with other human beings. Thus from a *christological* perspective, martyrdom was understood as a way of sharing in Christ's destiny: his death, obviously, and also his resurrection. From a *theologal* perspective, martyrdom was variously understood as the highest expression of love for God, and as the maximum expression of God's grace. From the perspective of *Christian praxis*, it was considered the maximum expression of love for the neighbor. And from a *soteriological* perspective, it was seen as effectively offering salvation to the martyrs' survivors. In short, understanding and appreciation for martyrdom gradually developed in complexity and richness.

We should emphasize that these are historical reflections on martyrdom. They are ways of conceptualizing the fundamental intuition of the Christian excellence of such deaths. But as has happened with many other theological conceptualizations, here too a single, precise, and even canonical notion of martyrdom was imposed, absolutized, and maintained right up to the present. So the prevailing official definition[7] of martyrdom can be described as follows: "the free and patient acceptance of death *for the faith* (including the moral teaching of the faith), as a whole or with respect to a specific doctrine (as part of the totality of the faith).[8] Taken together, as the catechism of the Catholic Church affirms, martyrdom is seen as "the supreme testimony to the truth of the faith, until death,"[9] death that is inflicted specifically out of *odium fidei*.

So martyrdom has been understood as witnessing to the truth; this is a viable and useful way of expressing the excellence of this type of death. But it is, we would now insist, only *one* way of understanding the excellence of the violent death that Christians may suffer. As an understanding, it can and should be updated and broadened; not to do so would lead to limitations and even absurdities, as Rahner noted in the article quoted above. María Goretti, murdered for defending purity in 1902, was canonized a martyr only after the official definition was broadened: In addition to the elements of death for witnessing to the faith and *odium fidei* as the cause, it now includes witnessing through moral conduct. Conversely, a failure to broaden the official definition led to the surprising canonization of Maximilian Kolbe as a confessor but not as a martyr.[10]

We believe we are facing the same situation today. In recent years a large number of Christians have been assassinated in Latin America and throughout the Third World, for being—to use a broad generalization—"followers of Jesus unto death." The people recognize them as martyrs, but they are not necessarily martyrs under the canons. This anomaly can only be overcome by broadening the concept of martyrdom, making it more analogous. Not only that, but we see a need to change the *analogatum princeps* of martyrdom. This is not mainly an academic problem, but an historical and existential one. It is not about shaping the reality to fit a prior concept, but quite the opposite: It is about the concept doing justice to the reality.[11]

The "Jesuanic" Conception of Martyrdom

Second proposition. The violent death of many Christians, especially in the Third World, has led to a rethinking of the meaning of martyrdom. Martyrs are those who follow Jesus in the things that matter, live in dedication to the cause of Jesus, and die for the same reasons that Jesus died. They are the "Jesuanic" martyrs.

Let us begin with an obvious fact. In Latin America, many Christians have lived a way of life and, especially, a praxis like that of Jesus. They have proclaimed the gospel of a kingdom for the poor, and have prophetically denounced the anti-kingdom that oppresses and represses the poor. This indeed is the great historical difference in comparison with other ways of being Christian, which have also led to martyrdom in other times and places. In principle, they have done it all out of love for the poor, God's privileged ones. In life they were like Jesus *in this way,* and like Jesus, they were killed *for this reason.* In this interpretation, the martyr is the person who dies as Jesus died because his or her life, love, and praxis were structurally—in different degrees, of course—like those of Jesus. In other words, the necessary material condition for martyrdom is a violent death, but the formal condition is that such a death must be, in some way, an *expression* and (without falling into sterile casuistry) the *culmination* of a praxis of defending and loving the poor and oppressed, as Jesus' death was.

This means that these Christians today are not, formally and historically, killed out of an explicit *odium fidei,* nor because they publicly professed a faith or doctrine in opposition to other religious faiths or atheistic ideologies or churches, as normally happened in the past. On the contrary, the people who kill Christians today in Latin America are baptized, they think of themselves as Christians, and sometimes they even justify the assassinations as a defense of the Christian faith.[12] Thus *odium fidei,* the main cause associated with martyrdom, is not explicitly present in these martyrdoms, although rejection of the God of justice, of the poor, of the victims, is always implicitly present.

But there is another, more important difference. In the martyrdom we describe as Jesuanic, we see the martyr in a different relationship with Christ: The Jesuanic martyrs are not only, or even mainly, those who die *for* Christ or *because of Christ,* but those who die *like* Jesus and *for Jesus' cause.* Thus martyrdom is not only death in faithfulness to some mandate or demand of Christ (a doctrine or commandment), which hypothetically could be different from the reality of Jesus of Nazareth, even an arbitrary demand. Martyrdom, rather, is a faithful reproduction of Jesus' death and the events that led to it. It follows that an affinity with the life and death of Jesus is essential to martyrdom, and helps bridge any possible distance in the martyr's relationship to Jesus. What makes one a martyr is following Jesus, commitment to the cause of the kingdom of God, and faithfulness to God's demands to the very end, more than the practice of specific virtues.

We believe that the assassinated Christians' "resemblance to Jesus in life and in death"[13] requires us to redefine martyrdom in Latin America. It also requires a decisive methodological change (making it consistent with Latin American christologies, which take Jesus of Nazareth as their starting point): A martyr's death has to be understood in the context of the death of Jesus. And that is what has happened. L. Boff describes "Jesus Christ as the original sacrament of martyrdom."[14] This methodological choice also leads to some changes in the traditional concept of martyrdom. One of these is to accept an alternate formulation of *odium fidei* as *odium iustitiae* (which is also consistent with Jesus' praxis).[15]

The important thing is this conclusion: What enables us to declare the excellence of the death of the assassinated Christians in our time is that it is like the death of Jesus. And what enables and requires us to call them martyrs is that we understand Jesus' death as a martyr's death. From this perspective, the analysis of contemporary martyrdom should not begin with—let alone center on—an analysis of the word *martyr,* which means witness; rather it should be an analysis of the *reality* of "faithfully following" Jesus, of "being like" Jesus. This is already expressed, with varying degrees of clarity, in the New Testament.

The gospel of Matthew speaks several times of persecution and death for the followers of Jesus, and the reason for that is in *the reality of Jesus himself:* his followers will be persecuted for his sake, for being and doing like Jesus. "And you will be hated for my name" (Matthew 10:22). "Then they will hand you over to be tortured and will put you to death, and you will be hated by all nations because of my name" (Matthew 24:9). "Blessed are you when people revile you and persecute you . . . on my account" (Matthew 5:11). That "on my account," on the one hand, personalizes the reason for persecution and martyrdom, but it also—and more importantly—refers back to Jesus' cause: proclaiming the kingdom and denouncing the anti-kingdom. We must not forget that Jesus himself sent his followers on a mission like his, to proclaim the kingdom, to cast out demons, and for that he warns them that they will suffer persecution (Matthew 10:16). My point here is that our understanding of martyrdom must break through a certain "distance" from Jesus, a distance that does not disappear simply by affirming that one is witnessing to Christ. To bridge the distance we need to affirm the "affinity" of the martyr with Jesus, that he or she is "like Jesus."

John's theology says the same thing in different words, and perhaps in greater depth. Jesus clearly describes what will happen to faithful followers: "They will put you out of synagogues. Indeed, an hour is coming when those who kill you will think that by doing so they are offering worship to God. . . . But I have said these things to you so that when their hour comes you may remember that I told you about them" (John 16:1–4). And he clearly explains the reason: "If the world hates you, be aware that it hated me before it hated you" (John 15:18). Putting it even more clearly, Jesus says: "'Servants are not greater than their master.' If they persecuted me, they will persecute you" (John 15:20).

In addition to its emphasis on being like Jesus as a cause of persecution, Johannine theology developed another tradition regarding the Christian excellence of death: "to lay down one's life for one's friends" (John 15:13; cf. I John 3:16). (St. Thomas also referred to this in his own understanding of martyrdom: Love is the formal element that bestows excellence on martyrdom.)[16] This, it seems to us, anticipates and makes explicit the two fundamental elements of today's "Jesuanic" martyrs. One is that they loved and defended their brothers and sisters, the poor. The other is that they acted on that love and carried out that defense of the poor in the same way that Jesus of Nazareth did.

These brief reflections lead to the conclusion that the persecution and death that will come upon Christians are fundamentally caused by their "being like Jesus," imitating his life and his praxis. In this sense, death comes upon the followers of Jesus when they take on the essential dynamism of his life. Putting it as simply as possible: (1) Jesus is murdered because he gets in the way; (2) Jesus gets in the way because he attacks the oppressors; (3) Jesus attacks the oppressors in order to defend the poor; and (4) Jesus defends the poor—to the end—because he loves them.

Yes, Jesus is a "witness," witness to the truth (John 18:37). But in the logic of his existence, prior to being a witness he is a "prophet" against the oppressors, and prior to that he is a "defender" of the poor, because he loves them. In judicial terms, Jesus gives testimony (he is a *martyr*) to God's preferential, free love of the poor. But he gives that testimony, above all, by *making that love real* and by *making real* his defense of the poor. In this sense—although our choice of words is not the most important thing—to fully describe the Jesuanic martyrs we should call them "defenders" of the poor before we call them "witnesses." Jesus is the good shepherd who defends the sheep: he does not leave them, as the hired hand does, but lays down his life for them.

Jesus witnesses by his death, but they do not kill him for being a witness; they kill him for being a prophet and defender of the poor. We are not denying that the language of "witness" can include "being like Jesus," but it does not do it justice. We also are not separating the element of "testifying to the truth" from that of "laying down one's life for one's friends." But strictly speaking, they are not identical. And conceptually, the idea of martyrdom has evolved in the direction of testifying to the truth, than of laying down one's life for one's friends.

In order to turn it back toward the Jesuanic element of love, let us remember how Johannine theology unifies and prioritizes the duality expressed in the double line of life and truth: *charis kai aletheia,* grace (life) and truth. They both go together, but *charis* (life) takes precedence. The same is true in reverse: the devil is a murderer (against life) and a liar (against truth)—in that order (John 8:44).[17] In the same way, we can say that the martyr is a "defender of life" (defender of the poor) and a "witness to the truth," but in that order.

The name we have given to this understanding of martyrdom, as the kind that happened to Jesus, is "Jesuanic." Objectively—although there is no need to separate the two kinds—there is more Jesuanic reality in dying because one lived like Jesus, than in dying because one has confessed Jesus as the Christ. To recognize this type does not detract from the fact that there can be different historical forms of martyrdom, in different times and places: that of María Goretti, mentioned above; of St. Andrés Bobola, horribly martyred in the seventeenth century for maintaining his ties to the Catholic Church; of those who refused to offer sacrifice to Caesar in the first three centuries. That is why we insist that martyrdom is analogous. And it certainly does not detract from the subjective holiness of the different types of martyr, nor does it establish degrees of holiness among them.[18] But it does underline something that we consider important: There is a "Jesuanic" type of martyrdom; that type is "more like" the historical form of Jesus' death and its causes; and that type of martyrdom is especially abundant in modern Latin America and the Third World (but let us not forget Martin Luther King and Gandhi).[19]

The Jesuanic Martyrs and Theology

Third proposition. The Jesuanic martyrs are a clear sign of the times, although theology, in general, has not taken them into consideration. But these martyrs are a source of theological knowledge; they contribute a certain spirit and a basic conceptual content to theological activity.

A Paradox Worth Thinking About

The Jesuanic martyrs are massively and unconcealably present in the Third World, and therefore constitute an obvious sign of the times in the historical-pastoral meaning of that term (cf. *Gaudium et Spes,* 4). Together with the reality of "the crucified peoples," martyrdom distinguishes our age both temporally and quantitatively: it is happening now, massively, which was not true before. And above all, it distinguishes our age qualitatively: in these martyrdoms reality has spoken a final word, not only with superficial changes, but with life and death, the horror of sin and the fascination of grace.

But the Jesuanic martyrs and the crucified peoples are practically not present, except in liberation theology and a few others,[20] which leads to three questions. The first, general question is whether today's theology—even progressive theology—is taking into account the signs of the times in its own activity, as *intellectus veritatis.* The second is more concrete: whether it is taking into account the undeniable sign of the times, the martyrs. And since that is in fact not happening as it should, a third question arises: whether paradigm shifts have already made the martyrs obsolete, a subject for historical investigation and for piety, but not for theoretical consideration—as if theology had more important concerns than the martyrs and crucified peoples. In that sense, Pedro Casaldáliga's lament has become a classic: "Some people believe it is time for a change of paradigms. They even think that the martyrs are a distraction for postmodern or postmilitant memory."[21]

One might perhaps object that some theologians do occasionally mention the subject by talking, if not about the Jesuanic martyrs, at least about the crucified people. For years people have been asking "whether and how it is possible to do theology after Auschwitz," a challenge raised by visionary pioneers like Metz and Moltmann. But in reality, even Auschwitz seems not to be very present in today's theology, and when it is mentioned, the accent tends to fall on the word "after." Moreover, to focus on Auschwitz—a barbarity that occurred half a century ago—may lead us to overlook contemporary Auschwitzes. In the same way, those who today remember Dietrich Bonhoeffer think more about his secularizing ideas—living *etsi Deus non daretur*—than about his own martyrdom.

But today's martyrs and crucified peoples are still bringing the problem to our attention. As Casaldáliga has said, the problem for us is not "how to talk about God after Auschwitz" but "how to talk about God inside Auschwitz."[22] Without going into grisly comparisons—whose holocaust was worse—we must remember that much of what happened at Auschwitz has also happened, very recently, in Latin America and throughout the Third World. Meanwhile the holocaust of injustice and poverty remains unchanged, as we can see in the annual reports of the United Nations Development Project.

In short, here is a flagrant sign of the times that theology is not taking seriously; this is a grave paradox for any theology that calls itself Christian. In effect, the "Jesuanic martyrs" and "crucified peoples" are also signs of the times in the historical-theologal sense, because in them "the presence or the plans of God" (*cf. GS*, 11) are made manifest. This is certainly not a fanciful interpretation of the faith; it is supported by the Old Testament tradition of God's intimate relationship with the suffering servant, "my" servant. It is even more clearly supported by the New Testament tradition of God's presence in the cross of Jesus: "God was on the cross reconciling the world to himself" (II Corinthians 5:19), or "Truly this man was God's Son!" (centurion's confession at the foot of the cross, Mark 15:39).

If God's presence is in the martyrs and crucified peoples, then theology should take them into account. And in doing so it should make them central, not reduce them to case studies in contextual theologies. Why should a phrase from Augustine in the fifth century have universal theological significance, and not the reality of today's martyrdoms?

The Jesuanic Martyrs, a Source of Theological Knowledge

The martyrs pose a challenge for theology, as they do for the Church and for every human and ecclesial activity. I mention this only briefly, since it will be the subject of another article. Let us move on to an analysis of their positive contribution.

From one martyr to another: a few days after Archbishop Romero's assassination, Ignacio Ellacuría said, "God passed through El Salvador with Archbishop Romero." Of the Salvadorans who were dying slowly and violently, he said they were "the presence of the crucified Christ in history." In other words, the martyrs (as persons and as peoples) not only *take us back* to theological concepts of God and Christ, but above all they *make them present*. In this way the martyrs become a source of theological knowledge.

This means that theology is confronted not only by reflection-texts (the reflections of the theologians, beginning with those inspired by Scripture), but also by reality-texts. If that is true, and not merely pious rhetoric, theology needs to take these reality-texts very seriously. Moreover, it should give precedence to the *reality* over the *text*, and to the *present* over the *past*, since much is irreversibly lost in the transition in each case—and that is especially true in the case of martyrs and victims.

Martyrs and victims are important to faith, but also to epistemology. The historical reality of the cross and its theologal correlate, a crucified messiah, so disturbs our intelligence that no text, no matter how important, can pacify it. Obviously, for theology we need to use *texts from the past*. In the case of martyrs and victims, there are important traditions like those of

Paul and Mark, Hegel's "speculative Good Friday," Bonhoeffer's "only a God who suffers can save us." But texts are not enough, for the victims themselves are a question that keeps echoing in the *present*—indeed they are a question *of the present,* which cannot be satisfied by answers from the past. Moreover, normally not even the most vigorous *texts*—from the past or present—are able to galvanize human spirit and belief in a search for answers. Only *reality* can provide the necessary energy for asking and answering the question. And it is the reality of the martyrs that endows theological activity with a certain spirit.

By being martyrs, they require and enable theology to be stirred up by that spirit. It is, first, a *theo-logal* spirit, that is, a spirit of ultimacy. The martyrs are not taking us back to mere conceptual categories, but to what is ultimate for human beings: life and death. They ask whether it is true that the kingdom of God has the last word, and therefore whether life is possible for the poor, the privileged addressees of the kingdom; whether God truly raised a victim, Jesus, from the dead and did justice to him, and thereby gave hope to the victims of this world.

It is, second, a *dialectical* spirit, for in their very reality the martyrs show the existence of victims and victimizers, justice and injustice, grace and sin. They show the existence of the kingdom of God and the anti-kingdom, the God of life, *Abba,* and the idols of death. They show that Jesus is truth and life, and that the Evil One is a liar and murderer. Theologically, this means going beyond the simple juxtaposition of truths (although that is still a risk, even if we invoke the hierarchy of truths). The martyrs in their own flesh show the dialectical and conflictive aspect of reality. That is why theology must both proclaim and denounce; it must be at once *eu-angelica* and prophetic.

Third, it is a *soteriological* spirit. The martyrs are—or can be—the basis of our hope for salvation in the cross (and life and resurrection) of Jesus. The texts on the cross of Jesus are a scandalous invitation to faith and also to hope within history; they are an invitation, definitively, because the cross is an expression of love. But this need not remain in history as "pure," unverified faith, as if the real existence of crosses as an expression of love, and therefore of hope and salvation, were an historically irrelevant point. The Latin American martyrs (taken together, I repeat, as Jesuanic martyrs and crucified peoples) shine a light on the truth of our world and express love for the poor of this world. In this way they "verify" the truth that there is salvation in the cross of Jesus.

Finally, it is a *mystagogical* spirit, for the martyrs bring theology face to face with mystery. In negative terms, they bring clarity to the problem of theodicy and anthropodicy. In positive terms, they express ultimate hope in God's future. The martyrs confront theology with the existential need to be theologal, and to place under a *reductio in mysterium* all its conceptual categories.

The Jesuanic Martyrs and the Content of Theology

The Jesuanic martyrs require and enable a certain spirit in theology, but they also shed light on important issues of content.

Christology. The importance of the Jesuanic martyrs for christology is obvious. They shed light on the figure of Jesus and the fundamental structure of his life; hermeneutically at least, they are essential to an understanding of Jesus. In their life and death, they reproduce the incarnation-abasement, the proclamation-denunciation, the destiny of cross-resurrection (the latter more as analogy, of course, but in the certainty that an Archbishop Romero "lives"). Historically and existentially, the martyrs are the best mystagogy for christology.

Like Jesus, the martyrs are nothing more than human beings, as we know historically from the fact that men and women, bishops and peasants, journalists and teachers, lawyers and students, Salvadorans and foreigners, have all been murdered. Exercising their humanity, and nothing else, caused their death: not their country of origin, not their social standing. But although they are only human, the martyrs—like the mediator in the Letter to the Hebrews—make their humanity real and historical in the form of mercy (defending the weak), faithfulness (martyrdom is normally the culmination of a process of defamation and persecution), commitment (not only sharing their own lives, but giving them up), and solidarity (on behalf of and together with the people they call "brothers and sisters," the poor). The martyrs are an expression of pneumatology *in actu:* They show the power that God's Spirit gives, historically and in the present, to be like Jesus.

Ecclesiology. With regard to ecclesiology, the martyrs are "creators of Church."[23] And the Jesuanic martyrs are martyrs in the same paradoxical way that Jesus was: They create Church by dying for others, not for what is theirs. Thus, strictly speaking, the Jesuanic martyrs are not martyrs of the Church, or more precisely, they are not only martyrs of the Church—just as Jesus, obviously, was not.[24] Formally, they are "martyrs of the kingdom of God,"[25] martyrs of a poor and oppressed humanity.

On March 24, 1980, when Archbishop Romero was assassinated at the altar, historians thought they had found a precedent in Thomas Becket, archbishop of Canterbury in the twelfth century. But there is an important difference between these martyrdoms. The archbishop of Canterbury was assassinated for defending the legitimate interests of the Church against the ambition of the crown. Archbishop Romero was assassinated for defending the rights of the poor and oppressed against oppression and repression by the powerful—and for nothing else. The Jesuanic martyrs express the extrinsic, decentralized essence of the Church, which it needs in order to carry out its salvific mission.

Today, it is the martyrs who show the best face of Christianity and give credibility to the Church—the problem of ecclesial relevance. And it is they who make Jesus of Nazareth present, overcoming the church's recurring temptation to distance itself from him: "Go, and come no more," in the words of the grand inquisitor.

The Mystery of God. The Jesuanic martyrs bring us back to the mystery of the ultimate reality, the mystery of God.

• *The God of life.* The first thing the martyrs express is the way in which the ultimacy of reality puts to the test the willingness to give up everything, even the person's ultimate reality. In this sense, historically and religiously, martyrdom is not something specifically and exclusively Christian. Any human being may be challenged by God—by the ultimacy of conscience, by the ultimacy of reality—to the point of having to sacrifice life. Martyrdom expresses the creature's willingness to let God be God, by accepting his or her own death. This kind of martyrdom includes all those who have died in order to give life.

What the Jesuanic martyrs have done is to make clear the reason for that challenge: God may require them to give up their lives so that there will be life, liberation, brotherhood (which is not explicitly required in other martyrdoms—for instance, such as giving one's life to defend a particular dogma). Martyrdom happens, then, because of faith in *that* God, but with the specific understanding of a *praxic* faith that corresponds to that God: "He judged the cause of the poor and needy. . . . Is not this to know me?" (Jeremiah 22:16; cf. Hosea 6:6). In the last analysis, the way to witness to the God of life is *by giving life.* This Jesuanic understanding of martyrdom—partial as it is—is paradoxically what makes it universal and ecumenical.

• *The God who struggles with other gods.* The God of life is actively opposed by the idols of death. For that reason, to witness for God is simultaneously to witness against the idols; justice in God's favor is simultaneously accompanied by a struggle "to the death" against the idols. As the prophets and Jesus conceived of them historically and in the present, the idols are mammon, the greedy accumulation in a few hands of the necessary resources for the life of the human family, the use of repressive power and violence. For Jesus the kingdom of God and the anti-kingdom, the God of life and the idols of death, represent contrasting and conflicting totalities. It is each against the others; that explains the intrinsic logic by which death must be inflicted on those who defend life.

This is expressed in total clarity by the Jesuanic martyrs. The dialectic we have just mentioned is not found only in the religious sphere, but above all in historical reality. The Jesuanic martyrs are dying today at the hands of those who accumulate military, economic, political power. These are the idols which must have victims in order to survive. And as Archbishop Romero said, "Woe to anyone who touches the idols! They are like a high tension wire. Those who touch them will be burned." From a theologal viewpoint, it is hardly surprising that oligarchies, superpowers, and armies kill.

• *The God of the poor.* The God of the Jesuanic martyrs is a God of the poor; he is "the God who loves the life of the poor simply because they are poor." It is these martyrs who have best introduced the poor and their life into the theologal sphere (just as it was theology, especially that of Paul, that introduced sinners and justification into the same sphere). The martyrs express and radicalize the depth of the option for the poor, raising it to a theologal level. They make real *in actu* the words of Puebla: "For this reason alone, the poor merit preferential attention, whatever may be the moral or personal situation in which they find themselves. Made in the image and likeness of God to be his children, this image is dimmed and even defiled. That is why God takes on their defense and loves them" (n. 1142). It is the "Jesuanic" martyrs who best illustrate the Jesuanic principle: they love the poor to the end, simply because they are poor.

• *The mystery of God.* Finally, the Jesuanic martyrs express God's will to accept the cross for the salvation of the poor. They express the ultimate scandal that God, by taking the side of human beings, ends up at the mercy of human beings. They express the God of resurrection, keeping alive the hope that the murderer will not triumph over his victims. They show a humble walk with God through history up to the end, when God will be all in all.

All the martyrs, in every form of martyrdom, endow theology with sources of knowledge, spirit, and content. The Jesuanic martyrs do not exhaust those gifts, but because they are "like Jesus," they give a Jesuanic specificity to theology that we believe is very important in our time. When theology distances itself from Jesus of Nazareth, and especially from his cross, it becomes bourgeois.

The Crucified People: Reference Point of the Jesuanic Martyrs

In our time the Jesuanic martyrs show the excellence of a Christian death; they must be considered together with the traditional martyrs who died because of hatred of the faith. But by analogy, we must also consider the nonbelievers who give their life for the kingdom of God. This includes even those Christians (and non-Christians) who for love of the people have used armed violence, as well as prophetic violence and social violence. St. Thomas saw no problem in considering a soldier's death as a possible form of martyrdom, because "the good of the republic is the highest of goods" and "any human good may be a cause of martyrdom when it is related to God."[26] Whether or not this last type of death is a form of martyrdom remains a *quaestio disputata,* and in the last analysis, God alone can judge which cases show a greater love.

All these forms of death show, or can show, the excellence of a Christian death (or a human one, anonymously Christian). They are not the same, so in this case we can speak of martyrdom only by analogy. But there is another type of death,[27] to which we have alluded only briefly: Those who die en masse, innocently and anonymously, having never used violence—not even violent words. These do not actively give up their lives in defense of the faith, not even to defend the kingdom in any direct sense. They are seen as "nuisances," and must be eliminated to facilitate the elimination of those who work more explicitly for justice. They are the peasants, the children, the women, and especially the elderly, who die slowly day by day or violently, cruelly, and defenselessly. They are, to put it simply, killed and massacred. They are not even free to escape death. They are Yahweh's servant, the crucified peoples.

If we wonder whether these are martyrs, in comparison with the Jesuanic martyrs, the answer is complex. If martyrdom is the response of the anti-kingdom to those who struggle *actively* for the kingdom, then the *analogatum princeps* is being like Jesus, as exemplified in Archbishop Romero. If martyrdom is bearing the burden of the sin of the anti-kingdom, then these defenseless majorities—killed innocently, massively, and *passively*—are the *analogatum princeps*.

Compared to the death of Jesus, the deaths of these majorities can be described as less expressive of the active struggle against the anti-kingdom, and they were accepted with less explicit freedom. On the other hand, they are more expressive of "historical innocence," because they did nothing to deserve death except being poor, and of defenselessness, because they had no physical opportunity to avoid it. Above all, it is these majorities who unjustly bear the burden of the sin that has been annihilating them little by little, first in life and then, definitively, in death. It is these majorities who best express the enormous suffering of the world. Without intending and without knowing it, they "fulfill in their flesh what was lacking in the passion of Christ." They are the suffering servant and the crucified Christ in today's world. It is they who most tragically show the passion of the world in all its blackness.

And now we wonder: Where is the *greater Christian excellence*—in the death of the Jesuanic martyrs or in that of the crucified people? I honestly do not have the answer. The death of the Jesuanic martyrs is pleasing to God, because it expresses love. The death of the crucified people evokes greater love from God. We must use ultimate Christian words to stammer, as a way of speaking about the excellence of a death. With regard to the death of the crucified people, the ultimate word is silence, or incarnation in that death. We have already mentioned an analogy between the deaths of active martyrs. That is the *lesser* analogy. Now we are comparing the Jesuanic martyrs with the crucified people; that is the *greater* analogy.

Christian faith scandalously affirms that there is excellence in both deaths; this is more scandalous when applied to the death of the crucified people than in the case of the Jesuanic martyrs. It is only by analogy that we can connect the excellence of both kinds of death, but it may be useful to ask which one gives meaning to the other. Definitively, it is the crucified people that gives meaning to the Jesuanic martyrs. They have actively and freely joined in the death of the crucified people; they have done so to save the people, and they have been saved by them.

And what gives meaning to the death of the crucified people? This goes to the depth of the mystery of Christian faith, and in faith—faith accompanied by love, faith made productive in love—it has only one answer. The answer is that God loves them, that they are the privileged ones of God.

Personally I cannot go beyond that answer, but I want to insist on the excellence of the death of the crucified people; it is much less well known than the death of the Jesuanic martyrs, and is sometimes totally silenced. In the Church, in the traditions of the religious orders, we know what to do with the active martyrs; one almost never knows what to do with the crucified peoples. And we are all the poorer for that.

There are passages in the synoptic gospels, for example, that know what to do with the disciples and followers of Jesus, but not with the multitudes that came to him from all sides: the poor, the sick, sinners, women, publicans. Yet the kingdom of God, Jesus says, will be theirs. I sometimes say, not in irony but from reflection, that two or three billion human beings have been chosen to live in poverty and have been placed with the Son—even without having meditated on the *Spiritual Exercises* of St. Ignatius. We know what to do with the followers who ask to be placed with the Son, but we often don't know what to do with those who have been crucified with him, "placed" with him without asking or even knowing it.

Something similar may be happening with the martyrs. In some places we know what to do with the "Jesuanic martyrs," but we often don't know what to do with the "crucified people." What the Jesuanic martyrs ask of us is to stand beside the cross of the crucified people; to deeply respect their mystery, which at once hides and reveals the mystery of God; to allow ourselves to be graced, forgiven, saved by them. And to pour out our lives, even unto giving up our lives, in the effort to bring them down from the cross.

—Translated by Margaret Wilde

Chapter 6

The Latin American Martyrs
Challenge and Grace for the Church

In the last third of this century there have been many martyrs in Latin America: peasants, workers, students, lawyers, doctors, teachers, intellectuals, journalists, catechists, priests, religious sisters, bishops, archbishops, and they all remind us of the crucified Jesus. There have also been groups from the poor majority, murdered in great massacres, totally defenseless, anonymous, who remind us of Yahweh's suffering servant. We have good reason, therefore, to speak of a martyr Church.

In this martyr Church there has also been a generation of bishops of exceptional evangelical quality, religious men and women like those in CLAR, and many priestly renewal groups. This Church gave us a theology—the theology of liberation—which has focused its faith, hope, and charity on the poor. Finally, in this Church there arose base Christian communities, communities of the poor, lay men and women, who brought the people of God to maturity.

This martyr Church, we think, has produced the finest evangelical fruits in many centuries. But the martyr Church is not the subject of this article. Rather, we shall take it as a starting point from which to analyze today's Church, and the ways in which the martyrs of the past thirty years can help to shape it. More concretely, we shall look at those martyrs as a challenge and a grace for the Church today. Both the challenge and the grace are central to the "call to sainthood" that is expressed in the document *Ecclesia in America*.

The Need for a Challenge to Today's Church

First thesis. This challenge to the Church is necessary and healthy. It is the martyrs who can challenge it most vigorously, because they constitute a powerful historical mediation for the challenge that comes

First published in *Revista Latinoamericana de Teología* 48 (1999), 307–330. This was written as a response to *Ecclesia in America*, Pope John Paul II's post-synodal exhortation of 1999 following the Synod of the Americas.

from God. A central element of the challenge is the ecclesial decline that has been occurring since Medellín.

This first thesis will serve as an introduction to the body of the article; it is important to understand the Church's *need* to be challenged and the martyrs' *competence* to do so.

Why the Church Needs to Be Challenged

Today's martyrs are a direct challenge to historical reality, including its economic, political, ideological, and other structures, and their agents. The fundamental challenge consists of holding them to account for their past, present and future actions toward the crucified peoples. But this questioning goes unheard. Normally the people being challenged do not see it as addressed to them, but rather try to defame the martyrs—or at least to bury them forever, as has happened and in some ways is still happening in El Salvador. The tragedy is that this kind of society impoverishes itself; it deprives itself of the humanizing potential of the martyrs.

Thus the underlying challenge is addressed to the sinful world, but the Church is also being challenged. The possibility and need for that challenge are well known. The Church considers itself to be *semper reformanda* (as Vatican II acknowledged); or, as the fathers called it in stronger words, it is the *casta meretrix*. Moving from words to reality, we might debate whether the Church in general is better or worse today than before. There have been clear improvements, compared with the Church of a half-century ago. But compared with the Church that emerged from Vatican II and Medellín, there has been an undeniable decline.

The Church has held on to good things, sometimes very courageously amid many obstacles, and even created new ones, but the signs of deterioration are unconcealable, and that is the direction in which we are moving. The challenge that concerns us now is not so much in the limitations and sins that always affect the Church—recurring scandals throughout history and in our own time—but rather in the loss and decline of the good things that were once real, which are now dying the death of a thousand details. We could formulate the challenge to the Church in biblical words: "Where is your first love, where the audacity of Medellín, where the courage to risk everything to save the poor of this world?" For the sake of self-examination, let us mention some examples of this decline.

Within the Church there has been a decline in *intra-church brotherhood*, an excessive insistence on hierarchical control and a fear of the popular base lay people, and especially women. There is a decline in *promoting the maturity* of the people of God; rather there is encouragement or toleration for internalizing movements that turn away from God's creation, becoming esoteric and, above all, infantile. There is a decline in *catholicity* and *collegiality*. A Church that once promoted ecclesial localities, in order to be

universal in the catholic way, not uniformist, and that promoted a generation of local bishops in Latin America, comparable only to the prophetic
bishops of colonial times, is once again part of an excessively centralized
and uniformist Church; it lacks the honor to acknowledge its need for that
kind of bishops and the audacity to seek them out, and very often does just
the opposite. And with the decline of collegiality, such bishops have little influence in the leadership of the universal Church.

With regard to mission, there is a decline in the *option for the poor,* in
the option for popular awareness, praxis, conflict, prophecy, and all that
that entails. In spite of many good words and documents it has ceased
to be a Church of the poor, committed utopically to their defense and
prophetically to the denunciation of their oppressors, and become instead
a Church that understandably seeks to return to normalcy—to make
peace with the powers of this world, which co-opt the Church even as it is
criticizing them.

Finally in terms of Christian essentials, there is a decline of *creaturely humility,* so that even when it engages in dialogue with the world, the Church
tries to hold on to its leading role, as if it were above all other creatures.
There is a decline in the *theologal creaturely awareness* that is needed to let
God be God, amid the newness of the signs of the times—lay people and
women, new theologies, experiments in inculturation. There is a decline in
following the evangelizing and prophetic Jesus, as if the Spirit—let us exag-
gerate a little—could give us today a Christianity that no longer needs Jesus.

This is a simplistic description; there is still commitment, solidarity, accompaniment and even martyrdom, as Bishop Juan Gerardi reminds us.
There are inspiring social encyclicals, and, above all, there are the things
done every day by the communities. But adding it all up—the points of emphasis and the trends, the things that are supported and discouraged, especially at the high leadership level, and the moments of anti-commitment and
anti-solidarity—it seems to me an objective description. The "ecclesial
winter" is real. The following words of J. Comblin are strong, but lucid and
necessary in order to work for the conversion of the Church. He compares
today's Church with that of Medellín, saying:

> These days, one gets the strong impression that the Church, as seen in
> the majority of its members, pastors and sheep, is returning to the
> past. It uses the same language, but its practice is different. It is re-
> turning to the sacristies and to the parish houses. It no longer hears
> the voice of the poor majorities, but listens instead to its traditional
> constituency, the people who attend worship. The Church is once
> again preoccupied with itself. It seeks to regain positions of cultural,
> political, and even economic power. It is again exploiting religious
> feelings, emotions. It does not lack for clients, because the neoliberal
> model has increased the anguish, the despair, the insecurity, the bewil-
> derment of the people.[1]

The Martyrs' Competence to Challenge the Church

So the Church is in need of change and conversion, but left to its own iner-
tia and to its administrative and canonical mechanisms, it finds that difficult. On the one hand it badly needs to be challenged, but on the other, it
has a hard time allowing itself to be challenged. The Church can always say
it is not accountable to anyone but God, so that only God can challenge it.
It now asks forgiveness, but it does not seem to be sincerely open to any
challenge from human beings. No doubt there are always exceptions, but
the very idea of enjoying a special status that protects it from challenge is
dangerous and impoverishing. Therefore the important question is whether
anyone is competent to challenge the Church.

Let us begin as always with the essential: with the God in whom the
Church believes, and who can indeed challenge it. Now this is not just any
God, transcendent and therefore distant, but a God who became humanly
real in Jesus Christ; thus the problem of God's challenge is translated into
the challenge that Jesus Christ makes to the Church. No one can deny that
possibility, although the words of the Great Inquisitor to the Lord ("Go,
and come no more") show our fear that Christ might come near us. But the
problem does not end there; Christ, now lifted on high, could only confront
us existentially and vigorously by means of historical realities.

The presence of Christ in these historical realities is traditionally accepted in the Church, although different confessions interpret it in different
ways. Christ is present in the eucharist, in the preaching of the word, in the
community, in the pastors. Furthermore, according to the gospel and the
orthodoxy of the Latin American Church, Jesus Christ is most present—and
most challenging—"in the poor" (Matthew 25:31–46). Medellín reminds
us of that (*Peace*, 14), and of "their cries that go up to heaven" (*Justice*, 1).
And Puebla proclaims it as clear as day: "And with particular tenderness he
chose to identify himself with those who are poorest and weakest" (n. 196).
It is in the poor that Jesus Christ can challenge the Church, and the Church
has no defense against that challenge.

But we can go one step further. The reality of the poor comes to its highest
expression in the martyrs, those who have suffered the greatest impoverish-
ment. From the standpoint of Latin American reality, martyrs are (a) those
who have lived as Jesus did and have been murdered for the same cause as
Jesus (for example, Archbishop Romero); and (b) those who have been massacred, massively, cruelly, unjustly, and defenselessly, because their death was
necessary for the perpetuation of injustice (the massacres of El Mozote,
Guatemala, Haiti, Rwanda, etcetera).

It is those martyrs who challenge the Church; or to put it differently, if
they cannot do so, it is doubtful that anything can. Quantitatively, there are
too many of them to be ignored. Qualitatively, the horror and the love they
express is sufficient to shake us and inspire us. Moreover, they make it impossible to excuse ourselves by saying that "only God can challenge the

Church," since they are the presence of Jesus Christ with us today. They are Yahweh's suffering servant, who bears the sin of the world and of the Church. They are the crucified Christ. Their blood explains the shedding of Christ's blood, as Irenaeus said: "If the blood of the righteous had not been shed, in no way would the Lord have had to shed his blood. . . . The blood shed by all the righteous and the prophets from the beginning . . . would have been repeated in his person" (*Adv. Har.* V, 1, 1, 7 ff.)

Obviously not only the martyrs can challenge the Church. It can be done by a peasant or a contemplative monk, an assembly plant worker or a laborer. But the purest challenge comes always in the presence of blood unjustly shed. "What have you done? Listen; your brother's blood is crying out to me from the ground!" (Genesis 4:10). And by its very nature, the concrete content of the challenge is shaped by the identity of the challenger. The martyrs have a *specific challenge* to raise in our time, which is fundamentally a time of decline. They can shake the Church as only love and blood can do, and they show the path we must follow to return to the Church of the poor, for they are its most excellent representatives. "We too need someone to serve as a prophet calling us to conversion, preventing us from being enshrined in a religion as if it were untouchable," said Archbishop Romero.[2]

Now we shall describe the fundamental content of the challenge—and the offer of grace—that the martyrs present, following the christological schema of incarnation, mission, cross, and resurrection.

Incarnation: "Overcoming Unreality"

Second thesis. Medellín helped the Latin American Church become an incarnated Church, a "real" church. Today that is a serious, fundamental problem: a Church that is not real does not meet its obligation of incarnation, and does not possess the dynamism of incarnation. It falls back into docetism, and loses identity and relevance. The martyrs challenge and enable the Church to be a "real Church."

The Church must let itself be challenged on whether or not it is a Christian Church, the Church of Jesus, sacrament of salvation. But a more essential question is whether the Church is—let us say, for lack of a better term— "real." That is the first challenge of the martyrs.

The Starkness of Being Real: Unjust Poverty

We shall mention this point only briefly: poverty and injustice are not the whole of reality, but they represent a failure of the human species and the human family, and are at the heart of any challenge to the Church. We know from everyday experience and from the annual reports of the United Nations Development Program, that unjust poverty is the deepest wound in our world.

On the Latin American continent, and all over the planet, the majority of people—especially women—are poor. In qualitative terms, the poor are *bent down (anaw)* under the weight of existence, for their most important and hardest task is simple survival. They are *silenced,* robbed of dignity and words to speak; they are *im-potent,* powerless to claim and use their rights; they are *disdained,* for they cannot do what the imposed culture requires of them; they are *in-significant,* counting for nothing; and they are increasingly *non-existent* within the machinery of economic production. The poor are *non-beings,* who have become poor because everything was snatched away from them. In Jesus' time the poor were the pitiable, the sick, women, sinners/publicans. Today we must add to their ranks the marginalized, members of certain races and cultures, and emigrants—especially the women in each group.

Quantitatively, two statistics tell the story. First, 1.5 billion human beings are forced to subsist on less than a dollar a day. And according to the United Nations Development Program, the ratio between rich and poor families was 1:30 in 1969, 1:60 in 1991, and 1:74 in 1999.

That is not the whole of reality; in the midst of these aberrations there is kindness, commitment, hope, and even joy. But it is the starkest side of reality. Ellacuría the philosopher understood reality as inhuman poverty above all, as the cruel and unjust death of the majorities, so sharply that he dared to challenge Heidegger: "Perhaps instead of asking why there is being rather than nothingness, he should have asked why there is nothingness—nonbeing, unreality, untruth, etcetera—instead of being."[3] And Ellacuría the theologian used to ask what was *the* sign of the times, and answered: "That sign is always the people crucified in history."[4]

This same vision of reality is the precious inheritance of the Latin American Church. Medellín begins with these words: "the misery that marginalizes large groups of people, [expresses itself as] injustice that cries out to heaven" (*Justice,* 1). In the words of Puebla: "So we brand the situation of inhuman poverty in which millions of Latin Americans live as the most devastating and humiliating kind of scourge" (n. 29). With or without globalization, with old paradigms or new ones, this reality not only isn't going away; it is intensifying at the beginning of the twenty-first century.

It is this reality that raises the question: do we live in this world, and thus are we real? Thence comes the challenge to incarnation, the only way for the Church to recover its dignity and overcome the shame of living in an artificial world. And it is not just a matter of being physically in this world, but being shaped by its reality. In other words, if Sumpul and El Mozote, Zaïre and Rwanda do not shape our knowing, our doing, our hope and celebration, if they do not move our intelligence and our heart, we are not living in reality at all; that means not only that we are not human, ethical or Christian, but more radically, that we are not "real." We shall have fabricated an alternative reality (historical, cultural, religious), in which to take refuge and protect ourselves from the true reality. In Kantian terms, we are still immersed in a dream of unreality.

"Unreality" as Ecclesial Docetism

Perhaps it will help to remember that from the beginning of Christianity, "unreality" was a serious problem in the form of "docetism." Docetism, which denied the humanity of Christ, was a serious problem—if not the most serious—in the early Church. And it was the hardest to overcome; as a result, it took the Church much longer to define the true *humanity* of Christ (at Chalcedon, 451 A.D.) than his true *divinity* (at Nicaea, 325 A.D.), even though his humanity was evident in the New Testament.

Now, docetism is also an ecclesial problem. That seems odd, because the Church's problem usually seems to be just the opposite—that it is "too human," even sinful. But that appearance is deceiving. The Church is factually in the world, but it has a recurring tendency and temptation to create its own environment of doctrinal, pastoral, liturgical and canonical reality that distances and protects it from the world. In terms of what we have just said, the Church's tendency and temptation consist of being in a world of poor majorities, without substantially affecting its faith, its mission, its theology, its internal organization, its dimension as people of God. Some more concrete examples would be its way of naming bishops, or its masculine and a-feminine understanding of priestly ministry. The Church is accustomed to considering the poor as addressees of social-pastoral practices and some ethical practices; but at the essential levels, where ecclesial "identity" and true ecclesial "power" are at stake, the Church does not give the impression of being "real" because it is not a Church of the poor.

This is not only a serious problem for the Church's relevance in a world of poor people, but also for its identity. The prologue to the Gospel of John expresses God's "will to be real," a will that consists not only of factually becoming flesh, but in becoming weak flesh. In the language of later christology, the reality that the Son takes on is not only *humanitas* (humanity), but *sarx* (the weakness of the flesh). And as we see in the christological debates of the first centuries, *humanitas* alone (what we call factuality) does not radically overcome docetism. To truly overcome it, Jesus had to become *sarx*.

And that is still a serious problem: *humanitas* without *sarx*, *factuality* without *reality* (in the world of the poor). To give a few examples: one often gets a feeling of unreality from homilies, documents and messages that do not make central—although they may mention it—the poverty of reality, the injustice and corruption that cause it, and the cover-up that accompanies it. The feeling of unreality comes especially from the lack of commitment to get involved in the conflict, to struggle against injustice and to suffer the consequences. *Words, words, words,* as J. Comblin calls such messages in the article mentioned above. At another level, one gets the same feeling of unreality from a seminary formation that protects the seminarian from reality; or from the spiritualities and pastoral practices promoted or tolerated by movements that lead the human being into an a-historical transcendence, with infantilizing consequences.

Important ecclesial events, like a papal visit, are often organized in such a way that they too produce a feeling of unreality. In the Pope's 1996 visit to El Salvador, it is true that most of the people who attended were poor. But all one could see of their reality was their religious enthusiasm, more or less effectively organized. One didn't see their poverty, their fears, their discouragement and helplessness, not even their true faith and hope; one didn't see their reality. As the event was organized, the poor served more as a backdrop than as the reality of the country; in the foreground were minorities that do not represent the reality: the government, legislators and politicians, the rich and powerful, and the Church beside them. The Pope's visit neither reflected reality nor, to judge from the consequences, had any important effect on it.

This docetism, as we have called it, has several consequences. The option for the poor no longer has ultimacy; rather it lives in balance with another option, which at the moment of truth seems to be far more forceful and more real: the option for peace with the powers that be. The Church does not see its being and doing in the context of the poor, but in other contexts—which may be necessary and even good, but are unrelated to the Church's essence. At the moment of truth such things as institutional organization, the struggle with the sects, maintaining church attendance and an alienating religiosity, obsessive faithfulness to the magisterium, and a long list of etceteras, count for more than the reality of the poor.

This unreality—more than any possible theological exaggerations—places at risk the deepest identity of the faith. To put it in slightly technical language, without living reality as it is, the Church can hardly obtain the perspective and the *hermeneutic* it needs to understand the essentials of faith: the in-carnation of the word in the weakness of reality, and the salvific dynamism of that kind of incarnation. Unreality leads in the opposite direction: to dis-incarnation from poverty and incarnation in centers of power, to the search for salvation not in the weakness of the flesh, but in power.

The Challenge and Grace of the Martyrs: To Be "A Real Church"

The truth of what we have been saying varies from one time and place to another, of course, but in general we believe the danger of unreality is undeniable. The way we are now, it seems that the official Church and many groups and movements have fallen into a dream state, unable to be actively and truly present in reality. It is in this situation that the martyrs challenge us, as Antonio Montesinos did five hundred years ago: "How can you sleep such a deep, lethargic sleep?" How can you be so detached from the suffering of the majorities, or relativize them? What happened to the homilies and pastoral letters of the 1970s and 1980s, that put the truth of reality into words and analyzed its causes? What happened to denunciation and confrontation, not only social doctrine and dialogue, with the sinful world? Above all, what happened to living with the poor, sharing their powerlessness and their destiny, sharing all that you are and have with them?

The challenge of the martyrs is fully credible. We cannot ignore them without falling into hypocrisy, because they were above all "real." Certainly that is true of the passive, anonymous martyrs, who lived directly and immediately the reality of poverty, insignificance, powerlessness. It is also true of the active martyrs, those who placed their words at the service of the wordless, their power at the service of the powerless. For that specific reason, the martyrs can hold the Church to account for its own reality or unreality. Their martyrial destiny makes their challenge all the more radical.

The martyr Archbishop Romero offers an example, better than any words, of what we have said. Monseñor built a "real" Church. It had limitations, errors, even sins, but there was never any doubt that it was a Salvadoran, a real Church. In his often-quoted words: "Brothers and sisters, I am glad that the Church is persecuted, precisely because it has taken a preferential option for the poor, and has tried to incarnate itself in the interests of the poor" (September 15, 1979). And even more clearly: "It would be sad if, in a country where people are being so horribly murdered, there were not also priests among the victims. They are witness to a Church incarnated in the problems of the people" (June 24, 1979).

But the Church of Archbishop Romero was real also because it was incarnated in the positive realities of the people. Seeing their resilience and resistance, he told the Christians: "If they should ever take away our radio station, suspend our newspaper, forbid us to speak, kill all the priests and the bishop too, and if you are left as a people without priests, each of you must be a microphone for God, each of you must be a messenger, a prophet" (July 8, 1979). Amid the generosity and the commitment of the people, Archbishop Romero took pride and joy in his Church: "You are a Church so full of life," he said, "a Church so full of spirit!"

These were not only words of piety, nor only of commitment, but also of lucidity: to know whether or not a Church is real. Archbishop Romero's Church was real. On the other hand, a Church cannot be real that is not poor in times of poverty, not persecuted in times of persecution, not murdered in times of murder; a Church that is not committed in times of commitment, and does not encourage commitment in times of indifference; that is not hopeful in times of hope, and does not encourage hope in times of discouragement. "To overcome unreality," it seems to us, is the martyrs' first challenge to the Church today. But they are also a grace for the Church. Their example and their memory are an inspiration for the task.

Mission: "Salvation of the Reality"

Third thesis. The Latin American Church has sought salvation for the crucified people as a whole. Now it is more concerned about internal, individual salvation. The martyrs are challenging and encouraging it to turn back its history and save those peoples.

Martyrs and the Salvation of a People

The martyrs we have called *active,* like Jesus, established concrete signs of salvation and were concerned with the salvation of people. But they also lived for the salvation of peoples: an historical, popular, and structural salvation. We want to emphasize that aspect now, because these days structural salvation is viewed with suspicion and is being forgotten, even as theory.

The martyrs, however, did not see it that way. From martyr to martyr: Ignacio Ellacuría described Archbishop Romero not only as a good man and a holy priest, but as "one sent by God to save his people"[5]—a salvation which for that reason has an essentially historical, popular, and structural dimension. In Archbishop Romero's own words, to save is to tell the truth in the name of the whole people: "these homilies are meant to be the voice of this people" (July 29, 1979); to save is to give hope to a whole country: "the glory of the Lord will shine over these ruins" (January 7, 1979). In the words of Ignacio Ellacuría, to save is "to turn back history," not only to mend it; it is to promote justice, to proclaim utopia, the civilization of love, which in order to be real must be a "civilization of poverty"; it is to proclaim to the people that "the saving God, the liberating God, is watching." Salvation and history, salvation and the people, were intertwined realities for the martyrs.

A Deficit of Popular and Totalizing, Salvific Pathos

These quotations are important because they express essential and totalizing dimensions of the Church's mission. They are words of encouragement and *pathos,* often forgotten in our time. The Church no longer speaks, as it once did, of transforming structures, of saving a people, of historical utopia, of bringing in the kingdom of God. It tends to focus on and promote individual or at most family salvation—which is also good and necessary—rather than the salvation of a people: internal rather than historical salvation. And its salvific activities tend to be more charitable than liberating; the Church acts in support of the weak, but does not enter into confrontation with the oppressors. This is an understandable tendency, given the enormous difficulties, urgencies and concrete needs of the poor, the discouragement and abandonment into which they have fallen. But it is dangerous: the mission of the Church is losing sight of what the magisterium, in sparse but important language, used to call integral liberation—the totalizing, and therefore historical, salvation of a people.

It is not that the martyrs who sought "the salvation of a people" ignored or minimized the salvation that comes specifically from a personal encounter with God. "I wish, dear brothers and sisters, that as a result of today's preaching each of us would come to know God," said Archbishop Romero (February 10, 1980). "To be a man one must be more than a man," Ignacio Ellacuría used to say in the words of St. Augustine. It is a malicious lie to say that those who sought the liberation of the people were fundamentally reductionist.

Indeed reductionism, in the opposite direction, is a problem of today's Church—a serious problem. That individualistic and internalistic reductionism places at risk the Church's relevance in a world of poor peoples, who urgently need salvation and also identity. A Church that is not committed to the salvation of those peoples will turn into a closed sect, a modern equivalent of the Essenes. Or it will become a massive institution, ignoring reality and alienating the people—a new experiment in sociocultural Christianity, albeit gentler and more vacuous.

We shall not go into detail here on what it would take for the Church's mission to overcome this deficit of salvific popular and structural *pathos*. It is enough to mention the importance of holding on to what Medellín made central: the struggle against injustice, in favor of a just and humanizing society, which Ellacuría called "the civilization of poverty," and for which he and others proposed at least modest solutions. New tasks need to be added today, or at least new dimensions of the perennial task: to struggle against the lie, to liberate truth, to unmask our world's gigantic cover-up; to promote an appropriate "spiritual ecology," that is, the needed purification of the air that the human spirit breathes in today's (pseudo) culture; to join in the battle to protect the hope of the poor from being snatched away from them.

We cannot analyze each of these tasks, but any description of the Church must emphasize two essential, now almost forgotten things. One is the *pathos* of historical *praxis* in the Church's mission—including, although it is not a popular topic today, the *agonistic*, struggling dimension of the Christian life. The other is the totalizing horizon of *praxis*: the kingdom of God, in evangelical language; the salvation of a people, in modern language. And let us remember that this totalizing liberation includes the full breadth of the life of the poor: the ability to form a home (*oikos*, from which comes the word economy), to be a fraternal family, to express themselves in culture and art, to speak and be listened to, etc. And the ability to be the people of God, not afraid of God because they are poor, but rather feeling embraced by God.

The Challenge and the Grace of the Martyrs: "To Save a People"

Why do we need the martyrs to challenge the Church on its praxis of historical salvation? Don't we have inspiring texts from the Bible and the magisterium to do it? The answer is that the martyrs' challenge is especially forceful because—in our time—there is *a close connection between the martyrs and the salvation of a whole people.* This is something new and very important, for the Church and for the peoples, which has seldom if ever been seen in history.

On the one hand the very reality of the passive and anonymous martyrs, the great majorities, the crucified peoples, constitutes an absolute demand to the Church to work, not just for any salvation, but for the "salvation of a people." And on the other, the active martyrs are a challenge to praxis because it was for the sake of that praxis, and in it, that their lives were taken. It is oversimplistic to ask whether they gave their life for Christian or political reasons, for their faith in God or for their commitment to the people. They gave their life as Jesus did, for the love of a people, to save a people, so the people might become a people of God in the kingdom of God.

One might object that this language was appropriate in other times, but that the present situation requires a realistic approach to integral liberation, to the salvation of a people. That is partly true. But however secular and ecclesial attitudes may be changing, the martyrs' questions should not be silenced. They are asking the Church whether its mission is going down the slippery slope of privatism and ahistoricalism, and thus losing its social impact; whether it is satisfied with doing good things but not liberating ones, with palliatives where a problem needs to be rooted out; whether it has succumbed to a postmodernism without utopia, or to a neoliberalism against utopia, which tolerates religion as long as it does not question the reality—and may even support it as long as it stays on the right side, while the poor never realize what is happening.

Now at the beginning of the twenty-first century, the martyrs are returning to ask the Church whether it has allowed itself to suffer with the crucified peoples to the end, without reservation, without holding back. They are asking about the Church's faithfulness to the heritage of Jesus and to the heritage that they, the martyrs, so generously left us: to live, and to pour out one's life, to save a people.

And they not only challenge, but also enlighten and encourage us on a crucial point. Crucial, because we must clearly understand that the Church does not create the mission; the mission creates the Church. It is not a pre-existing Church that decides what it should doing, but the Church takes shape as a particular Church in the process of working for and conveying salvation. The kind of Church it will be depends on the way it works for and conveys salvation, on the kind of salvation it wants to bring to the world. Thus we must be as clear as possible about the nature of that mission; it takes precedence over problems of pastoral practice, liturgy, and canons.

We talk a lot these days about pastoral plans and methods—and with good reason—but we have little to say about mission; there almost seems to be a fear of seriously addressing that theme. At best we assume, simplistically, that the question was already settled at Vatican II and Medellín. But that clearly is not the case, for there is no evidence that mission is being defined from that viewpoint; rather mission is sometimes defined quite independently of Vatican II and Medellín, and other times against them.

In this situation we must return to the martyrs and their mission. The martyrs did not give their life for a few good deeds or for small liberations, but for something much deeper and broader: for the salvation of a people, and within it, for the salvation of persons. That mission generated a kind of

Church that had a lot in common with the Jesus movement. So the martyrs are asking—and challenging—us, whether the Church's mission today is focused on the salvation of a people, and whether it is giving birth to a Church that looks like Jesus. Again, the martyrs give us the spirit and grace to meet the challenge.

Cross: "Bearing the Burden of Reality"

Fourth thesis. The Latin American Church has borne the weight of reality, carrying out its mission in the presence of the anti-kingdom and in opposition to it. Today it seems to be ignoring the structural conflict, and the burdensome part of reality. It thereby loses "reality," "salvific capability," and "credibility." The martyrs challenge and inspire the Church to take up the cross of reality.

Reality as the Death-Giving Anti-Kingdom

It is not masochism to talk about bearing the weight of reality; indeed that should be obvious in an historical reality like ours. The passive and anonymous martyrs show it clearly, and show their helplessness in the face of the cruel reality that hangs over them. They are the *analogatum princeps* of what it means to "bear the burden of reality."

But we are more concerned here with the active martyrs. Bearing the burden of reality was not masochism in their case either, nor a purely mystical and intentional desire to identify with the crucified Christ, as it is sometimes presented; rather it was honesty with regard to reality. If we look carefully, Jesus' demand—"take up your cross and follow me"—is tautological; to follow Jesus, to live as he lived and do what he did, leads to carrying what he carried, the cross. What we must clearly understand about the martyrs' challenge is what the cross means, and why we are called to carry it.

The cross is not only the suffering caused by our human limitations, although that suffering obviously deserves respect and compassion, and efforts to eliminate or relieve it. The cross is the suffering expressed in anguish, illness, failure, discouragement, incomprehension, bereavement, the fear of one's own death—all these painful things, which can sometimes become even more subjectively painful than the martyr's cross. Yet in formal terms all of this, though it expresses the limitation of human reality, is not yet a "cross." We stress this because the Church has a long tradition of alleviating these types of suffering, and participating in them in order to alleviate them for others, which is meritorious and Jesuanic, but it does not yet mean the same as "bearing the cross."

Directly speaking, the cross is the death that comes from defending the oppressed and struggling against the oppressor. By analogy, the cross is the suffering caused by that elemental struggle: harassment, slander, persecution, exile, imprisonment, torture, etc. In other words, the cross speaks of injustice; in a world without injustice there would doubtless still be suffering, but there would not be a cross. In this context, subjectively, the cross comes from the willingness to be incarnated in the conflictiveness of history. Objectively, it presupposes a conflictive structure of reality. This understanding may or may not be common to philosophy, sociology and politics, but it is clear in the Christian vision: it is the historical-theologal structure of reality, dialectical and conflictive.[6]

The Bible, which knows little of sociology, economics and politics, still offers this great insight on the structure of reality which is seldom found anywhere else—and which is potentially so revealing that it is ignored and covered up, even by many Christian theologies. In Johannine language, the Evil One is a murderer, and reality is infused with that murderous evil. It is thus hardly surprising that human beings who are honest about reality, and committed to transforming it, are murdered. It would be abnormal if they were not, because it would mean either that reality is no longer murderous, or that in the Church and the world there are no longer believers and human beings who are honest about that reality.

The Church's Temptation: Avoiding Conflict

In Latin America today there is little real confrontation—although there are verbal debates—between the Church and the world of sin. It is said, by way of simplistic justification, that "things have changed." But there is a serious lack of analysis about what has changed, and above all there is a lack of logic, as if all conflict between the God of Jesus and the idols would automatically disappear whenever the situation changes (without necessarily changing anything fundamental). It is bad enough for neoliberal theoreticians to celebrate the present situation, but it is indeed serious when the Church falls into the trap of ceasing to denounce the underlying conflict and ceasing to become directly involved in it. Evil is not only a bad thing; by its very nature it generates conflict, it "goes against." The Church must take a stand against an evil that is conflictive, even if that causes serious complications for the Church.

It is true that there have been verbal confrontations about the right to life, between the Vatican and international governments and organizations. But in other areas—economics, human rights, the arms race, etcetera—the Church's denunciations, however ethical and accurate, are normally co-opted; there may be textual conflicts, but not real conflicts. The Church is not carrying any important cross as a result of saying such things. The situation was very different in the time of Archbishop Romero, Dom Helder Camara, Enrique Angelelli, Don Sergio Méndez Arceo, and Leonidas Proaño, to name only bishops who have died. Their denunciations were not co-opted; they had to fight for them.

Today in several countries, certainly in El Salvador, some nominations of bishops have been planned to avoid conflict and renew the good relations of fifty years ago between the civil and ecclesiastical powers. There are worthy exceptions among the bishops, but statements from the bishops' conference use denunciation sparingly in comparison to the magnitude of the tragedy; they sometimes use vigorous language to describe the reality, but they do not analyze its causes or identify specific perpetrators. As a result, they do not generate conflict. In my opinion the Church today cannot be compared with Socrates' gadfly, or with Ellacuría's unmasking pen, or with the incorruptible word of Archbishop Romero.

Let us not be anachronistic, people say. But as Christians we also should not be uncritical, and we should neither deceive nor be deceived. In any case we should hold on as best we can to the *parresia* of Paul: courage, audacity and confidence, and not fall into cowardice. We should not offer a watered-down, bland Christianity that talks in the same tone with the victims and with their murderers—and we shouldn't even think about talking more with the murderers than with the victims, more with Pinochet than with the disappeared ones, even if we do it elegantly, and in order to avoid greater evils. We must not offer "cheap grace," which Bonhoeffer called the greatest danger for Christianity. And although the phrase should be used carefully, without sacrificialist overtones, we should recall the New Testament insight about "the cost of salvation," so as not to trivialize the Christian life: "You know that you were ransomed . . . not with perishable things like silver or gold, but with the precious blood of Christ. . . ." (I Peter 1:18–19).

Our Church and our faith are based on a conflict, a cross, and therefore on a resurrection. To forget that would be the end of Christianity. "The times have changed," some say, thus subliminally telling the believer that the cross (and resurrection) are good and necessary in the liturgy, in private devotion and in personal life, but cross and resurrection have nothing ultimate and serious to say to the reality that the Church seeks to evangelize. That is not true. There have been changes in the political scenery, but it would be a serious mistake to confuse that scenery with the true reality. Changes in the political superstructure have no effect on the deeper theologal or metaphysical structure of history; there the confrontation continues. It is fortunate that in some countries this confrontation is no longer as warlike and brutally repressive as it was a few decades ago. But that does not mean that the historical conflict no longer exists, or that the Church no longer needs to be engaged in it. In any case the Church in practice should not be playing by the rules of the system, acting as if everything were substantially improved or, at least, moving in the right direction.

The Challenge: "There Is No Salvation Except by Bearing the Burden of Sin"

Without bearing the burden of the world's sin there is no incarnation, of course, but without it the Church also cannot bring salvation or possess credibility. It is not a philosophical but a Christian truth that without a struggle against sin from within, bearing the weight of sin and its consequences—there will be no redemption. As much as we need to guard against spurious sacrificialism in theory, and as much as things have changed in practice, it is still true that a grain of wheat does not bear fruit unless it falls to earth and dies, but if it dies it bears much fruit. This is what the martyrs have told us, without a word, simply by being martyrs. But some of them also made it explicit.

At the ceremony to confer an honorary doctorate on Costa Rican president Oscar Arias, in the midst of a political speech in the presence of ambassadors and ex-president Cristiani, Ignacio Ellacuría quoted these words in Latin: *"Sine effusione sanguinis, nulla redemptio"* (there is no redemption without bloodshed), and added: "The salvation and liberation of the peoples passes through very painful sacrifices."[7] We need to understand this well, and commit it to history in less warlike times. But the thesis still holds: unless it is willing to engage in the conflict of reality, to bear its burden and pay a price, the Church cannot bring salvation. It also will not possess credibility. When even United Nations reports on the world situation speak of tragedy and inhumanity, the Church will have no credibility unless it is at least willing to struggle against those things and accept the consequences. And finally, there will be no way to verify that the Church is acting in a Christian way: if none of the things that happened to Jesus happen to the Church, there is no evident reason to understand and accept it as the Church *of Jesus*. Archbishop Romero said that very clearly: "A Church that doesn't suffer persecution, but enjoys the privileges and support of all the land, that Church should beware! It is not the true Church of Jesus Christ" (March 11, 1979).

The martyrs challenge the Church to bear the cross, because they themselves did so. But they also show that in this way the Church brings salvation to the poor majorities, it gains credibility, and it is embraced and loved—by the poor—as the Church of Jesus. By their example, they inspire us to do the same.

Resurrection: "Letting Reality Carry Us"

Fifth thesis. We can say, by analogy of course, that the martyrs "have appeared to the Church." They are still challenging it, encouraging it, and enabling it to live today as a Church resurrected in history, in freedom, joy and hope.

In the previous theses we have looked historically at the Church's incarnation, mission and cross, through the lens of the martyrs; that can be done easily. Now we turn to the resurrection, which places us in a different type of reality; here our analysis must be done by analogy. Nevertheless, we shall offer two reflections on a "risen Church." One is that the martyrs are a very special grace, analogous to an appearance by the crucified-risen one, so that we can speak of an ultimate gift that has been given us, and of ourselves being carried by reality. The other is that the martyrs, now resurrected, triumphant over negativity and death, are inviting us to live as a Church resurrected in history.

Grace: "Something That Has Been Given Us"

The New Testament proclaims that Jesus has been resurrected by the Father and has appeared to the disciples, women and men. Two things are of particular interest here. The first is that Jesus "lets himself be seen," *opthe*. That is, the appearance of Jesus and the Jesus who appears are a gift and a grace: the one who lets himself be seen is good, and the fact that he lets himself be seen is grace. And the second is that the fact that the risen one lets himself be seen, does not alter the fact that during his lifetime Jesus also "let himself be seen." Although the New Testament does not use this language, we might say it is talking about an historical *opthe*: the Jesus who came doing good is the one who let himself be seen. The appearance of the risen one was the greater grace, we might say, but through it the disciples understood that Jesus' coming was also a grace: "in him the kindness of God appeared." To put it simply, in the total "appearance" of Jesus, historically and eschatologically, something good has been given us: we have been introduced into the dynamic of kindness in reality, and it is carrying us.

This is important for our analysis of the martyrs' importance to the Church. By analogy, we might say that throughout history there have been "appearances;" *opthe* happens again and again. Archbishop Romero said simply: "If they kill me, I will rise again in the Salvadoran people," and indeed many have seen Monseñor and other martyrs in that way. But just as with Jesus, the martyrs' resurrection breaks in alongside their life in history: Archbishop Romero's word of truth, his praxis of justice, his strength under persecution, his unconditional love for the poor to the very end, were also a grace—in them, he "let himself be seen." From an existential and experiential viewpoint, martyrial death helps the Church to open its eyes to the goodness of the martyrs. And the goodness seems to overflow, flooding over us, inviting and enabling us also to be good. This is the original grace of reality, which carries us and, by doing so, graces us.

That is the fundamental point of this final section: the challenge-invitation to the Church to let itself be graced by the martyrs, and to live as a risen Church in history. We shall return to the latter, but here we want to emphasize the moment of "letting ourselves" be graced, "letting ourselves" be carried. This "letting" always runs up against the danger of *hybris,* or human arrogance. So let us pause for two reflections on that danger. By way of example we shall briefly analyze what can happen in the canonization process, which greatly interests us now that the process has begun for Archbishop Romero.

The martyrs as grace for the Church. The martyrs, above all, are a grace for the Church; they are an original mediation of the crucified and risen one. For that reason any canonization process should express the grace that the martyrs represent for the Church. This does not detract from the need to regulate (canonize) such processes, but the process should never hide the grace—or make it appear, if we may say so, that the Church "graces" Archbishop Romero, "does him a favor," when in fact it is he who "graces" the Church, both local and universal. In this sense, we believe it is more important to analyze whether Archbishop Romero's life, work, and martyrdom have been recognized and embraced by the people of God—which is true beyond any doubt—than to analyze his virtues, orthodoxy, and ecclesiastical obedience. Grace does not live by the canonization process, but quite the reverse.[8]

Holding together the totality of the martyrs. The second reflection is that we must hold together the totality of the grace expressed in the martyrs. That is, the final, formally martyrial moment must be held together with their life and their *praxis*, remembering moreover that for the Latin American martyrs, martyrdom has often been the culmination of a whole life. A dialectic is involved here: their life explains their martyrdom, and their martyrdom expresses their life. This is an important problem in our time. The powers of this world clearly want to bury the martyrs, albeit elegantly. But at some ecclesiastical levels there is also an effort to domesticate them, precisely because of what we have been saying in this article: they are the historical mediation of the challenge from God.

Let us come back to Archbishop Romero. I hope it won't happen, but there is a risk of canonizing someone who is not the "true" Monseñor: a nice, pious, zealous, priestly, but "watered-down" Monseñor. We need to hold on to the "true" Monseñor who lived to bring justice to the poor and glory to God, and who also for that reason struggled against injustice and against the gods of death. That was the whole Archbishop Romero, the "true" Monseñor. It was he, and not another Archbishop Romero, who ended up a martyr.

If the official Church canonizes a martyr, no one can say it has forgotten him; but we might ask what part of him the Church wants to continue living and acting in history. In order to avoid corrupting in memory the man he really was, the canonization should stay close to the facts—as in his case it very well may; it is equally important not only to remember the moment of his death, but also to value and hold up as a model the martyr's *life*, which really made him a witness to God, to truth, to life, and which finally led to his martyrdom.

The New Testament teaches us about this way of proceeding: The risen Christ—even after moving into eschatological reality—let himself be seen with the wounds of the crucified one, as the one who gives pardon and peace and who prepares a table for sharing, all typical aspects of the living Jesus of Nazareth. We need to see today's martyrs that way too. Moreover, the New Testament warns against the risk of diffusing and manipulating the risen one. The gospels were written to avoid that risk, and it is important that they tell the life story of the particular Christ who was Jesus. That life—consummated forever—is what the evangelists reported as good news, and as a life that must continue. By analogy, this is what should be done with the memory of the martyrs.

Living as Risen in History

We have said that in "resurrection" something appears to us, something is given: life in abundance. But resurrection also has an essential dimension of "triumph" and "victory" over negativity. Let us conclude by asking what "triumph" and what "victory" are expressed today in the life of the Church, so that we can now live as risen within the conditions of history. In my view there is an historical echo of resurrection in freedom, joy, and hope. That is the invitation offered by the martyrs.[9]

Freedom as triumph over self-centeredness. Freedom reflects the "triumph" of the risen one, not by removing us from our material reality, but by introducing us into historical reality, so that we can love without being conditioned by material reality. In Christian terms, free people are those who love—in the last analysis who only love, without being distracted from love by any other perspective. In paradoxical terms, freedom is being bound to history in order to save it, but in such a way—to continue the metaphor—that nothing in history can bind or enslave people to keep them from loving.

In history there are different kinds of love. Many people—some at least—can sincerely say they have dedicated their lives to poor people and victims, and that they truly love them, but normally that love is accompanied by ties that bind them to other loves, including legitimate ones: a political party, a popular revolutionary organization, a religious congregation, an ecclesial institution. These loves almost always mitigate, condition, or distort their love for the poor; more so when they are *bound* by ambition for wealth or power. To that degree one might say that although there is real love, it is not total love because the "ties" remain, even when some of them are understandable and legitimate in themselves. But there are other people, like Archbishop Romero, who loved nothing more deeply than the poor, without mixed motives, without other loves—even legitimate ones— to distract them from that fundamental love, and without caution in the face of the risks they incur by loving.

In this kind of love—deeper in some than in others, but real in the martyrs—there is freedom. Christian freedom, in the last analysis, is freedom to love. It is the freedom Jesus himself showed by affirming: "No one takes [my life] from me, but I lay it down of my own accord" (John 10:18). It is the freedom Paul showed in becoming "a slave to all, so that I might win more of them" (I Corinthians 9:19). This freedom has nothing to do with escaping history; it has nothing to do directly with one's own right to freedom, even though that right is legitimate and urgently needs to be exercised in the Church. The freedom expressed in the triumph of the risen one consists of not being bound to the enslaving aspects of history (fear, paralyzing caution); it consists of love's highest freedom to serve, without limits or obstacles to that love. The martyrs, especially the majority whose death came as the culmination of persecution, challenge and encourage us to be free.

Joy as triumph over sadness. The other triumphant dimension of resurrection is joy, and joy is only possible when there is something to celebrate. To live joyfully means being able to "celebrate life"; the question is whether there is anything to celebrate. This is another paradox, in situations of such terrible suffering as that of the crucified peoples, but indeed there is celebration. Gustavo Gutiérrez once heard a base community member say, "the opposite of happiness is sadness, not suffering."

That life can be "celebrated" with joy is fundamental to living as a risen people, and such joy is possible. It is the joy of communities which gather in spite of everything to sing, to recite poetry, to show that they are happy because they are together, to study the Bible and celebrate the eucharist. To be true to their own life they feel the need also to celebrate it. This is the joy of Archbishop Romero, harassed by the powers on all sides, who nevertheless took joy in visiting the communities—and who said rhetorically but truly, "with these people it is not hard to be a good shepherd." It cost him his life, but the people gave him a joy that no one could take away, and the triumph of resurrection was historically present to him in that joy. The martyrs challenge and encourage us to feel that joy.

Hope against resignation. Nothing more fully expresses resurrection than the triumph of hope. "You killed him, but God raised him up," Peter says in Acts. God did justice, not to a corpse, but to a victim. Thus is fulfilled the desire that "the murderer will not triumph over the victim."

Hope is, and continues to be—perhaps increasingly so—hope against hope. But a hopeful Church is a Church already living the resurrection. The martyrs—by expressing the blackness of murder—may be the greatest test for hope, but also its greatest source, because they also express the brightness of a death for love. Indeed that is how the Church began; hope did not die with Jesus' death, but a fuller hope—though still a crucified hope—emerged. That also happens today, so I want to end with I. Ellacuría's words on hope, shortly before his martyrdom:

All the blood of the martyrs, spilled in El Salvador and throughout Latin America, far from causing discouragement and despair, has brought a new spirit of struggle and a new hope to our people. In this sense, we may not be a "new world" or a "new continent," but we are clearly and verifiably (and not necessarily by outsiders) a continent of hope; that is a very interesting mark of a future society, in the eyes of other continents that have no hope—only fear.[10]

Freedom, joy and hope are realities that triumph over the negativity of history. The martyrs encourage us to think of them as forms of historical resurrection. And a free, joyful and hopeful Church is already living as a risen Church.

The Latin American Church has been a persecuted and martyrial Church. Objectively, its martyrs are like Jesus because they followed Jesus to the end, and were killed as a direct result of defending the oppressed, as Jesus was—thus, as witnesses to the God of life. They are martyrs of the kingdom of God and of humanity.

Today at the turn of the millennium, in different situations, the Church of Jesus still needs the spirit and the *pathos* of its martyrs. Its identity, and its relevance, are at stake.

As we look at our world, scattered with the human debris and victims of an iniquitous system, only a Church that holds on to the heritage of the martyrs will have credibility among the poor and those who care about them.

And as we look at God, at faith in God which is often hard to keep alive in our times, only a martyrial Church is able to speak God's name with credibility. Vatican II was already aware that "believers can have more than a little to do with the birth of atheism . . . [when they] conceal rather than reveal the authentic face of God and religion" (*Gaudium et spes,* 19). Scripture says the same thing more sharply: "because of you the name of God is blasphemed among the nations."

In contrast, the martyrs have not used God's name in vain; rather in life and in death they have showed the true face of God. The name of God is not blasphemed in martyr churches; it is blessed, or at least respected. So I want to close with these words of gratitude to the Latin American martyrs: "because of you the name of God is blessed among the poor."

—Translated by Margaret Wilde

Chapter 7

The Crucified Peoples

Yahweh's Suffering Servant Today

In Memory of Ignacio Ellacuría[1]

Ignacio Ellacuría admired Jürgen Moltmann's well-known book *The Cruci-fied God,* but he made a point of stressing another much more urgent theo-logical idea: the crucified people. This was not just for historical reasons (our reality is like this), but also for theological ones (God's creation is like this). It is necessary for us to speak of these crucified peoples in relation to 1992, as well, in order to recall their historical causes. The sole object of all this talk must be to bring them down from the cross.

The Crucified Peoples: A Horrifying Fact

The obvious is the least obvious, Ellacuría used to say. And this is our start-ing point for talking about the crucified peoples. When what is obvious in others—the crucified peoples—shows us what we are, we tend to ignore it, cover it up, or distort it, because it simply terrifies us. So it is understand-able that we should ignore the evidence of the crucified peoples, but we must at least suspect—especially in the Western world, which boasts it has been schooled by the great masters of suspicion—that this ignorance is not mere ignorance, but a will to ignore and cover up. So let us start by dis-covering the covered-up reality of our world.

That creation has turned out badly for God—another provocative phrase of Ignacio Ellacuría's—is confirmed by economists. Terrible poverty is in-creasing in Latin America. It is estimated that by the end of the century, some 170 million Latin Americans will be living in dire poverty and another 170 million in poverty critical to life. To this inhuman poverty, we must add the victims of repression and the wars it has caused. In Central America alone, the victims are estimated to be a quarter of a million.

Reprinted from Jon Sobrino, *The Principle of Mercy* (Maryknoll, N.Y.: Orbis Books, 1994), 173–185.

The Latin American bishops have said so. What characterizes Latin America is "the misery that marginalizes large human groups," which "as a collective fact is an injustice crying to heaven," (Medellín, *Justicia*, no. 1, 1968), "the situation of inhuman poverty in which millions of Latin Americans live" (Puebla, no. 29, 1979). And John Paul II repeated it again in *Sollicitudo rei socialis* (1987).

Whether we look at it from the worldly or the Christian point of view, both agree about the tragedy. Looking at the present situation, which we can see and touch in one way or another, helps us to grasp what happened centuries ago. At the origin of what we call Latin America today there lies an original and originating sin. To give one single fact: Some seventy years after 1492, the indigenous population had been reduced to 15 percent; many of their cultures had been destroyed and subjected to anthropological death. This was a colossal disaster, doubtless due to various complex causes, but nevertheless a really colossal disaster. "For some time . . . I have felt the disappearance of whole peoples as an absurd mystery of historical iniquity, which reduces me to the most abject sort of faith," says Casaldáliga.[2]

So there was a historical disaster, and we have to give it a name. Our current language calls these peoples "Third World," "the South," "developing countries." These designations are attempting to say that something is wrong, but such language does not communicate how wrong. Therefore we need to speak of crucified peoples: metaphorical language, of course, but language which conveys much better than others the historical enormity of the disaster and its meaning for faith. At any rate, it is much better at avoiding the cover-up operated by other languages.

Crucified peoples is useful and necessary language at the real level of fact, because cross means death, and death is what the Latin American peoples are subjected to in thousands of ways. It is slow but real death caused by the poverty generated by unjust structures—"institutionalized violence": "the poor are those who die before their time." It is swift, violent death, caused by repression and wars, when the poor threaten these unjust structures. And it is indirect but effective death when peoples are deprived even of their cultures in order to weaken their identities and make them more defenseless.

It is useful and necessary language at the historical-ethical level because *cross* expresses a type of death actively inflicted. To die crucified does not mean simply to die, but to be put to death; it means that there are victims and there are executioners. It means that there is a very grave sin. The crucified peoples do not fall from heaven. If we followed the metaphor through, we should have to say that they rise from hell. However much people try to soften the fact, the truth is that the Latin American peoples' cross has been inflicted on them by the various empires that have taken power over the continent: the Spanish and Portuguese yesterday, the U.S. and its allies today; whether by armies or economic systems, or the imposition of cultures and religious views, in connivance with the local powers.

Colonialism

It is useful and necessary language at the religious level because cross—Jesus suffered death on the cross and not any other death—evokes sin and grace, condemnation and salvation, human action and God's action. From a Christian point of view, God himself makes himself present in these crosses, and the crucified peoples become the principal sign of the times. "This sign [of God's presence in our world] is always the historically crucified people."[3]

Crucified peoples exist. It is necessary and urgent to see our world this way. And it is right to call them this, because this language stresses their historical tragedy and their meaning for faith.

The Crucified People as Yahweh's Suffering Servant

In Latin America, the fundamental theological statement affirms that the crucified people are the actualization of Christ crucified, the true servant of Yahweh. The crucified people and Christ, Yahweh's servant, refer to and explain each other. This is what two Salvadoran martyrs did, who knew very well what they were talking about. Monseñor Romero told some terrorized peasants who had survived a massacre, "You are the image of the divine victim,"[4] and in another sermon he said that Jesus Christ, the liberator, is so closely identified with the people that interpreters of Scripture cannot tell whether Yahweh's servant proclaimed by Isaiah is the suffering people or Christ, who comes to redeem *us*.[5] Ellacuría said the same. "This crucified people is the historical continuation of Yahweh's servant, whom the sin of the world continues to deprive of any human decency, and from whom the powerful of this world continue to rob everything, taking everything away, even life, especially life."[6]

This theology of the crucified people has become established in Latin America, whereas in other places it may seem exaggerated, unjustified, or unscientific pious language. This is because hermeneutics seeks not only common horizons of cultural understanding between the present and the past, but above all common horizons of reality. This common reality appears clearly in Latin America. The theology of the crucified people as Yahweh's suffering servant includes not only the servant as victim—which people in other situations can understand—but also the servant's saving role in history: historical soteriology, as Ignacio Ellacuría insisted, which is more alien to the theologies of other latitudes and difficult even to imagine if the reality is not seen.

However, to grasp this theology, we need only read the songs of Yahweh's servant with the text in one hand and our eyes on the crucified peoples. So let us do this in the form of a meditation.[7]

What do the songs say about the servant? Above all, he is a "man of sorrows acquainted with grief," and this is the normal condition of the crucified people: hunger, sickness, slums, frustration through lack of education, health, employment. . . . And if their penalties are innumerable in normal times, "peace time," as it is called, they increase even more when, like the servant, they decide to "establish justice and right." Then repression falls on them and the verdict, "guilty of death." Massacres occur, as at Sumpul and El Mozote in El Salvador or Huehuetenango in Guatemala and so many other places. The people become even more like the servant with "no form or comeliness . . . no beauty." And to the ugliness of daily poverty is added that of disfiguring bloodshed, the terror of tortures and mutilations. Then, like the servant, they arouse revulsion: "Many were frightened by him because he was disfigured and did not seem to be a man or look like a human being." And people "hide their faces from him," because they are disgusted, and also so as not to disturb the false happiness of those responsible for the servant, or unmask the truth hidden behind the euphemisms we invent daily to describe him.

Like the servant, the crucified people are "despised and rejected"; everything has been taken from them, even human dignity. And really, what can the world learn and receive from them? What do they offer the world for its progress, apart from their primary materials, their beaches and volcanoes, their folklore for tourists? They are not respected, but despised. And this contempt reaches its height when ideology takes on a religious tinge to condemn them in God's name. It is said of the servant: "We esteemed him stricken, smitten by God, counted among the sinners." And what is said about the crucified peoples? As long as they suffer patiently, they are regarded as having a certain goodness, simplicity, piety especially, which is unenlightened and superstitious, but nonetheless surprises the educated and secularized people from other worlds. Yet when they decide to live and call on God to defend them and set them free, then they are not even recognized as God's people, and the well-known litany is intoned. They are subversives, terrorists, criminals, atheists, Marxists, and communists. Despised and murdered in life, they are also despised in death. It is said of the servant: "They made his grave with the wicked and his tomb with evildoers." This is also the crucified people's epitaph. And sometimes they do not even have this, because though ancient piety denied no one a grave, the crucified people sometimes do not even have this. This is what happens to the disappeared: corpses thrown on rubbish heaps, clandestine cemeteries.

It is said of the servant that "he was oppressed and he was afflicted yet he opened not his mouth," that he died in total meekness. Today not all the crucified die like this. Monseñor Romero was able to speak in his lifetime, and his death shook many consciences. So did the deaths of priests and nuns, and recently that of Ignacio Ellacuría and the other five Jesuits in the UCA. But who knows the seventy thousand assassinated in El Salvador and the eighty thousand in Guatemala? What word is uttered by the children of Ethiopia and the three hundred million in India living in dire poverty? There are thousands and millions who do not say a word. It is not known how they live or how they died. Their names are not known—Julia Elba and Celina are known because they were murdered with the Jesuits. Even their number is not known.

Finally it is said of the servant that "he was taken away defenseless and without judgment" in total impotence against arbitrary injustice. Again this does not apply altogether to the crucified people. Many fight for their lives, and there is no lack of prophets to defend them. But the repression against their struggle is brutal. First they try to discredit the prophets and then coopt them for a civil and ecclesiastical society that presents them as tokens of freedom and democracy—with well-calculated risks—until they become really dangerous. Then they kill them too. Is there a real court to defend the cause of the poor, that at least listens to them and does them justice? No serious notice is taken of them during their lives, and when they die, their deaths are not even investigated.

The crucified people are this suffering servant of Yahweh today. This fact is covered up, because like the servant, the people are innocent. "He had done no violence and there was no deceit in his mouth." The servant not only proclaims the truth of the crucified people, but also the truth about their killers. All of us can and must look at ourselves reflected in the crucified people in order to grasp our deepest reality. As in a mirror, we can see what we are by what we produce.

And we have to be very aware of this in 1992. Some will recall the advances in science and democracy that the Western world has brought, and the church will remember the preaching of the gospel. Others will add that things are not as simple as that, that we cannot blame others entirely for the crucifixion. But at the hour of truth, unless we profoundly accept the truth of the crucified peoples and the fundamental responsibility of successive empires for their crucifixion, we will miss the main fact. That is, that in this world there is still enormous sin. Sin is what killed the servant—the Son of God—and sin is what continues to kill God's children. And this sin is inflicted by some upon others. In a typically Spanish turn of phrase, Ellacuría summed up what successive empires have done to the Latin American continent: "they have left it like a Christ"—they have made a Christ of it.[8]

The Salvation the Crucified Peoples Bring

The foregoing theology is fundamental, and to some extent it is usually adopted in other theologies, especially as an expression of the current problem of theodicy, "how to do theology after Auschwitz." However, in Latin America, we add a second perspective belonging more specifically to liberation theology: We must bring the crucified peoples down from the cross. This is the requirement of an anthropodicy by which human beings can be justified. This can only be done by bringing the crucified peoples down from their crosses.

This is the marrow of liberation theology. And what we want to stress now is that the crucified people themselves are bearers of salvation. The one chosen by God to bring salvation is the servant, which increases the scandal. We sincerely believe that theology does not know what to do with this central statement, unless it seeks in the servant's "vicarious expiation" a theoretical model for understanding Christ's redemption on the cross. But this model does not illuminate what salvation the cross brings, far less what historical salvation the cross brings today. Yet if we abandoned the salvation brought by the servant we would be throwing out something central in the faith. Liberation theology has tried to analyze what salvation and what historical salvation is brought by the servant, and Ellacuría did so with great rigor and vigor in his work *The Crucified People,* which he subtitled "an essay in historical soteriology." Understanding what salvation is brought by the crucified people's suffering is not only or principally a matter of speculation and interpretation of texts. It is a matter of grasping the reality.

The Light the Crucified Peoples Bring

God says of the servant that he will set him up as a "light for the nations" (Isa. 42:6; 49:6). Today this light is to show the nations what they really are. Which is no small benefit. Imprisoning the truth by injustice is the fundamental sin of individuals and also of the nations. Many evils derive from it: among others, the darkening of the heart. A light whose power is capable of unmasking lies is very beneficial and very necessary. This is the light offered by the crucified people. If the First World cannot see its own reality in this light, we do not know what can make it do so.

Ellacuría expressed this graphically in various ways. He said bluntly, using a medical metaphor, that in order to test the health of the First World it was necessary to do a "coproanalysis," that is, to examine its feces, because it is the reality of the crucified peoples that appears in that analysis, and their reality reveals that of those who produce them.

He also said that the Third World offers a great advantage over the First World in throwing light on where we ought to be going.

> From my viewpoint—and this can be one that is both prophetic and paradoxical at once—the US is much worse off than Latin America. Because the US has a solution but in my opinion it is a bad solution, both for them and for the world as a whole. On the other hand, in Latin America there are no solutions, there are only problems. But however painful it is, it is better to have problems than to have a wrong solution for the future of history.[9]

The solution offered by the First World today is factually wrong, because it is unreal; it is not universalizable. And it is ethically wrong, because it is dehumanizing for all, for them and for the Third World.

Finally he said that the Third World offered light on what historical utopia must be today. Utopia in the world today can only be a "civilization of poverty,"[10] all sharing austerely in the earth's resources so that they can stretch to everybody. This sharing achieves what the First World does not offer: fellowship and, with it, meaning of life. He proposed as the way to reach this utopia a civilization of labor as against the current civilization of capital, in all its capitalist and socialist forms.

This is the light given by the crucified peoples. If it is allowed to shine, 1992 will be a very beneficial year. Undoubtedly it will produce panic and disruption, but the light will also dispel the darkness and heal. Instead of the "discovery of America" we shall see the cover-up that has been done there and that what 1492 discovered was above all the reality of the Spanish and Portuguese empire at the time and the Catholic Church at the time: a tragic but fruitful discovery. It will also produce the light of utopia: that true progress cannot consist in what is offered now, but in bringing the crucified peoples down from the cross and sharing the resources and everybody's goods with all.

The Salvation the Crucified Peoples Bring

The crucified peoples also offer positive salvation. Obviously, this is scandalous, but unless we accept it in principle, it will be pointless to repeat that there is salvation in the servant, that the crucified Christ has taken upon himself and got rid of the sin of the world. What we have to do is verify this salvation historically.

Above all, the crucified peoples offer values that are not offered elsewhere. We may discuss whether they create these values because they have nothing else to hold on to, and whether these values will disappear when their present economic and social circumstances disappear and are devoured by the Western capitalist world and its "civilization." But they are there now and are offered to all (and those who work to bring the people down from the cross also work to prevent these values from disappearing).

Puebla said it with chilling clarity, although Western countries and churches have taken very little notice: The poor have evangelizing potential. This potential is spelled out as "the gospel values of solidarity, service, simplicity and readiness to receive God's gift" (no. 1147). In historical language, the poor have a humanizing potential because they offer community against individualism, co-operation against selfishness, simplicity against opulence, and openness to transcendence against blatant positivism, so prevalent in the civilization of the Western world. It is true, of course, that not all the poor offer this, but it is also true that they do offer it and, structurally speaking, in a form not offered by the First World.

The crucified peoples also offer hope, foolish or absurd, it might be said; because it is the only thing they have left, others argue. But once again, it is there, and it must not be trivialized by other worlds. That it is hope against hope is obvious, but it is also active hope that has shown itself in work and liberation struggles. What success these have is another matter, and the Western world appears to emerge triumphant and suffocate them all. We should not hail this as a triumph but mourn it as a disaster, because it is crushing the hope of the poor and thus depriving itself of their humanizing potential. In any case, the very fact that hope arises and re-arises in history shows that history has a current of hope running through it which is available to all. The bearers of this current of hope are the crucified peoples.

The crucified peoples offer great love. It is not masochism or an invitation to suicide, nor making a virtue of necessity, but it is simply true that Latin America's innumerable martyrs show that love is possible because it is real, and great love is possible because many have shown it. And in a structurally selfish world based on selfishness and making a virtue of it—not in so many words, of course—that love is a great offer of humanization.

The crucified peoples are ready to forgive their oppressors. They do not want to triumph over them but to share with them. To those who come to help them, they open their arms and accept them and thus, even without knowing it themselves, they forgive them. In this way they introduce into the Western world that reality which is so humanizing and so lacking, which is gratuitousness: not only what you get for yourself, but also what you are given unexpectedly, freely, and without having to earn it.

The crucified peoples have generated solidarity—human beings and Christians mutually supporting one another, in this way and that, open to one another, giving and receiving one another's best. This solidarity is small, quantitatively speaking; it is only between church and human groups. But we must stress that now it is real and that it did not exist before. On a small scale, it offers a model of how people and churches can relate to one another in a human and Christian way.

Finally, the crucified peoples offer faith, a way of being the church and a more genuine, Christian, and relevant holiness for the world today, that gives more of Jesus. Again, this is more like a seed than a leafy tree, but it is there. We cannot see any other faith, any other way of being the church, or any other holiness that humanizes any better or is a better way of bringing it to God.

It is paradoxical, but it is true. The crucified peoples offer light and salvation. Both can be had in 1992 by those who declare themselves their discoverers, although they have mostly been their coverers-up. Not to receive them would be ungrateful and idiotic; it would be the most radical way of ruining the 1992 "celebrations." Receiving them and letting this gift become a new impulse to bring the people down from the cross would be the best—and the only—proper celebration. Liberated and given grace by the crucified peoples, the First World could become grace and liberation for them. And then there really will be something to celebrate: solidarity of human beings, mutually supporting one another in universal fellowship.

I wish to end with the words with which Ignacio Ellacuría concluded his reflections in 1992. He was not in the least inclined to ahistorical idealism or purely transcendental statements that could not be located in history.

I wish to state the following. Far from causing discouragement and despair, all this martyr's blood spilt in El Salvador and the whole of Latin America infuses our people with a new spirit of struggle and new hope. In this sense, if we are not a "new world" or a "new continent," we are clearly and demonstrably a continent of hope, which is a highly interesting symptom of a future new relation to other continents which do not have hope—the only thing they have is fear.[11]

—Translated by Dinah Livingstone

Part Three

THEIR LEGACY

Chapter 8

Monseñor Romero, a Salvadoran
and a Christian

The most essential thing about the life, faith, praxis, and destiny of Monseñor Romero was this: he was a real human being, in a real world and a real church, with a real faith, real hope, and real commitment. This is what I wish to affirm when I say that Monseñor was, simply and above all else, a Salvadoran and a Christian. I want to recall this clearly so that Monseñor Romero will not be relegated to the void—to *la nada*. This is what many of those who, in his day, hated him and killed him would like. Many of those who even today do not know what to do about him would like this, too. I want to recall his realism, above all, in order that Monseñor not be relegated to a kind of unreality, to appearance or to Docetism, or turned into a figure on a pedestal who offends no one. It is the profound realism of Monseñor Romero's spirituality that has affected me the most. But before reflecting on that spirituality, I want to say something first about the problems I have with using this word, and why.

I must confess that the word "spirituality" makes me uncomfortable and even scares me somewhat. The reason for this is that spirituality comes from Spirit, and the Spirit is something that is not visible and is often contrasted with what is material and historical. For this reason, to speak of spirituality can and often does carry us, one way or another, off to an invisible world, or even to an unreal one. This danger is clearly present whenever we speak about spirituality, but it is especially tragic that it becomes manifest when one is speaking about Monseñor Romero's spirituality, because if there is one thing that Monseñor did not do, it was to live in an unreal world or insulate himself from the reality of El Salvador. Quite the contrary. Without a doubt Monseñor maintained an intimate relationship with God, the great Invisible, but that did not lead him to confuse the world of spirituality with the world of the invisible. Rather, it led him to incarnate

Originally published in *Revista Latinoamericana de Teología* 49 (2000), 24–35. English translation first published in *Spiritus* 1 (2001), 143–155, © 2001 by The John Hopkins University Press.

167

spirituality extremely deeply and radically in the reality of El Salvador. He was, ever increasingly, a "real" archbishop, Christian, and Salvadoran. Spirituality never carried him off into an unreal world.

In the final section I will return to Monseñor's relationship with God. But at this point I simply want to emphasize that he did not fall into this danger and trap—typical of many spiritual persons—as we often see in the history of the Church. Many years ago a French author observed, in denouncing this error, "Because they are not of this world, they think that they are heavenly beings. Because they don't love human beings, they think they love God." Perhaps these are harsh words, but they are useful and necessary, because they put us on our guard against a spirituality that is false.

What am I saying, then, about Monseñor Romero's spirituality, if this spirituality did not carry him off to an invisible or an unreal world? Basically, I would like to say that Monseñor lived his life in the sight of God and of human beings, and that his work, suffering, and dreams were characterized by power and energy. This is quite proper, because power and energy are both signified by the word "spirit." Monseñor Romero was a spiritual person because he was filled with the power of God, with the Spirit of God. But once again, to avoid falling into the error of attaching wings to the Spirit, let us remember that this Spirit is the Spirit of Jesus, and none other. The Spirit molded Monseñor Romero into a likeness of Jesus.

If we ask ourselves, before beginning our reflection, where Monseñor Romero got this power and energy, and how he was able to bring his life into harmony with the Spirit of Jesus, several things may be said. Without any doubt prayer, and reading and hearing the Word of God, were important "places" where he immersed himself in that Spirit. But prayer and meditation can be done in many places and in many ways. I believe that what was unique about Monseñor was that the special place from which he prayed and meditated was the reality of El Salvador, filled as it is with both sin and grace, with both injustice and hope. To put it in the most human terms, reality for him was the poor of Salvadoran society. It was there, amongst the poor, that he made contact with God and immersed himself in the Spirit, in the power of God.

Monseñor opened himself up to the Spirit of God and let himself be carried along by his compassion for this Salvadoran reality—the terrible suffering, the heroic solidarity, and the poor people's incredible sense of hope. Love for God and the Gospel did not cause him to distance himself from what was real; they did not become some kind of drug he took to help him drift off to sleep. Quite the opposite. Love of God and the Gospel turned him back to face the reality of his people, and from there he drew light so that he might know God better, and he drew power and energy from that place to put the Gospel into practice. Monseñor Romero was a *real* Salvadoran and a *real* Christian, and this, I believe, was the most essential thing about his spirituality.

With regard to Monseñor's spirituality I will reflect on four elements that follow the outline of the life of Jesus: incarnation, mission, cross, and resurrection. Spirituality, for Monseñor Romero, consisted in living out—in reality—these four critical moments in the life of Jesus.

Monseñor Romero Was, Like Jesus, "Real" in His Incarnation within the True Reality of El Salvador

I think we all remember a time when, if you wanted to praise someone, it was common to say they were very "human" or "Christian" or "authentic." However, I do not think such words are sufficient in this case. Nor do I think it is enough to say that "he was a saint" or "he was very spiritual." Someone might be all these things and still not be real—in our case, not be Salvadoran. For example, in a country where there have been persecutions, if these do not bespatter us with any dirt, then people might say all the beautiful things about us mentioned above, but we are not real. Indeed, we have become unreal.

Let us recall Monseñor Romero now and ask ourselves, what was the reality of his time? Actually, things have not changed much since then. There were *anawim* in El Salvador then, those "bent beneath the weight of heavy burdens," as the Scriptures say. There were poor people, for whom to be of service was the greatest ambition, and whose most likely fate was often death from hunger or from violence at the hands of the state. There were— and still are—those who had no dignity, who had no significance, those who did not count, those who were excluded. There were those who were silenced, those who had no voice. There were those who were powerless, who did not have the ability to defend their most basic rights. There were also those considered to be of no account because they did not follow the cultural dictates imposed on us.

That was the reality then, and all these groups of persons (Neoliberalism would today add to the list those "who do not exist"—those who cannot even be considered cheap hand labor—because they are unemployed, and it is impossible that they will ever be employed) were oppressed by that reality. Additionally, we are more aware of the oppression, hidden for centuries, of women, of children, and of whole races of people. In the days of Monseñor Romero there also was cruel and inhuman oppression—today it no longer takes the abhorrent forms it did then. As he would say, "Hacking people down with machetes, torture, exile, throwing people into the air (from a helicopter). . . . That is a Satanic empire."

The question we must ask about Monseñor Romero's spirituality, then, is what did he, as a man and as a Christian, do within that reality? Let us begin by remembering what he did *not* do. Although it might seem obvious, one thing that Monseñor Romero never did was to distance himself from that terrible reality. To elucidate this, we might begin by recognizing his limitations, including things he did that may have been mistakes. Still, one thing Monseñor never did was to distance himself from the reality in which he lived—and that is the first step of what Christians call incarnation. When we speak of the flesh that Christ assumed in the Incarnation, the Gospel does not speak simply of "flesh," but of *sarx,* which is to say, "the debilities of the flesh." Monseñor Romero did the same thing: he did not simply incarnate himself within Salvadoran reality; he also took on the debilities of that reality: the pain, poverty, suffering, and oppression of the poor, and the violence directed against them by the state.

I begin my analysis of Monseñor Romero's spirituality in this way because, in my opinion, one of the greatest dangers in the Church today, especially in the Salvadoran Church, is the absence of true incarnation in reality. The danger we face is that of falling into unreality, and thus we end up living outside this world, and never making the real life of the poor of this country our own. The Church might say that its reality has other parameters, which is obviously true—it has its evangelization parameters, liturgical parameters, doctrinal parameters, and canonical parameters. The Church accepts that it can play a role only in the social sphere, not in the political sphere. It reiterates that its true purpose is bringing God's salvation. But what worries me is that by appealing to these arguments—which are of questionable validity—or others like them, the Church ends up distancing itself from the reality of El Salvador.

Let us consider a relatively recent example, which I mention with all respect due such matters, but I mention it because of the way it illuminates the theme of incarnation. In 1996, we were visited by the Holy Father. If we look beyond what was an understandable and inevitable mixture of devotion and euphoria, of Christian message and folk expression, the question becomes, how and where was the reality of this country made visible within the context of that visit? In other words, where were the poor? Of course, they could be seen on the sidewalks all along the route taken by the papal procession, but they were there more as part of the background than as something that is central to our reality. The most "real" aspect of that reality—their poverty and suffering, as well as their hopes and pleasures— was not made a central theme. It would seem that, according to the organizers of the Holy Father's visit, making that reality visible was not truly important. It was certainly not the most central issue. So, in this way, the Church, without meaning to do so, created the appearance of many things at once: of being well organized, and of being close to the leadership of the country and to the media. It did not, however, give the image of being a Salvadoran Church, or a Church of the poor, or a Church that is "real."

With Monseñor Romero, things were not like that. The reality of the poor moved him passionately and he let that passion absorb him, not for superficial sentimental reasons, but because he saw in it the endpoint of pain and of hope, and the endpoint of his own faith: the presence of God and of Jesus. I often say, because it impressed me so deeply, that many things could be said about Monseñor Romero's Church. You can say that his Church had limitations, that it made many mistakes and committed many sins. But what you cannot say about Monseñor Romero's Church is that it was not Salvadoran. I do not mean this in a populist sense. Nor can you say that the Church was not "real." The majority of the poor, the peasants and the workers, did not feel that this Church was alien to them. They did not see it as separate from themselves. They saw it as Salvadoran, as real, and as theirs.

Monseñor Romero expressed this, above all, in his daily routine. But every once in a while he would also let slip some audacious and beautiful remark that captured his great dream, which was that the Church might be Salvadoran. For example, Monseñor Romero would make statements that still amaze us today, such as, "I am glad, brothers and sisters, that the Church is being persecuted." Someone might think that these are the words of a mystic, or a saint, but that would be a mistake. These are simply the words of a Christian and a Salvadoran. He explained the reason he felt this paradoxical gladness: the Church was persecuted "because it tried to become incarnate in the interests of the poor." Monseñor Romero was pleased that the Church was persecuted not because of some precipitant mysticism, but because this made the Church a Salvadoran Church, a Church that was real. Using even stronger words, he sometimes said, "It would be sad that in a country in which there are so many horrible assassinations there were no priests counted among the victims."

These are the words of a great Christian. I would even go so far as to say that they should be sufficient to canonize him and make him a doctor of the Church. But the important thing is not the inspiration or the genius of the formulation, but the depth of the conviction of Monseñor Romero, and of his passion to "be real." Certainly the priests who were assassinated are testimony to a Church that is incarnate in the problems of the people. They were not perfect; Monseñor recognized this. They had their faults, but they were assassinated for living in and trying to create a Salvadoran Church, a Church that was real.

It is also important to emphasize, not only to correct any suggestion of masochism but also to understand Monseñor Romero's passion for a Church that was real, that he wanted this Church to express the positive aspects of Salvadoran reality, the pleasures and hopes of the poor, as the beginning of *Gaudium et Spes* says to do—but he wanted this to be taken seriously. When he witnessed the tenacity and long suffering of the people, he would say, speaking to Christians, "If someday they take the radio away from us and shut down the newspaper, if they refuse to let us speak, if they kill all the priests and even the bishop, and you are left alone, if only the people remain, without any priests, then each one of you must become God's microphone. Each one of you must become a messenger. Each one of you must become a prophet."

These words spoken by Monseñor Romero about his Church reflect what he himself was: a man possessed by the spirit of incarnation, a spirit of solidarity with reality and with its poor. I imagine that if there was one thing that would have made Monseñor ashamed, it would have been a Church that was not bespattered by the dirt of Salvadoran reality. Likewise, he would never have suggested, even within his own heart, that the Church should be exempt from the dangers of our reality. This error, so often accepted without a thought, he would have denounced as Docetism, which is what it ends up being. This type of thinking goes something like this: "Although unjust and regrettable, it is understandable that the labor unions have their microphones confiscated or their buildings bombed, or that the peasants be oppressed and attacked. What is not acceptable is that the Church be treated in this way, because we are not like everyone else." Monseñor Romero would say just the opposite: "I am glad that they confiscated our microphones! We are like everyone else, and we are going to show the same tenacity and longsuffering as everyone else."

I come to the end of this reflection. The Church of Monseñor Romero, with him as its head, was Church that was real. By way of contrast, a Church that in a time of poverty is not poor; that in a time of persecution is not persecuted; that in a time of assassinations is not subject to assassination; that in a time of solidarity does not manifest solidarity nor dares to do so in times of indifference; that has no hope in a hopeful time nor dares to hope in a time of hopelessness, simply is not a Church that is real. Perhaps it might be considered "spiritual" by other measurements, if you permit me this irony, but it would not have the "spirit of reality" Monseñor Romero had—and which Jesus of Nazareth had, too.

Monseñor Romero, Like Jesus, Fulfilled His Mission, Which Was the Evangelization of an Entire Nation, of All of Reality

Monseñor Romero evangelized through the Word, announcing the good news of God's love to the poor, denouncing the oppressor, and writing pastoral letters to bring light to the nation. He also evangelized through his deeds: by seeking through dialogue to bring about peace, by supporting the work of Judicial Aid and the Social Secretariat, and by opening the first shelters when the war began. He also evangelized through his person; his way of acting was itself gospel, good news, for the majority of people in the country and for many others beyond our borders. All this is well known. What needs restating, in terms of spirituality, is, in the first place, that Monseñor did all these things in a spirit of mercifulness. In the second place—and this I want to emphasize—this was a mercifulness that was extended to an entire people. Monseñor Romero sought the salvation of an entire nation.

I want to recall this because today there are all kinds of ecclesial movements that seek to bring salvation to married couples, to young people, to university students—we also try to do the same things here at the University of Central America—and we all know how necessary this work is. But we must be clear that the reality of our situation is greater than these things. Reality, of course, includes these things, and it tells how important they are. For example, in our countries the youth issue is decisive. However, we must not forget that reality includes the entire people. Perhaps this sort of language seems outmoded or naive, because there have been many changes in the Church since the days of Monseñor Romero. But if we wish to recall Monseñor, then we must also remember the popular majorities. We must remember the people.

Ignacio Ellacuría, who is very knowledgeable regarding Monseñor Romero and is anything but naive, was asked, shortly after Monseñor's death, to write an article about him. He began it with these words: "Monseñor Romero, the man sent by God to save his people." With regard to the mission of the Church, this reminds us that Monseñor's desire was to work out the salvation of the people. With regard to spirituality, it reminds us that he was inspired to include everyone, the whole nation. "I want these homilies," he would say, "to become the voice of those who have no voice," that is to say, of the majority, of the common people. When he witnessed violations, horrors, and the countless occasions of suffering in the country, he would say, "Upon these ruins will shine the glory of the Lord."

When, in compassion, he would look on the people, he said, like Jesus said, "They are like sheep without a shepherd." What am I trying to say by this? That in following Jesus and carrying out the mission of the Church, Monseñor Romero kept the majority of the people and a complete view of reality ever before him. He could not bring salvation all by himself, of course. The Church cannot do that, either. However, he never fell into what I regard as the "triple error." The first error is to place boundaries on the scope of the Church's evangelization, taking care to not overstep the limits of normal ecclesial concerns, and making oneself smaller to stay within those limits, thus reducing the scope of the Church's mission, saying, "This is political, this is *not* political." It is as if, by determining what is and what is not reality through the use of definitions, the primary responsibility of the Church and of all human beings, which is to bring salvation to all of reality, might be made to disappear. The second error is to lower and hold down the horizons of the Church's mission; by satisfying itself with the doing of good deeds the Church is thus absolved of its responsibility. The third error is to agree to an "abridged version," in which the totality of situations is not recounted, such as whole peoples crucified, hopes dashed, and the laborious task it is to try to take them down from the cross. In this regard, Monseñor Romero breathed the spirit of the epic narratives.

Monseñor Romero was not mean-spirited, not a man of pettiness, not the "save what you can" type. In the professional sense, as an archbishop, he was well aware of what his duty was and was not. However, the horizons of his mission were clear: salvation must reach everything and everyone. In this regard, Monseñor Romero was a man with a largeness of spirit, a man of strength when the hour came for decisions to be made. His pastoral letters—

and here it must be noted that in the intervening years since his time no pastoral letters of importance have been written regarding this country—his letters considered how problems would impact the entire population. His denunciations, as we all know, were heard around the world. And this happened even though he mentioned, in fact *because* he mentioned, all the cases of human rights violations. His dominical homilies were unparalleled and exemplary; they amounted to a massive pastoral pronouncement on everything, and they reached everyone. This did not happen by accident; rather, it was what he desired and then brought to fulfillment in the light of conditions that made such a massive pastoral pronouncement necessary. It proceeded from serious biblical reflection in preparation for giving a homily that would truly bring light to shine on the country's reality. It was reflected in the credibility of his words, the decision to continue "forever" despite the slander, the many types of interference, or the destruction of the bearer of the Word.

Monseñor Romero's hope was to evangelize the structure of society—something seldom even considered these days. He wanted to change the economic and political infrastructure, as well as the legal institutions, the health care institutions, and the media. He also wanted to change—to evangelize—the ecclesial infrastructure, with its curia, parishes, religious congregations, educational institutions, and internal politics. When he saw serious problems in the country—the violence, the problems faced by grass-roots organizations, and, toward the end of his life, the imminence of war—he tackled these in a responsible fashion. He always acted in the country's best interests. Sometimes he uttered threats of punishment, like the prophets of ancient Israel, but never against this or that person, but rather against an entire class of people guilty of oppression. "You rich, remove your rings, because, if you don't, your hands will be cut off" (quoting, of course, from Paul VI).

Monseñor Romero also perceived that, within the errors I have mentioned above, there are other errors of the opposite sort, too, such as becoming involved in politics as an entity with political power, or trying to do so much that you end up accomplishing nothing. However, he did not regard these as major issues. He did not allow himself to be walled up in a sacristy, or in a pastoral letter, or in a mission with limited horizons.

He accomplished all this with an exceptional creativity that combined real closeness with people in their communities. In making his pastoral visits, he dealt with the reality of the entire archdiocese, and he did not lose the perspective of the country as a whole. If Monseñor Romero went to a specific town or a village, this act would have larger implications. If he spoke on the radio, many communities were able to participate and hear what he was saying. When he opened a shelter—with great symbolism, in the building that housed the seminary—he did much more than to simply open "one" shelter; he started a whole shelter movement.

What am I trying to say? I believe that Monseñor Romero undoubtedly had an idea what evangelism meant—in 1977, he organized a conference for priests on Paul VI's *Evangelii nuntiandi*. The most innovative aspect of this for me was that he wanted to evangelize the country in its totality—everyone: individuals, social groups, and infrastructures—and to evangelize a country in which there was terrible oppression and state-sponsored violence, kidnappings, disappearances, and killings; where there was poverty and injustice but also hope, solidarity, strength, faithfulness, and martyrdom. I repeat, Monseñor was a man of courage, of Pauline *parresía*. "Evangelize" meant, "to bring salvation to a people." There is a deficit of such thinking in the Church these days.

Monseñor Romero Bore the Burden of Reality: Like Jesus, He Died on the Cross

This is a well-known fact and it need not detain us. I merely want to make clear that Monseñor's spirituality was not a spirituality of suffering, to be understood either ascetically or mystically, but rather a spirituality of honor in the face of reality, and thus, necessarily, a spirituality of bearing the burden of reality. Monseñor could easily have toned down his denunciations; he could easily have reached an understanding with certain authorities, or left the country—and done so with ample justification. But his sense of honor led him to bear the heavy burden of reality and not seek to escape from it. Above all, it must be said that he never invoked God or the Gospel as an excuse for fleeing from his obligations.

Bearing the cross is not some sublime experience. Rather, it is the most absolutely obvious task if one wishes to behave honorably in the face of reality. I say this because this conviction has become eroded lately. There is a deficit in this country generally, both among politicians and within the Church, of this sense of honor and readiness to bear the burden of reality.

It is commonly said today that things have changed, and it is true that there have been important innovations. But in this country there has been no change in the fundamental reality of poverty and injustice—although they may take on different forms—nor has violence been curbed to any major extent. At the level of world statistics, the annual United Nations reports show that the planet has remained mired in violence to a horrendous extent; there has been no substantive change in the amount of social conflict or the need for its unmasking and resolution. There has been no change in the need to engage in this conflict. What has changed, in many places and also in this country, is the willingness and resoluteness to see and say the truth, as well as to engage in the conflict.

In the days of Monseñor Romero, the Church came into conflict with the powers of oppression when it defended the majority of the people against oppression and state-sponsored violence. We know that this stance created great suffering and, in the long term, that this stance is hard to maintain—and, of course, not all situations in the long term of history are equally serious. However, it would seem that today one tries to avoid anything involving conflict as if on principle, as if some better way has been discovered, some way of being Church and remaining on good terms with other powerful entities in this world, even when these entities continue to create victims.

When this is the case, reality is neither a burden nor something onerous, and there is no need to bear its burden. But then one hears the quiet echo of Monseñor Romero's words: "A Church which does not suffer persecution, but in fact enjoys the privileges and the support of the world, is a Church which should be afraid, because it is not the true Church of Jesus Christ." He said such things at a time when the persecution of the Church and of grassroots organizations was harsh and pitiless, and today that is no longer the case. However, to think that not suffering persecution is more Christian, or that the most desirable arrangement is for the Church to be on good terms with the powers of this world is an error, if considered in light of the Gospel—and in light of Monseñor Romero.

In society there are many real conflicts, and the Church will find itself facing many other potential conflicts if it is truly fulfilling its mission of prophetic denunciation and maintaining a preferential option for the poor. To face such conflicts, the Church must have a spirit like Monseñor Romero had, a spirit of integrity with regard to reality, a spirit of strength to join in the conflict and a spirit of resolve to bear the burden of that reality. This is what it means to carry the cross today.

Monseñor Romero Accepted the Burden of Reality and Experienced the Grace of Living as if Already Participating in the Resurrection

Shortly before he died, Monseñor Romero said these well-known words: "If I am killed I will resurrect in the people of El Salvador." And one can say that this has come to pass in many ways: Monseñor lives on in our sense of hope, in the celebrations of individuals and of communities. He lives on, above all, in many Salvadoran hearts, as in the hearts of people all over the world, whenever anyone decides to live as he did, and as Jesus did.

Since we are speaking about the spirituality of Monseñor Romero, I would like to conclude with some reflections that are normally not included. It is true that reality is harsh and one must bear with that harsh reality, but reality also bears with us and helps us to walk within history. In Christian terms, we can say that in reality there is both gift and grace, that there is something we receive. If I were to use even more audacious language, I would say that we can live within reality like persons who already participate in the resurrection. When history no longer binds us down and we are able to triumph over those elements within it that enslave us, then we reflect in some way the triumph of the resurrection of Jesus. What is expressed is a fullness, and it shows forth when, through following Jesus—

and remaining focused on love—liberty, joy, and hope appear. That is what showed forth in Monseñor Romero.

Reality—that is, the people, with their example of solidarity and generosity—made Monseñor Romero act freely, and made him a man of freedom. This was not the freedom of the liberals, which comes from selfishness. Rather, for Monseñor Romero, as for Jesus, freedom meant that no obstacle could stand in the way of the need to do good. This is what it means to be a free man. And this freedom came to him from the people. The suffering he saw in his people and the love that his people showed him caused him to lower all his defenses. It made him free. It was for that reason that he was able to say, like Jesus, "No one takes my life from me, because I give my life up freely."

Reality—which means, again, simple people and their love—taught him also to rejoice in living and serving. Monseñor was a nervous type of person by temperament, and was sometimes weak and restless. However, I believe that, paradoxically and in the midst of so many difficulties, he lived in peace and joy. Sometimes you glimpsed this in the smile on his face, especially when he was surrounded by children, by peasants, or by simple people. Once, he expressed it in these beautiful words: "With people such as this, it is not hard to be a good shepherd." In truth, being a good shepherd did cost him a great deal. In accepting the burdens of the people, he took on the burdens of the cross as well. And yet, the people also accepted his burdens. For this reason Monseñor Romero had to suffer, but he was not overcome by sadness. Like Jesus, he felt the profound joy of realizing that it is the little ones who understand the kingdom of God.

And finally, there was hope. His well-known denunciations of the country's abominations would have driven anyone to a feeling of impotence or resignation. Nevertheless, Monseñor Romero was a man of hope: "Many times I have been asked, 'is there any way out of this?' And I, feeling full of faith, not just a divine faith, but also a faith in humanity, say, 'yes, there is a way out of this!'" Monseñor was triumphant over resignation, lack of faith, and disillusionment.

From that Salvadoran reality, before which he lived with honor, and all the while being immersed in it, desiring to completely change it, and bearing its burden, there also sprang grace, freedom, joy, and hope. In that regard Monseñor lived like someone who was already resurrected, although still living within history. This is vital to recall today, when there is no such abundance of freedom, joy, or hope in the churches. The key here is having a spirituality of grace, which requires the opening up of oneself to grace.

These I believe to be the main points of Monseñor Romero's spirituality. What I have tried to emphasize is that these points are attitudes, convictions, and practices that were taken up by him in response to reality.

Perhaps this way of interpreting spirituality seems strange, because it is not an analysis of his relationship to God. At this point all I can say is that for Monseñor Romero, God was very real. In the depths of his heart—in the inner "cells of the heart," as he would say—God was present. I have absolutely no doubt about that. I would only like to add that being able to discern God's presence in the heart of another person is, on the one hand, a mystery. But, on the other hand, God's presence can be seen in the way a person conducts himself in reality, in what he does with it, in his willingness to bear its burden and let it bear his burdens. When that exterior self is like that of Jesus, then within the interior self of the person the God of Jesus must be present, too.

Monseñor Romero, a Salvadoran and a Christian. I hope we can continue to regard him in these terms. And I hope that we do not put asunder what God has joined: that which was Salvadoran and that which was Christian, that which was best in the country and that which was best in the Church were united and spoke to us in the person of Monseñor. These parts were joined together not by any jealousy of one part for another, but by *bringing* one part over to *meet together* with that other part.

—*Translated by Michael O'Laughlin*

Chapter 9

Archbishop Romero: Requirement, Judgment and Good News

March 24 [2000] was the twentieth anniversary of the murder-martyrdom of Archbishop Romero, and the celebrations have brought to light several things that are worthy of reflection. The first reflection is on Monseñor's presence in these celebrations, twenty years later, in spite of all the obstacles. The second is on Monseñor's identity, how he got the courage to speak as he spoke and to live as he lived—which keeps him alive into our time. The third is about the need to carry on his cause, today and throughout history, in the midst of efforts to bury him and co-opt him. And finally, there is the perennial question about what Archbishop Romero represents today, for our country and our world.

These reflections are addressed to everyone. Perhaps believers are the ones best able to grasp the nuances of the religious concepts and language. But we think everyone who works for the life of the poor, and who holds on to hope, can understand. Institutions can also understand. As we write we are thinking especially of the churches, but clearly any institution (transnational corporations, international political bodies, governments, armies, banks, political parties, the media, labor unions, etc.) can and must wonder sometimes—or shamefacedly suppress the question—what to do with Archbishop Romero.

Let us begin with a word about the title. Monseñor was a rich figure, hard to synthesize in a few words. We have decided to call him "judgement," "requirement," and "good news." Clearly he is "good news" for the poor of this world. It should also be clear that Monseñor is for us a "requirement," to bring the poor down from the cross. And in his death, he is also "judgment" on a murderous world which continues to produce death in the [African] Lake Region; in the economic boycott against children, women, and the elderly in Iraq; in the barbarity now occurring in East Timor and Chechnya. "Judgment on the world" is not a widely accepted phrase these days, but without it Monseñor's figure would be distorted and

First published in *Revista Latinoamericana de Teología* 50 (2000), 191–207.

co-opted—as would that of the crucified Christ, whom we remember now
during Holy Week.

Monseñor's Presence in This Anniversary

First proposition. This celebration of the twentieth anniversary has
shown that Archbishop Romero is still present among the poor, and
among their partners in solidarity in many parts of the world. His
presence is not obvious, but it is a "triumph," for he is here in spite of
the powerful forces that are trying to bury him.

In an interview three weeks before his assassination, Archbishop Romero
spoke these famous words: "If they kill me, I will rise again in the Salvadoran people. I say this without pride, with great humility." Twenty years
later it is clear that he was right, and the twentieth anniversary celebration
leaves no doubt about it.

These have been days of cultural and artistic celebration, of academic
and theological events. But they have been above all days of pilgrimages to
the "little hospital" and to the crypt, days of heartfelt eucharists and, we believe, of commitments made in the secret places of people's hearts. People
from this country and around the world have taken part. There were tens of
thousands of them, in what was perhaps the largest popular demonstration
since his tragic funeral on March 30, 1980. The people came into the
streets, and their respect and devotion, their happiness and joy, were unconcealable. And let it be understood that their joy, especially that of the
mothers and relatives of victims who had taken mortal risks in the days of
repression and war, their joy was not from denial and forgetting, but remembrance and a word of gratitude that cannot be forever silenced. Archbishop Romero's twentieth anniversary was "full of grace and truth," as
John's gospel says of God's coming into our world.

So Monseñor was right, and these days have only served to universalize
his resurrection. "St. Romero of the Americas," Dom Pedro Casaldáliga
wrote of him soon after his martyrdom. Now he is rightly called a "universal saint." He has truly risen in the crucified peoples' hunger for justice, dignity and life; in the commitment of men and women everywhere who have
not become completely immune to the shame of living in this cruel world,
but who rather are trying to change history.

That said, we must also be aware that his resurrection is not obvious,
given the existing balance of power. The conditions have not been favorable; practically all the powers of this world were against it. For twenty
years the oligarchies, military leaders, governments—here and in the United
States—as well as some ecclesiastical powers, bishops, and cardinals have
been trying to silence and bury Monseñor. On his side were groups of followers and their partners in solidarity, and a people who have kept him

alive by dint of their hope and their nakedness—as in the painting by Benjamín Cañas which shows a peasant woman delicately holding him up with one hand, while with the other she lays a flower on his body.

If that is true, then the finger of God is here. And if Monseñor is still present, in spite of and against so many powers, then he was right to use the word "resurrection," which means not only life but triumph over death. Indeed the Monseñor who lives today has triumphed over slander in his life, and over the cover-up that surrounded his death. He triumphs today over efforts to forget him and to manipulate him. Those who wanted to bury him have lost a battle, which they fought intensely and with no holds barred—but in vain. Even the Legislative Assembly, which has repeatedly blocked the search for justice and truth, which proclaimed an unjust and conspiratorial amnesty, was finally forced to declare him a "meritorious citizen," and to recognize him as a pastor who struggled for justice, freedom, democracy and peace. So Monseñor has not only risen but triumphed over his adversaries, and yet he continues to hold out the hand of reconciliation. He is not an inflated myth, as some wish; he has imposed himself gently but inexorably, by his own reality. And that explains the joy of the poor: for once their defender has triumphed over their oppressors.

This is the first point to emphasize from the twentieth anniversary: Archbishop Romero "was right." There is not a touch of *hubris*, nor a glint of arrogance, in that affirmation. Nor is it the last, cold comfort of a people who can say "at least we were right" after years of being denied not only life and justice, but also truth and rightness. Rather it is the joy of sometimes, miraculously, seeing good come out of our usually cruel and secretive history: the joy of seeing that God has done justice to a victim, that the murderer has not triumphed. There is hope for the victims of this world; that is good news in a country of 70,000 victims.

There is also another hope, in other memorable words spoken by Archbishop Romero in the same interview. These words gave his people hope "that my blood may be the seed of liberation," and gave hope for the Church: "I hope they will realize they are wasting their time. One bishop may die, but God's Church, which is the people, will never die." And with regard to reconciliation, Monseñor did not speak in terms of hope, but of reality: "You may say that if they should kill me, I will forgive and bless those who do it."

Monseñor's Identity: Identification with the People and with His God

Second proposition. A decisive change took place in Archbishop Romero, which shaped his deepest identity: a total identification with his people, with their sufferings and hopes, and total trust and faithfulness to the mystery of God, as God of the poor.

Archbishop Romero was right, but his words still leave us speechless; we wonder how he could say such things, where he got the lucidity and conviction to say what no one else dared say, and to say it so naturally. Understanding this, we believe, helps to understand his most intimate identity—to know what made him a Salvadoran and a universal Christian. Let us see how Ignacio Ellacuría understood Monseñor's deepest roots, as one martyr to another. This is what he said on March 22, 1985, when the Central American University posthumously awarded Archbishop Romero an honorary doctorate:

> Archbishop Romero's hope was supported by two pillars: an historical pillar, his knowledge of the people, who he believed had an inexhaustible ability to find a way out of the most serious problems; and a transcendent pillar, his conviction that ultimately God is a God of life and not death, that the ultimate reality is good and not evil (*ECA* 437 [1985], p. 174.)

The Mystery of a Suffering and Hopeful People

Let us begin by analyzing the "historical pillar." We can debate whether what happened to Monseñor was a change or a conversion, but there can be no doubt that at some moment in his life—very shortly after he began his ministry as archbishop—the people, "their poorness," came into his heart and mind and made of him a new man and a new believer, a flawless human being and a man of faith.

That essential turning toward his people became second nature to him, or rather, became the true and definitive nature that he could no more take off than his own skin. And I believe that turning explains the radical newness of Monseñor's way of being, doing, and speaking, as he said in his own words, without rhetoric but with complete authenticity:

> The people are my prophet (homily of July 8, 1979). With these people it is not hard to be a good pastor (November 18, 1979). You see, the conflict is not between the Church and the government. It is between the government and the people. The Church is with the people and the people are with the Church. Thanks be to God! (January 21, 1979). First I have to listen to what the Spirit says through the people; then I can meet with the people and analyze it, and—together with the people—use it to build the Church (September 30, 1979). May my death be for the liberation of my people (interview, March 1980). My life is not mine, but yours (August 21, 1977).

Some say that in the Church's twenty centuries there have never been homilies like Monseñor's. This might seem exaggerated, or at least surprising.

But clearly the profound truth in that affirmation is explained by the impact that his people's suffering and hope caused in Archbishop Romero. "The people made you a saint," Casaldáliga said from the beginning. Archbishop Romero was graced, blessed, freed from himself by the Spirit of God, but the historical mediation of that fundamental, foundational grace was "the people who loved you so," as a popular song put it. Once that grace was consummated, Monseñor came to be, to do, and to speak in a very different way—as if something had awakened in him, at last and irreversibly, the depth and simplicity of his humanity and Christianity.

Something new was given to Monseñor with that change, without detracting from the good that was there before. He was given freedom, so that nothing would hinder him from serving the people: "Pray that I may be faithful to this promise, that I will not abandon my people, but with them I will accept all the risks that my ministry requires" (November 11, 1979). He was given compassion, so that nothing would distract him from the people's suffering: "It is my job to go around picking up assault victims and cadavers" (June 19, 1977). He was given hope, so that the last word would always be good news: "The glory of the Lord will shine over these ruins" (January 7, 1979).

And perhaps the deepest grace that he was given was his passion for nearness and identification with the people. That is the meaning of these words, which one seldom if ever hears from a bishop:

> I rejoice, brothers and sisters, that our Church is persecuted (July 15, 1979). . . . It would be sad if in a nation where people are being murdered so horribly, there were not also priests among the victims. They are the testimony of a Church incarnated in the problems of the people (July 24, 1979).

These are not the words of a mystic, and certainly not of a masochist. They are the words of a graced, Christian man, someone who wants to be real in and with his people. "We don't want to be different," Archbishop Romero seems to be saying, in defiance of centuries of ecclesiastical tradition. Given the depth of his identification with his sheep, it is not at all surprising that the sheep heard his voice and recognized themselves in Monseñor's voice.

The God of the Poor, a Holy and Unmanipulatable Mystery

Let us turn now to the "transcendent pillar." Throughout his life Archbishop Romero was an honorable believer, but—in the midst of his people—God took over and reshaped him in a different, radical way. Monseñor became a believer who reminds one of Abraham and Jeremiah, of Mary and Jesus. In that God, Archbishop Romero discovered his own depth.

God was a holy mystery for Archbishop Romero, something beyond all humanity and yet present in the depth of humanity. He was the God who judges severely, but above all, the God who humanizes, who saves without enslaving, and gives without diminishing. So for Archbishop Romero, turning to God was a source of salvation. He said this with total conviction, in words that coming from others would sound like facile pietism. We remember some of his words, whose depth is evident from the context in which he spoke them. Six weeks before his murder, on February 10, 1980, Monseñor harshly denounced the reality of the country:

> Undoubtedly aided by elements of the national army, in violation of their promise on October 15, the illegal arrests have continued; investigations have been delayed; there has been negligence—not to mention ill will—in investigating all the operations and criminal actions of the extreme right.

And in the same context of the country's reality, with the same conviction and energy, Archbishop Romero rose to transcendence and spoke of what is truly humanizing and salvific in God: "I wish, dear brothers and sisters, that as a result of today's preaching each of us would come to know God, and that we would rejoice in his majesty and our insignificance!"

That mystery of God, unspeakable and invisible, began appearing to him in different ways, with different faces. It showed itself most certainly in the face of the poor, as the God of life, God of justice, God of the victims, and also the God of hope and resurrection. And this new faith, taking shape within him, could also be seen on the outside of Archbishop Romero's life.

Although an experience of God is never fully verifiable—certainly not another person's experience of God—it was clear to everyone that the same Monseñor who never knew what to do with Medellín, although he accepted it formally, was beginning to feel at home with Medellín. This caused astonishment among those who had supported him before, precisely because he was not a "Medellinista" (whereas Archbishop Rivera and others were perceived as such). What happened is that Medellín began to speak to Monseñor of the poor and of their God, so that he rediscovered the scriptural God who had always been "the father of orphans and widows"—the one described in these words about God, which express the faith of Israel according to the experts: "In thee the poor find compassion."

And that explains (although we can only mention it briefly) how Archbishop Romero—a Christian and a bishop of whom people rightly expected orthodoxy and faithfulness to ecclesial tradition—naturally and joyfully rediscovered in that tradition the God of the poor, the poor who cry out to God. Thus Monseñor paraphrased the saying of St. Irenaeus, the second-century bishop of Lyon: "the glory of God is the poor person who lives." He practiced daily—to the point of martyrdom—what was required of bishops in the sixteenth century: "to be, *ex oficio,* defenders of Indians," following the Old Testament principle that Yahweh is the *goel,* "defender" of the poor and "restorer" of what has been taken away from them. He focused his ministry on the absolute supremacy of the life of the poor: "a living Indian is of greater value than a dead convert," as bishop Bartolomé de las Casas used to say. He also adopted Las Casas' central christological insight: "I leave Jesus Christ, our God, in the Indies, flogging and afflicting and slapping and crucifying him, not once but thousands of times, all in the name of the Spaniards who are laying waste and destroying those peoples." In the same tradition, with the same energy and devotion, Archbishop Romero called his people "the pierced of God," "the crucified Christ," "Yahweh's suffering servant," who bear the sins of the world on their shoulders.

God and the poor, the poor and God, who were united from the beginning but who have often been separated by the churches; Archbishop Romero brought them together in his person with unequaled depth. He identified with the poor people and gave himself to them, to the very end. He lived and walked always in total faithfulness before God and with God, and that gave meaning and joy to his life. "My life has only been one poem in God's project. . . . I have tried to be as God wants me to be" (April 13, 1979).

If anyone wonders why Monseñor lived, spoke, and loved as he did, we believe the answer is that it was given to him to "see" the people and their God, in their deepest reality. He was graced with an "appearance," like those that occurred at the beginning of Christianity. That is what changed him into the new Archbishop Romero.

The Real Tradition of Monseñor: To Carry On His Work and His Cause

Third proposition. Like all traditions, Archbishop Romero's can take different directions. The true tradition of Archbishop Romero is to carry on his work and his cause. Specifically, it consists of building an "ecclesial body" to "save a people"; these are necessary tasks, today neglected.

How to Remember Monseñor

We remember Archbishop Romero because he has generated a Salvadoran, Latin American, universal tradition. But we can remember him rightly, or wrongly. The question is, how can we remember him properly? The answer was given us two thousand years ago.

The night before Jesus of Nazareth was murdered—as a blasphemer and rebel, remember, as they also said later of Archbishop Romero—he gathered his friends for a farewell dinner. They talked about life as he had lived it, and how it should be in the future. Then Jesus took bread in his hands, broke it, and gave it to his friends. The symbolism is clear: to live is to be broken and shared, as Jesus' life had been. And since it was a farewell, Jesus went on to say: "if you want to make me present, live in this way," "do this in memory of me."

To "do" things right we must "remember," and to "remember" right we must "do." This is an ancient Christian truth, because remembering Jesus has always meant following Jesus; there is no Christianity without it. Something like that is true of Archbishop Romero: in order to celebrate him, to make him present, we have to follow him in our own life, in our way of looking at reality, in our way of hoping, doing, and celebrating. Without these things, the celebration can always be co-opted, manipulated and even distorted. With them, Archbishop Romero will remain present, generous and liberating, in the world and in the Church. And let us remember that this choice has been facing us since immediately after his assassination.

In the preparations for his funeral mass on March 30, 1980, talking about the homily, someone suggested that the celebrant (who turned out to be Cardinal Corripio, the archbishop of Mexico City) might speak first about the scripture readings and the figure of Archbishop Romero—but insisted that the second part of the homily should begin: "And now let us talk about the events of this week." The idea was that the preaching should be not only *about* Monseñor, but *like* Monseñor's preaching. It was to initiate the tradition of Archbishop Romero by talking not only *about* him, but *like* him.

The celebrant at that funeral mass on March 30 never had a chance to give a normal homily; the service was barbarously broken up with bombs. But those reflections on whether the focus and structure of the homily should be mostly *about* Archbishop Romero, or *like* his homilies, were not in vain. They established the structure and focus of what would become the future tradition of Archbishop Romero.

In the twenty years that have elapsed since then, Monseñor's tradition has gone in the right direction as long as "we said and did" as "he said and did." And it has gone in the wrong direction whenever we have been satisfied with "talking about him," not to mention when we "forgot to talk about him," or "talked in the opposite way from his." Today we are privileged to keep the tradition of Archbishop Romero, but we also have the obligation and responsibility to do it right. Monseñor Ricardo Urioste has recently insisted on that important point: it is not enough to admire Monseñor and sing his glories, but we must also carry on his cause. So remembering Monseñor entails both possibilities and dangers; let us begin by analyzing the dangers.

The Danger of an Adulterated Tradition

Obviously we can devalue Archbishop Romero's memory if we ignore him (it has now been twenty years of silence among the powerful) or distort him, sometimes intentionally and maliciously (as the daily press has done recently, especially *El Diario de Hoy*, in ways not seen for a long time). In any case, today it is practically impossible to go on as if Archbishop Romero had not existed, now that John Paul II has knelt to pray at his tomb (and Caritas International published thousands of beautiful posters of the event), now that Monseñor's statue stands at the main entrance to Westminster Abbey, in the heart of London. It is no longer easy to silence him overtly, but his memory can be devalued in many other, more dangerous ways.

One is by reducing him to a single dimension of his reality, especially if we do so consciously, by making of him a pious priest without a real, suffering, committed, struggling and hopeful people. This is the most common temptation for the churches. Or by seeing only his Salvadoran nationality, without the transcendence of a God who "raises his arm against oppression," who inspires history to give more of itself, who is a source of truth and grace, able to heal the just but negative side-effects of the struggles for justice. This is the most common temptation of some leftist groups, who see God as a source of alienation. In either case, the greatest danger is to declare him an object of private property—"Archbishop Romero is ours," as one sometimes hears in church offices—as if grace and truth had an owner and did not belong to everyone, thus projecting our human pettiness and jealousy onto God's fullness.

His memory can also be distorted—I pray this will not happen—in the process of beatification and canonization, by canonizing a watered-down Archbishop Romero instead of the robust and courageous Monseñor who walked through the Salvadoran villages, who challenged, denounced and unmasked all the country's powerful, who died at the hands of murderers. In the most radical distortion, Monseñor's beatification and his rise to the altars could be interpreted as an act of ecclesiastical kindness, a favor bestowed on him. The archbishop of San Salvador has rejected this possibility in his homily of March 24 [2000], referring to the "exceptional holiness" of Archbishop Romero, and adding that beatification and canonization "can add nothing to his glory." We have to insist on that point. It is not the Church that graces Monseñor, but Monseñor who graces the Church and elevates it, "so that they may see your good works and give glory to your Father in heaven" (Matthew 5:16), as Jesus said at the end of the beatitudes. (And we hope—although it could happen—that the beatification process will not be subjected to purely human calculations: whether or not this is the opportune time, or what benefits and problems will accrue to the church leaders and authorities as a result.)

Finally, Monseñor's memory can be distorted if we reduce him to an object of exaltation and enthusiasm, in the same way that the Christians in Corinth acclaimed the resurrected one and ignored the Jesus of Nazareth who had not come to be served, but to serve—which sometimes led them to do the opposite of what Jesus did. It is wonderful to let joy overflow, as happened at the twentieth anniversary; the people have every right to such moments of joy, which enable them to recover their hope and inner dignity. But exultation and joy are not enough. If that is all we remember, we dilute the true Archbishop Romero.

The Real Tradition: Building an Ecclesial Body for the Salvation of the People

Those are the dangers; now let us analyze what is the real tradition of Archbishop Romero, and what we must do today to carry on what he did in his day. Obviously the situations are not the same, but let us not be deceived. There is a certain isomorphism—a great deal of analogy—between the problems Monseñor faced and the ones we face in today's world.

In a nutshell, the world we live in today is still a world of cruel poverty, of terrible injustice, and of iniquitous inequality. Two statistics are sufficient: 1.3 billion human beings have to live on less than a dollar a day; and the ratio of rich to poor people grew from 1:30 in 1960 to 1:74 in 1997, and is still growing. The International Labor Organization recently reported that "80 percent of the population of Central America lives in poverty," and there is El Salvador with its poverty, unemployment, migrations in search of survival, corruption, etcetera. The warlike violence of the 1980s has disappeared, but everyday violence makes us the most violent country in the continent. The peace agreements are going nowhere; the economic ones in particular have never been implemented. Disenchantment is rampant, and in the elections last March, almost 70 percent of eligible voters stayed home. The Salvadoran people are still being crucified.

The Church, on the other hand, is not the Church of Archbishop Romero. In this judgment we must distinguish among individuals and groups, in order not to fall into unfair generalizations. But in general it is true that the Church does not understand its mission as bringing the people down from the cross, although there are important exceptions. Seen from within, the Church looks more like a scattering of movements than like a compact body, determined to struggle for the poor; more like a place of easy, infantilizing comforts than of reasoned, committed faith. Again, there are worthy exceptions, but in comparison to that of Archbishop Romero, the Church today seems to be sleeping.

We must avoid simplistic predictions about what Archbishop Romero would do today. Personally, I have no doubt that he would confront the new things that are emerging in history: ecology, interreligious dialogue, serious ecumenism, and above all, the situation of women in society and in the Church; he would be especially sensitive to injustice against women. But it seems most important to keep Archbishop Romero alive in the tasks to which he gave personal leadership, and which are still clearly needed today, in view of our national and ecclesial situation and the grave problems surrounding those tasks. Here is a partial list:

First, to tell the truth about reality. Remembering Monseñor means, above all, *telling the truth* in the following ways. The truth must be spoken as *denunciation* of a sinful reality (poverty, injustice, violence), and a dehumanizing reality (discouragement, feelings of abandonment, an alienating and infantilizing pseudoculture). The truth must be spoken to the powerful in *freedom,* without fear of the risks it entails, "because the darkness hates the light," and with the *clarity* of a word that everyone can understand and that does not become an abstract, ethically universal, easily coopted, and finally sterile word. The truth must be spoken with *partiality* to the poor, rather than hastily invoking a Church in which all are equal, which ends up being a Church of the few, the powerful. The truth must be spoken with strength equivalent to the magnitude of the evils we face. And finally it must be spoken with *credibility,* based on serious analysis and with courage in the face of attacks and persecution.

This is about giving the people back their own truth, and not playing along with those who would deceive them. It is about being, in Monseñor's words, "a voice for the voiceless." Or in Ignacio Ellacuría's words about the university, it is about being "a science for the voiceless, an intellectual support for those who have truth and rightness in their own reality, even though it has been taken away from them, but who do not have the academic reasons to justify and legitimate their truth and rightness." With all the necessary allowance for changing times and persons, it is about going back to the focus and structure of Archbishop Romero's homilies.

Second, to analyze reality and its causes. Remembering Monseñor means analyzing the causes of poverty, injustice, violence, and cultural dehumanization. In view of the current ecclesial silence in this area, it means going back to his pastoral letters, full of doctrine—on the gospel, on the social doctrine of the Church, on the best theologies and analyses. It means now, as it did in his time, gathering the knowledge of experts in economics, sociology, politics, theology, pastoral practice. It means—very especially—giving central attention to the people's understanding of reality based on their experience, and absorbing their wisdom. That is what Archbishop Romero did when he took an opinion poll in the parishes and communities before writing his fourth pastoral letter, and then made use of the answers.

Third, to demand structural change and work for it. Remembering Monseñor means taking seriously the structural dimension of reality, working for structural change, denouncing and combating neoliberalism and capitalism in all its disguises—knowing that God and the poor will hold us accountable for our inaction and silence, especially in this area. It means going back to Archbishop Romero who denounced the idolatries, the economic and military structures, which spread death and generate victims. It means going back to Medellín, which denounced structural injustice (also calling it "institutionalized violence.") It means going back to Ignacio Ellacuría, who spoke of the crucifixion of whole peoples, whom the Church (together with other people, of course) must bring down from the cross, and make that its principal task. It means making all possible efforts, some bold, others modest, to turn history upside down. Today it means urging at least that the peace agreements be fulfilled, as a way of defending the poor and defenseless majorities.

Fourth, to promote a liberating evangelization. Remembering Monseñor means going back to the liberating concept of evangelization, in words and deeds. It means trying to perform not only acts of charity—which produce good things—but liberating acts, which are also aimed at uprooting the evil things. All this, which used to be called "liberation," is dying the death of a thousand details, distinctions, and cautions. The word "liberation," like the word "popular," has been forgotten by the Church—as if it had never been the focus in Medellín and Puebla, in Paul VI's encyclical *Evangelii Nuntiandi,* and above all in the gospel of Jesus. It almost goes without saying that the mission of the Church should be liberating, if it wants to overcome the sin of the anti-kingdom and promote the kingdom of God. The problem is that this liberating mission requires a willing Church, and such a Church is hard to find. Archbishop Romero is asking us whether a Church at the service of the liberation of the poor really exists; whether after so many words have been spoken, the Church is making liberation its central mission. And he is reminding us that it was Jesus' central mission, and that far from separating us from God, that liberating mission brings us closer to the God of Jesus.

Fifth, to carry out a mature, not infantilizing, evangelization. Remembering Monseñor (especially in these days) means offering a mature and reasonable religion (especially to the poor majorities), not a merely enthusiastic and infantilizing one—as if any religion would do as long as it upholds the existence of God, though not necessarily the God of Jesus, and offers transcendence, though not in historical terms—even a religion that borders on irrationality and alienation, as often happens in the religious press and radio and increasingly on television, and in so doing plays the game of the powerful. It is understandable that the poor majorities seek a consolation in the Church that they do not find anywhere else, since the economy does not solve their problems, the politicians neither defend nor guide them, violence threatens them on every side, families are disintegrating and their members are scattered among other countries and continents.

All that is true, but let us remember that these problems also existed in Monseñor's time, sometimes more acutely. The difference is that then the Church offered consolation through its nearness, solidarity, and identification with the people in their suffering and hopes; that way it helped them to grow and mature, in their awareness as Salvadorans and in their faith. It did not infantilize them, as often happens now, and it would not have been satisfied with full stadiums. The Church went out to the poor and suffering, it did not wait for them to come to church. Today's pastoral problems are obvious, but we must not add another to the list: the failure to give serious, evangelical, Salvadoran pastoral guidance to the people. Let us repeat what we have said before: the Church must know and analyze its reality, above all its social reality as seen in families, labor groups, youth, migration, etcetera. Without doing our own analysis we can only borrow foreign pastoral methods, which are largely inadequate.

And if we may add a present-day reflection, let us remember that Archbishop Romero appreciated popular and liturgical celebrations and made use of them, but always in the service of a liberating evangelism. So it is fair to ask the hypothetical question: how would Archbishop Romero celebrate Jubilee 2000 today? What kind of conversion would he demand? For what sins would he ask forgiveness, personally and on behalf of the Church? From this viewpoint the Salvadoran Church, in this jubilee year, might well have sought forgiveness for its participation in the evils of the war, and for what it has not done to carry on Monseñor's tradition over the last twenty years. It would also have been appropriate for the Church in the United States, through the presence of the cardinal from Los Angeles, to seek forgiveness for the things its governments have done to the Salvadoran people and many other poor peoples in the third world. And for the Vatican to seek forgiveness, among other sins, for the way it treated Archbishop Romero and several other bishops, priests, theologians, and lay people during their lives.

Sixth, to build an ecclesial body. Remembering Monseñor means—and this may well be the most important condition for moving forward—building an ecclesial body in which we can all support each other and contribute our share to the mission and holiness of the Church. Archbishop Romero worked for a communitarian, creative Church. He encouraged the Church to witness—to the point of martyrdom—and thus to be credible. He admonished it never to let the scriptural warning come to pass: "because of you the name of God is blasphemed among the nations" (as Isaiah and Ezekiel said in the Old Testament, and Paul, James, and II Peter in the New). On the contrary, Msgr. Romero encouraged the Church to be salt in the dough and light in the darkness. This is how he put it: "You, a Church so alive, so full of the Holy Spirit." Remembering Monseñor means working to bring back a Church like his, a Church of the poor. It means, above all, bringing back an ecclesial body that is united, resolute, and proud of its mission.

Finally, to give hope to a suffering people. Remembering Monseñor means generating and maintaining hope. It is well and good to offer a more blessed beyond, especially when the here and now is iniquitous. It is well and good to bring comfort, especially the great comfort that everyone will come into the fullness of God—but there's no need to rush it. The Church should also, resolutely, encourage the hope that life is possible, that God's creation can be for us like the shared table that the martyr Rutilio Grande so often talked about. "If they take away the people's hope, they have taken everything," says Dom Pedro Casaldáliga. Remembering Monseñor means, then, that the Church becomes a faithful and unconditional guardian of the hope, the utopia of life. "We have to defend the minimum, which is the maximum gift of God: life," Archbishop Romero said in Puebla. "The hope of the poor will not perish," says the psalm. That is God's wager, God's utopia. That should be the mission of the Church.

The Salvadoran Church faces many other tasks, and we have mentioned some of them: to promote ecumenism, to find solutions for the problems of youth, the ecology, to restore the dignity and rights of women, etcetera. We have focused here on the ones that Monseñor was most concerned about, and which are still urgent. The most important, we believe, is to recover Archbishop Romero's perspective on the mission of the Church: to save a people. Monseñor did many good things, but he also tried to do something more all-embracing: to save his suffering and hope-filled people. In an article written a few months after Monseñor's martyrdom, Ignacio Ellacuría called him "Archbishop Romero, sent by God to save a people" (*Sal Terrae*, December, 1980).

This is the *pathos*—no longer present—that the Church must once more draw from the tradition of Archbishop Romero: to live, and be willing to die, for the salvation of the people. It must also take specific actions, of course. But this popular, all-embracing perspective in everything it does, including the small, specific actions, provides the beginning and foundation for its evangelizing mission and its identity as people of God. It is the "foundation" because many other things can be built on it: evangelization, liturgy, doctrine, theology, pastoral practice, morality, canon law, social service, etc. And it is the "beginning" because so much can grow out of it: faith and prayer, commitment and mystique, mercy and hope—all crowned by martyrdom, as was so splendidly shown by the Church that followed Monseñor.

Can this be done? We have mentioned the limitations, but we must also mention the available ecclesial resources. Many things have happened during this anniversary celebration that give us hope, if we can put them to use. The celebration showed the remarkable dedication of many people to make it possible and give it dignity: the presence of a large number of people, institutions, priests and bishops; the quality of the celebrations, the respect and devotion one felt in gatherings of thousands of people, the international solidarity—in Spain alone there are 32 Oscar Romero solidarity committees. There was also a remarkable number of retreats, workshops, lectures and papers whose purpose was to bring Monseñor to people's hearts and to the world of ideas, to encourage a more spirited and lucid mission. The charism and the words of Don Samuel Ruiz and Dom Pedro Casaldáliga were outstanding, to mention two examples, along with those of many other people, less visible but no less real.

And not only in the anniversary. In these twenty years there has been an accumulation of local traditions, activities, books and articles, forums, solidarity groups, base communities, and some bishops—without much peer support, as we have said—all of which offer great resources for remembering Monseñor as God wills. The love and the day-to-day persistence of the Salvadoran people are unfailing.

So we're not starting from scratch. An anniversary like this could not have been improvised. It could only come to flower because it came from reality—even a sometimes hidden reality, seemingly small as a mustard seed. And to keep spirits high, let us not forget the gospel teaching: to carry on Monseñor's cause, to keep his tradition alive, is demanding and burdensome. But this tradition is like the gospel: the more we carry it, the more the tradition carries us. The Romerian tradition that carries us is the great resource of the Salvadoran, Latin American, and universal Church.

Archbishop Romero: Prophecy, Judgment, and Good News

Fourth proposition. Today, most certainly, Archbishop Romero is good news for the poor and their partners in solidarity. But he is also a prophecy and judgment on this world which has killed, and continues to kill, righteous and innocent people.

Let us end where we began. Monseñor is a universal martyr and saint, and he has clearly been canonized by the people. Without much help from science and canon law, but with a great *sensus fidei* which grasps the presence of God in our world, the people—"their poorness"—have recognized him as a martyr and saint. They have blessed his day (March 24) and his places (the "little hospital" and now the crypt) with art, music, poetry, countless paintings, songs and popular refrains, and the streets and country roads with demonstrations and processions.

This is the most important fact: the people's canonization of Monseñor. It is not yet official, and we are waiting for that. But let us remember that the people's canonization gives life to the official one, and not the other way around. The people feel that Archbishop Romero has placed them in a different reality, at a higher level than the one we live in from day to day, and higher than any canonization process—as important as that is for other reasons. To call Monseñor a saint does not mean violating any norm, or defying any canon. It means experiencing and saying, gratefully, that something very special has happened: people have seen God passing through this world, they have felt the breath of the Spirit and have given thanks for the appearance among us of the good news of Jesus.

How do the people express this unique experience? I have often heard it in words like these, with their recurring, three-part rhythm: "Archbishop Romero told the truth. He defended us, the poor. That's why they killed him."

That "he told the truth," that he was a prophet, is unforgettably clear to anyone who heard his denunciations. He said to the rich: "The oligarchy is desperate, and is blindly attempting to repress the people" (February 24, 1980). To the military: "Stop the repression" (March 23, 1980). To the government: "When will you sanction the security forces that have committed so many violent acts?" (July 8, 1979). To the communications media: "The truth is missing from our environment" (April 12, 1979); "There are too many people with their pens paid for and their word sold" (February 18, 1979). To the U.S. government: "We are fed up with weapons and bullets. What we are hungry for is justice, food, medicine, education" (October 21, 1979).

People also remember his denunciations of the Church, when it "unfortunately served certain economic interests, but that was a sin of the Church, by deceiving and not telling the truth when it should have done so" (December 31, 1978). When it prostituted religion: "The Mass is subjected to the idolatry of money and power when it is used to legitimate sinful situations. . . . And not only the Mass; what is worse is to appear in the newspapers, to impose a merely political coexistence" (June 24, 1979). And drawing a conclusion from his denunciations of the Church, he said cuttingly: "The Christian who does not want to live in commitment to the poor is not worthy to be called Christian" (February 17, 1980).

That "that's why they killed him," and that he is a judgment on the world, is clear from the New Testament reflection on the cross of Jesus. That Archbishop Romero, a good and righteous man, was murdered means that this is a murderous world. Monseñor's death accuses it of murder, as do the children of El Mozote, the Indians of Guatemala, the women of the Congo, the 800 million people who are living in critical, biological poverty. Monseñor was a peerless prophet in his lifetime, comparable only to Isaiah, Amos, Jeremiah, or Micah. In death he is the crucified Christ, pronouncing judgment on the world which he accuses of sin. Archbishop Romero denounces, unmasks, and condemns its crimes.

That "he defended us, the poor" is the deepest of the things the people saw in Monseñor: It is good news. "Archbishop Romero is the only image we have of God," said an old man in a poorhouse. Gustavo Gutiérrez says that the great question for theology is "how to tell the poor that God loves them." Archbishop Romero answered that question with his whole life.

In conclusion: Archbishop Romero brought truth, compassion, and reconciliation into a world of lies, cruelty, and violence. He brought steadfastness and love into a world of triviality and selfishness. Into a world that doesn't need God, or infantilizes God, he brought a faith that trusts in the ultimate mystery, and is absolutely committed to God's will. We don't often see truth and compassion, steadfastness and love, trust and commitment in one person. So when such a person comes into our lives, it is like a breath of fresh air. To see judgment and good news together—the Monseñor who was at once steadfast, hard and implacable against death-giving oppression, and sensitive, tender and earnest with the weak—that is good news. This earnest Monseñor loved the poor, and let them know that he loved them more than anyone else.

One final word. There will always be great heroes, personalities, even saints. We may admire them, venerate them, perhaps thank them, but we seldom love them. But that is what happened with Monseñor, and that may be his unique characteristic. After all these years, his memory has not cooled, has not become a museum piece, but remains a warm and loving memory. To this very day the people, the poor, love Archbishop Romero.

—Translated by Margaret Wilde

Chapter 10

The Legacy of the Martyrs of the Central American University

It is a Christian truth that wherever there is death like the death of Jesus on the cross for having defended the victims of this world, and with a great cry, there is also resurrection, a word continues to resound and the crucified endure through history.

The martyrs of the UCA, Ignacio Ellacuría, Segundo Montes, Ignacio Martín-Baró, Amando López, Juan Ramón Moreno, Joaquin López y López, Julia Elba, and Celina Ramos, together with Monseñor Romero and so many thousands and thousands of Salvadorans, died like Jesus on the cross, and that is why they must stay alive like Jesus. If this were not so, our faith in the resurrection of the crucified would be in vain, but if it is so, we must ask ourselves what those crucified persons have left to us.

One year ago, just a few days after their murder-martyrdom, I tried to say what that was, with pain and passion at the time, but it is important to take it up again, although I may do so today more calmly and with the perspective that time affords.

As with all human beings, with their death they have left us what they were in life. Their legacy as academics has already been explored in depth,[1] and so I will not delve into this aspect. Rather I will focus on the human and Christian legacy they left us, reflected in their university work, and which also made that work possible. Seeing them as a whole, I would like to say that these martyrs were human, merciful, truthful, just, lovers of mankind, blessed and believing, and that is what they leave to us: humanity, mercy, truth, justice, love, blessing, and faith. Let us say a few brief words on each of these.

Reprinted from Jon Sobrino, *The Principle of Mercy* (Maryknoll, N.Y.: Orbis Books, 1994), 173–185.

The Incarnation Which Humanizes: Coming to Be in the Real World

We are born men and women, but becoming humans is not a simple matter. Above all, it means existing and being in the real world, and not in the exception or the anecdote of reality. It is easy to determine what the real world is in El Salvador, but it is essential to remember that, in order to understand the human side of our martyrs.

In contrast with other societies of plenty in the countries of the First World and in the First World enclaves in El Salvador, what characterizes our Salvadoran reality is the unjust poverty of the majority, which produces a slow daily death, to which can be added the speedy and violent death which occurs in the form of repression and war. The world which is more real and more Salvadoran is thus the world of poverty and injustice. This is in a quantitative sense, since the majority are poor, and it is in a qualitative sense, because that poverty is not only one dimension of reality among many, but the one which cries out the most.

Things being the way they are, for these Jesuits—as for all—to ask oneself the question of one's own humanity was to ask oneself a question about incarnation, the question of where to stand: on these islands of plenty and well-being, which have nothing Salvadoran about them—in fact, almost without exception, they are anti-Salvadoran—or in the midst of the reality of the poor and impoverished majority.

Faced with this reality, our martyrs exercised the option, above all, to live in the midst of the true Salvadoran reality. This was their fundamental option for the poor, demanded of Christians by the gospel and ethically required by history. But above all it was a primarily human option—we could say even metaphysical—in order to become simply real and human themselves.

Their principal work, and the greatest part of their time, were spent in the UCA, although the cries of the poor also physically reached the UCA, and several of the martyrs assiduously stayed near the reality of the poor. But although they worked in the UCA, they did not live life from the UCA standpoint or for the sake of the UCA, but rather from and for the reality of the poor. This reality is what guided their actions and options. They worked at their desks, but not from the standpoint of a desk and not in order to pile up writings on a desk. The "from" and "for" of all their work was the impoverished and hopeful Salvadoran reality.

Their death shows perfectly clearly that in life they became incarnated in that reality. Monseñor Romero used to say in thunderous tones: "In a land in which so many horrendous murders are taking place, it would be sad if priests were not among the victims," a prophecy which was fulfilled in the case of the six Jesuits. But the reason Monseñor Romero was even gratified by these martyrdoms was also translated into reality: "They are the testimony of a Church which is incarnated in the problems of the people." If our martyrs suffered the most real form of death in El Salvador, it is because they lived the most real reality of El Salvador.

Thus, death made them participants in Salvadoran reality, but that same Salvadoran reality is what humanized them in life. In El Salvador there is not only poverty and death, but the poor also possess and transmit realities and values which are very difficult to find outside their world: hope instead of senselessness, commitment instead of selfishness, community instead of individualism, celebration instead of simple amusement, creativity instead of culturally imposed mimicry, a sense of transcendence instead of the blunt pragmatism and positivism of other worlds. With these values, the poor shaped them as Salvadorans and made them human. "Their pain converted and purified them, they lived on their hopes and their love seduced them forever," I wrote shortly after their martyrdom.

This is the primary and fundamental legacy left us by the martyrs: They were real human beings in El Salvador. And it must be added that they became so in the face of the temptation *not* to become so, since to be an intellectual in a university and a religious person in an order which frequently moves in another world tends to generate a bit of superiority and human artificiality, a tendency to live above and beyond true reality. But this did not happen with these martyrs. In Christian terminology, they were incarnated in truth, like Jesus, in the reality of our world. In the words of Luis da Sebastian, "they were where they had to be." In the simplest terms, they became human beings.

The Heart Which Is Moved to Mercy

To live truly and humanly in El Salvador inescapably means, as Jesus said in the parable of the good Samaritan, meeting up with a wounded person on the way, and they met one. But they did not meet up with an individual, but rather an entire people, and not just with a wounded people, but rather with a crucified people. And this meeting is where the human part is decided: Either you make a detour around him, as the priest and the Levite of the parable did, or you heal his wounds.

Our martyrs made no detour. Even amidst grave danger, they did not leave the country. Within the country, they did not even settle in those artificial islands in which one does not want to see the crucified people. Nor did they make that subtle detour—frequent in these cases—of taking refuge in science, in the university, in the religious life—there are always good reasons to do so—to avoid doing what had to be done with the wounded person. They stayed within the country, amid countless attacks and threats, when they could perfectly well have found comfort and gratification in other places. They turned the university and religious life not into a pretext to avoid dedicating themselves firmly to healing the wounded, but into an effective instrument for truly healing them.

But the most decisive part is knowing why they dedicated their lives to healing the wounded. The answer is extremely simple, but extremely fundamental in understanding how human these martyrs were. Just as with the

Samaritan in the parable, in the presence of a crucified people, their hearts were moved and they were moved to mercy. They internalized the suffering of an entire people and responded to it. And they did all that without ulterior motives, without any more motive than the enormous suffering of the crucified people.

I like to think of these martyrs above all as human beings with compassion and mercy, for whom responding with effective love for the crucified people was the beginning and the end of existence. It is true that they worked and served in the university, in the Society of Jesus, in the church, but in the final analysis they were not serving and working for the good of the university, the Society of Jesus, or the church. They were working to bring the crucified people down from the cross, in the language of Jesus, to eliminate the anti-kingdom and build the kingdom of God. Thus, they did not use the poor as a means to further their academic or religious interests— an everpresent temptation, since we human beings manipulate for our benefit even that which is most sacred—but on the contrary, they used the latter as a means for practicing mercy.

This is what we mean when we say that mercy was the beginning and the end for them. These words should not surprise or shock us, as if in this way we were undervaluing the reality of the university, the Society, and the church. According to the gospel, the final goal is the kingdom of God, and for that reason, in the presence of the anti-kingdom, nothing can go beyond or before mercy. The Samaritan, who is presented as the perfect human being, acted only through mercy, and not to defend institutional religious interests or as a way to achieve his own perfection. The same thing is said in the Scriptures of Jesus and the Heavenly Father. If Jesus healed the sick and wounded, if God liberated an oppressed people, they did not do so with ulterior motives, but rather simply—as is said in both cases—because the cries of the poor moved their hearts.

Mercy was, therefore, much more for our martyrs than a feeling, or the willingness to alleviate some suffering or other, something which can exist in many people. It was a principle which guided their entire lives and work. Mercy was there in the beginning, but it stayed there throughout the entire process, shaping *them* as well. It is true that mercy is not everything for human beings, nor was it for our martyrs, since—as human beings—they were also necessarily confronted with knowledge, hope and praxis, as Kant said, and also with celebration. But the principle of mercy is what guided and shaped all that.

The Truth Which Defends the Victims

Mercy is what moved them to look at Salvadoran reality in order to understand it as it really is, and what guided their thought and knowledge. Moved by mercy, they sought the truth, analyzed it, and proclaimed it.

They did all this in an academic way, as we will see tomorrow in a here we would only like to emphasize one point.

We all know that truth does not abound in El Salvador, not only because ignorance exists, but because falsehoods prevail. Not only is the truth about reality unknown, but it is also covered up so that it may not see the light of day. In this way the realities of death and terrible massacres are unknown and relegated to oblivion, and very frequently fundamental truths are distorted to the point where the victims are portrayed as the executioners. This is not said as clearly today as before, but we should recall how Monseñor Romero and our martyrs were slandered, as if they had caused the violence instead of being its victims. In El Salvador, therefore, the same lie that provoked the terrible lament of the prophet Isaias, "Woe to you that put darkness for light, and light for darkness!" is repeated.

In this world of lies, finding the truth means not only overcoming ignorance. Our martyrs certainly dedicated their work to overcoming it, to obtaining the scientific and technological knowledge which is, of course, necessary to build a viable country. And they did so in research and teaching. But the first step they took, also in an academic manner, was to unmask the lie, because no just society can be built on that foundation, and with lies the necessary scientific and technological knowledge does not become liberating knowledge, but frequently becomes a new instrument of oppression.

Academically, they unmasked the original sinfulness of human beings which, as Paul said, consists in "oppressing truth with injustice," or in the words of John, in that "the devil is a liar." And they denounced that sinfulness as something real not only in the individual but also in society itself. A society which generates unjust poverty furthermore tends to cover up the fact, to justify it, even to try to portray it as something quite different, inventing euphemisms which cover over the fundamental sin. In this way, the Third World is often spoken about in terms of developing nations, of incipient democracies, without analyzing whether the Third World is really on its way to development or, on the contrary, if it is moving toward greater underdevelopment, or whether the democracies reach the "demos," the people, or not. And thus in El Salvador, although no one can any longer deny the tragedy of this country, they talk about democratic progress, progress in human rights, progress in the administration of justice, in the professionalization of the Armed Forces. . . . Pretty words to cover up the lie of reality.

To speak this truth in a country like El Salvador, above and beyond anything else, means to unmask the lie. But whoever does so not only speaks the truth, but automatically becomes a defender of the poor. The poor are those who contain and express the most fundamental truth in their own flesh, although they cannot make it prevail. From this standpoint, we can understand the epithets repeatedly applied to Monseñor Romero in his time—for clearly speaking the truth—and which today I would like to apply to our martyrs. They were the voice of the voiceless, the intellectual words of those who have no words, even though they possess the truth.

With this, we wish to say that their passion to seek, analyze, and speak the truth did not, in the final analysis, come from a pure wish to further their own knowledge, although they were well aware of the need to increase their rigorous knowledge. Above all, it came from the wish to defend the poor, who have the truth on their side, and at times that is the only thing they have on their side. The ability to seek and analyze the truth certainly came from their own intelligence, of course; but their passion for the truth was rooted in mercy. "Suffering precedes thought," said Feuerbach. These martyrs undoubtedly thought and tried to think in the best possible way, but they thought in order to defend the poor. A rare convergence of intelligence and mercy took place inside them.

Structural Mercy: The Paths of Justice

The wounded found along the way were actually an entire crucified people, not just an individual. For this reason, mercy took a certain shape in history and was not reduced to mere benevolent feelings or occasional help. It took the shape of justice, which is the expression necessarily taken by love for the poor majority, and took the shape of liberation, which is the expression of love for a majority who are unjustly and structurally oppressed. Returning to the parable of the good Samaritan, not only did they look at the wounded, but also at the highway robbers, those structures which necessarily inflict wounds. Not only did they wish to heal the wounded, but also to eliminate the causes of the wounds and propose the best solutions. In the final analysis, that is how they understood their university work, and they saw the university as an effective instrument for achieving their goals. All this is well known. What I would like to add is that their structural view of reality, the investigation into its causes and solutions, was guided by mercy, and that is why they always kept the concrete reality of the poor before their eyes.

This is also why, from a fundamental perspective of justice and liberation, which always guided their steps, they continually modified and changed their concrete views on how to implement those principles. And here they were very demanding in two aspects: in the rigor of their analysis, to avoid playing or experimenting with things which were such serious matters for the people, and in the creativity of their analysis to avoid falling into a dogmatism which always ends up prevailing over one's own preconceived ideas—as scientific as they may be—about the reality of the poor.

How they analyzed Salvadoran reality is well known. At this time I would only like to emphasize their willingness to change, to adapt their theoretical analyses to Salvadoran reality, and not vice versa. In simple terms, I wish to say that they were not dogmatic, although they were indeed firm in their positions. Nor were they purely pragmatic, much less opportunists, but they were flexible in order to be creative, and they were creative in order to respond to the demands of reality. It is sufficient to read the last twenty years of the magazine *ECA* in order to verify both assertions.

This is how they analyzed, as principles or at least as factors in a solution for the country, the elections of the 1970s, the coup of October 15, the revolutionary political-military solution, dialogue, negotiations . . . They analyzed the fundamental agents of social change, popular movements, the so-called and misunderstood "third force. . . ." Whether or not all their analyses were correct is open to discussion—and in fact some of their positions were at times criticized—but what is beyond discussion is the objective of that flexibility and creativity: to find a solution for the popular majority. They greatly valued, and used, a variety of philosophical, sociological, political, and theological theories, but they never turned any of their principles into dogma, but rather used them insofar as they "opened" paths to solutions. The reason for that is the primacy they assigned to the reality of the poor over and above any theory about the poor. Just as Monseñor Romero said, "the Church will support one political process or another, depending upon how well it serves the people," so were the martyrs eager to find knowledge, theories, analyses which would benefit the people. If they held any immutable dogma, it was that of the suffering of the crucified people and the urgency of bringing them down from the cross.

The creativity of their thought undoubtedly stemmed from their own intelligence, but it was the people's pain that put it into motion, directed its fundamental course, and continually drove it to seek out new paths. Their thinking minds instilled the necessary intellectual rigor into their feeling hearts, but these feeling hearts were those which put vigor into their minds and moved them to produce knowledge for the benefit of the people. In the language of Saint Ignatius of Loyola, consecrated by Ignacio Ellacuría, their great question was always: "what are we going to do to bring the crucified people down from the cross?" But that question—as Ignatius of Loyola requested—was posed before a people who were actually crucified.

Enduring Mercy: The Greatest Love

When mercy takes the shape of justice and liberation in history, no matter how rational and reasonable it may seem, it must confront those who do not allow themselves to be governed by the principle of mercy. There are those in history who overlook mercy: the priest and the Levite, which is already a tragedy; but there are others who are governed by the principle of active anti-mercy: the highway robbers of the parable, which is a greater tragedy. This is why active and effective mercy for a crucified people must be maintained as mercy in the presence of active anti-mercy, in order to be enduring mercy. This means necessarily stepping into society's conflicts, running personal and institutional risks. And when, out of mercy for the victims, one touches the idols which produce the victims, it means risking one's life. Enduring mercy is that which leads to the greatest love, that of giving one's life, and when one gives one's life it means that mercy has truly been present and active in one's lifetime.

This is how the martyrs were: endearingly merciful, until the end. Mercy for them was the beginning and the end, and they put nothing before it, not even their personal safety, not even—and this was perhaps the most difficult part—the safety of the institution. As we all know, during fifteen years they were the target of countless attacks, threats, and personal risks, and they also risked—but prudently—the institution, which was many times attacked and physically damaged, and always was threatened by the paralysis which is a product of the fear that some wished to instill into its members. Their deaths were thus the culmination of a process, and not the product of macabre and momentary madness.

But if this is so, our martyrs gave their lives freely—as did Jesus, as did Monseñor Romero—and they gave them in order to keep mercy enduring. Their deaths demonstrated, therefore, that what moved them in life was definitely their great love for the poor, and not any personal interest or hatred of anyone. Here is where, in the final analysis, their credibility lies. Their deaths, which they met consciously, are what convince the poor, more than any possible words, that they were with them, that in this cruel world there are human beings who have defended them and loved them.

The Joy of the Beatitudes

Joy and suffering also belong to the human world. These martyrs had some of each. The joy and suffering of daily life, when things turned out well or turned out badly, when—as persons—they felt gladness in their hearts or suffered tension, when they saw progress or setbacks in the processes they worked for. This joy and suffering were very real, and each one had his; but here we continue to move in a world of particular joy and suffering, not in that fundamental sphere which makes a life blessed or damned. Underlying, and going beyond, concrete and particular joy and suffering is the enjoyment of life or the pain of sadness.

Now at this level, in which the meaning of life is at stake, I would like to say that these martyrs were human beings who felt joy. This should be seen as a given, since if they were truly merciful, they were already blessed with one of the beatitudes of Jesus: "Blessed are the merciful." From this standpoint of the beatitudes—which we could call Jesus of Nazareth's theory of happiness—I would like to recall the joy they shared and offered to all.

"Blessed are the poor," says Jesus, and these martyrs shared—each in his own way—that joy. By carrying out their work from the standpoint and for the sake of the poor, they participated in their reality, which gave them a fundamental human dignity and filled them with joy. And their direct contacts in the refugee camps, poor parishes, and base communities filled them with a shocking happiness.

"Blessed are the clean of heart," says Jesus. By letting themselves be enlightened by the poor and see the world through purified eyes, they experienced the joy of holding the truth and serving the truth.

"Blessed are they who hunger and thirst for justice," says Jesus. By living and dying for justice for the poor, they found a superior food, one which satisfies the hunger of humanity and fraternity.

"Blessed are the peacemakers," says Jesus. By working to achieve peace amidst repression and war, even if they themselves were repressed, defaced, and slandered, they achieved true peace, not the kind afforded by the world but rather one upon which they could rest their hearts.

"Blessed are they who suffer persecution for justice's sake, for theirs is the kingdom of heaven," says Jesus. By stepping into conflicts and remaining with them until the end, until giving their own lives, they achieved the maximum joy, which is the maximum paradox. By giving their lives, they showed the greatest love, and that made them live.

Saint Ignatius asks the Jesuit to do everything "freely, without expecting any human payment or salary for your work," in somewhat ascetic language. Jesus says it to us in the language of the beatitudes: "It is more blessed to give than to receive." This is what was personified in our martyrs. They did not keep their lives for themselves, but rather gave their lives so others might live and live in plenty, as Jesus says. In this they lost their own lives, but by giving life to others they themselves came to life.

This is what their joy consisted of, and in this joy they were similar to the poor whom they served. Gustavo Gutiérrez often repeats these words he heard from a peasant: "The opposite of happiness is not suffering, but rather sadness. We have much suffering, but we are not sad." My brothers—I know it well—had much suffering, but I never saw them sad. And that joy of being human, that deep sense of life, is what they leave to all of us.

The Faith Which Walks Humbly with God through History

These martyrs were, finally, believers, and in a very concrete way. Their faith certainly did not separate them from being human, much less did it remove them from Salvadoran reality, as sometimes happens with people who, "because they are not of this world, believe that they are of God, and because they do not love men, believe they love God." The martyrs rather saw in Christian faith a requirement and the best opportunity for themselves to become human and humanize others, and they saw in it the great Christian principles which guide humanization: the kingdom of God as an ideal for society, and following Jesus as an ideal for human beings.

Thus, they verified and insisted upon the historical effectiveness of the gospel, but also believed in the gospel. In Jesus they saw the perfect human being, and believed that by following him one set into motion the essence of the truly human being, and all that we have said about them up to this point is nothing but concretizing in our time what it means to follow Jesus. But that following is also faith, since nothing—no philosophy, no ideology— can guarantee historically that following the path of Jesus leads to the right place. If, however, they followed that path until the end, it was because they believed in Jesus, because they were convinced that there is nothing more true than Jesus.

They felt attracted by the Jesus who says: "The spirit of the Lord is upon me, because he has anointed me; to bring good news to the poor he has sent me, to proclaim to the captives release, and sight to the blind; to set at liberty the oppressed . . ." (Luke 4:18). And to that Jesus they were true. That is why I wish to place on their lips these words taken from Paul:

> Who shall separate us from the love of Christ? Shall tribulation, or distress, or persecution, or hunger, or nakedness, or danger, or the sword? Even as it is written, "for thy sake we are put to death all the day long. We are regarded as sheep for the slaughter." But in all these things we overcome because of him who has loved us. For I am sure that neither death, nor life, nor angels, nor principalities, nor things present, nor things to come, nor powers, nor height, nor depth, nor any other creature will be able to separate us from the love of God, which is Christ Jesus our Lord (Romans 8: 35–39).

Our martyrs, perhaps because of their sober temperament which was Salvadoran, Basque, and Castilian, never used such lyric expressions to speak of Jesus, but they said as much in their daily stubborn efforts to follow his steps until the end.

Finally, by following Jesus, and like Jesus, they found themselves before the final mystery of personal existence and history: the mystery of God. God was, for them, a reality which must be reproduced in history, in a historical fashion, and limited to human beings, of course; but a reality which, in the final analysis, must be "practiced," as Gustavo Gutiérrez says. They saw that "practicing" of God as something very good for them and for history, but if they perceived it as good, it was because they believed in a just and good God, in a God the Father. Believing in God was for them an attempt to be in affinity with God.

Furthermore, God was for them a reality which was always impossible to embrace and manipulate, a reality whose word—whatever it was—had to be listened to and answered. God was the height of mystery, the greatest possible otherness, and to believe in God meant letting him be God. This presupposed standing before God, sometimes without hearing a word, asking God and crying out; "My God, my God, why have you abandoned me?" in one's personal life and, above all, faced with the tragedy of El Salvador, without hearing an answer. But it also meant standing before God in terms of the utopia of this mystery, the God who draws everything to him so that all would be more, so that there be life and plentiful life.

They too lived their faith in this *chiaroscuro* of all that is human, I think with more light than darkness, definitely so. Like all human beings, and like Jesus, they struggled with God, and he vanquished them. In the midst of such darkness in history, they let themselves be seduced by God, like the prophet Jeremias, and the burning flame they carried in their hearts was not extinguished. They sought rest in God the Father, but he never left them in peace. But true to the mystery of this God, they walked humbly with God in their own lives, as Micheas says, and thus they walked toward God.

I think this is the faith shared by our martyrs, this is the faith they proclaimed, and this is the faith they left to us. In their lives, in their work, and in their martyrs' fate they united the human and the divine. In the words used by the Jesuits to define our mission in the world of today—words inscribed on their tombs—they united faith and justice, God and the victims of this world. In their words used by the Letter to the Hebrews to describe Jesus, they united faithfulness to God and mercy for the weak.

In this way, along with "many other Salvadorans," they united what is Salvadoran with what is Christian, and strengthened both. To some they offered the God of the Salvadorans, God of the victims as opposed to the idols, so that their faith would not be alienating or obfuscating. To others they offered the mystery of God, so that their liberating practice would not reduce or make smaller that which is human, but rather open it up more.

Ignacio Ellacuría said of Monseñor Romero something that neither he nor his fellow martyrs would have said of themselves. But the truth is that, with Monseñor Romero, with many thousands of others, with Julia Elba and Celina and the six Jesuits of the UCA, God passed through El Salvador. They leave us their faith, therefore, but above all, they leave us the mysterious passing of God.

Martyrdom: A Cry Which Continues to Resound

All this has been left to us by the martyrs of the UCA. In its concrete execution they undoubtedly did it with limitations, and for this reason what I have said is not intended as a eulogy. But I do hope it contributes inspiration and courage so all of us can reproduce the fundamental structure of what is human and Christian. What martyrdom adds to their lives is, on the one hand, credibility, and on the other, a great cry to the world saying that *that*—and not so many other deceiving offers—is what humanizes and christianizes, that *that* is what is human and Christian.

"Death is more eloquent than words," said Monseñor Romero. And Don Pedro Casaldáliga said of Monseñor's martyrdom that "nothing will silence your last homily." On November 16, my eight brothers and sisters spoke their last homily. Let us finally take a look at what they said with that last cry of theirs, although briefly and somewhat schematically.

Above all, their martyrdom has shaken the world in such a way that this time it cannot be silenced. In many places, and in many institutions which usually overlook our reality (governments, universities, churches, political parties), people have finally had to look Salvadoran reality in the eye. "Something is very wrong in El Salvador," our martyrs cried. And many of those who have heard that cry—although not as many and not as profoundly as we might wish—have felt called upon.

Politically, for the first time, the United States—which bears such great responsibility for our tragedy—has been forced to take a hard look at these martyrs, and through them, at El Salvador. For the first time, the Salvadoran Armed Forces has felt strong pressures to renounce its aberrant practices. The cut in military aid and the way in which this contributes to a negotiated solution is a great contribution made by our martyrs. The same can be said of the Salvadoran negotiations now underway, whose pace has been accelerated by the murders.

Solidarity with El Salvador, so necessary and so difficult to maintain for the duration of the tragedy, and which suffers understandable discouragement on the part of some, has increased. The celebrations being held these days in El Salvador and in many places around the world—in the United States alone there were activities in over 200 cities—is strong evidence of this.

But beyond this shakeup and the important fruits the moment has produced, they leave us something more fundamental and lasting, since that cry—like the cry of Jesus on the cross—is also good news.

From their crosses, the martyrs are, paradoxically, feeding hope, and this was seen by the recent celebrations. There is weeping, but more from emotion than from hopelessness. There are songs of thanks, of commitment, and of hope.

From their crosses, the martyrs unite us as a Salvadoran people and as a Christian people. Around their crosses have gathered Salvadorans and people from many other countries, Christians of different churches, and even nonbelievers, intellectuals and peasants, religious workers and trade unionists. This true ecumenism is a great benefit for all of us, in human and Christian terms.

From their crosses, the martyrs tell us, finally, that in this world it is possible to be human, to be academics, to be Jesuits, and to be Christians. Although this may not appear to be exceedingly good news, it is. And they proclaim it decisively, because they tell us that it is possible to live with a great love in this world and to place all our human abilities at the service of love. My personal impression of the recent celebrations is that all of us who participated in them came out with greater firmness, inspiration, and courage to be a little better, a little more human, and a little more Christian.

At the beginning I said that all who die crucified like Jesus will rise again, and that is what is also happening with the martyrs of the UCA. One year after their deaths, they continue among us, and they are becoming—as Monseñor Romero said—a "tradition," a permanent source, already objectified in history, of inspiration and courage. Their names are already on schools and libraries, on streets and plazas of important cities, and in little villages and repatriate communities. But let us also remember how the resurrection of the crucified is described in the gospel: he appeared before "witnesses," not before mere "seers." That is what is now our task: To bear witness for our martyrs, pursue their cause, and in that way keep them alive in a world which so deeply needs what they were and did.

I would like to close by using, one year later, the same words I wrote just a few days after their martyrdom:

> My six Jesuit brothers now rest in the chapel of Monseñor Romero beneath a large portrait of him. All of them, and many others, would have given each other a firm embrace and would have been filled with joy. Our fervent desire is that the heavenly Father transmit that peace and that joy very soon to all the Salvadoran people. Rest in peace, Ignacio Ellacuría, Segundo Montés, Ignacio Martín-Baró, Amando López, Juan Ramón Moreno, Joaquin López y López, companions of Jesus. Rest in peace Elba and Celina, very beloved daughters of God. May their peace give us hope, and may their memory never let us rest in peace.

Chapter 11

Archbishop Romero and the Faith of Ignacio Ellacuría[1]

I was asked to write a foreword for this book in honor of Ignacio Ellacuría. I wrote it with pleasure, but it was not easy; I didn't know quite what to say, without repeating what is already in the articles. Finally I decided, with fear and trembling, to write about "the faith of Ignacio Ellacuría."

I made that decision for two reasons. First, I personally often wonder what a person's faith is like, especially those people who have been important to me. After the death of Archbishop Romero I wrote a long article, trying to sum up his person and his work,[2] in which I said: "It may seem like an understatement or oversimplification, to say that Archbishop Romero was *a man who believed in God.*" That was the beginning; before speaking of Monseñor the archbishop and Salvadoran, I spoke of Monseñor the believer. Years later, on March 9, 1991, in the funeral homily for Father Pedro Arrupe at the Central American University, I said: "What impressed me about Father Arrupe is that he never gave his heart with ultimacy to anything besides God. He very simply let God be God."[3]

The second reason for writing about Ignacio Ellacuría's faith—or better, his conviction—is that faith in God does not at all diminish, or overpower, other dimensions of the believer: mercy, the struggle for justice, honesty about reality, intellectual honesty, community, tenderness, hope. Rather, faith empowers these other dimensions—as we also know by remembering Archbishop Romero and Father Arrupe. It is true that faith in God shapes the believer's reality in a very specific way. We can debate just what faith "adds" to other aspects of the believer's historical reality, and how it empowers them, but for me at least, there is no doubt that faith in God gives a special flavor to everything the believer is and does. It is impossible to know people fully, without knowing their faith. That is why I write about the faith of Ignacio Ellacuría. I hope it will help the reader to know him

This appeared as the foreword to Ignacio Ellacuría, *Aguella libertad esclarecida* (San Salvador, 1999), 11–26.

"fully"—and also to overcome or counteract other presentations that have been made about him, some of which have resorted to manipulation.[4]

The following comments are based more on my personal perception from the 16 years we lived together, than on an analysis of his writings, although I shall mention some of his words.

Struggling with God

I have always believed on the one hand, that Ellacuría's faith must have passed through some kind of crisis and darkness; and on the other, that his fundamental honesty toward reality always led him back to a greater mystery. Like Jacob, he struggled with God.

In November 1990, on the first anniversary of his martyrdom, I wrote him a letter about this. In the letter I recalled that his faith could not have been naïve. His contact with modern philosophers (most of them non-believers, except for Xavier Zubiri), the environment in which he came of age intellectually, his own critical and honest way of thinking, his aversion to credulity, and the scandalous, unjust and perennial poverty of the Latin American continent must have made it hard for someone like Ignacio Ellacuría to believe in God.

Those were challenging times of secularization, demythologization, theodicy, and even the death of God. Ellacuría was absolutely aware of all that, and sometimes he showed it. At a 1969 meeting in Madrid, he said something I have never forgotten: "Karl Rahner carries his faith-doubts elegantly," meaning that he also did not think of faith as something obvious, but as a victory. Like many others, he had to learn to live "etsi Deus non daretur," as Bonhoeffer wrote in prison. So Ellacuría's faith could not have been naïve, because of the way he was and the times in which he lived.

But I think Ellacuría walked in faith over the rocky ground of wisdom. He was reserved about such things, but sometimes he "let it show." When Rutilio and Romero were murdered, he gave us glimpses of deep emotions and religious feelings about the ultimate truth of things. He spoke of Jesus and of God in the language of faith-hope. These were like "echoes" of a faith that he seldom talked about in public.

Among these "echoes" I remember the existential conviction—not what one would expect of a professional theoretician—with which he spoke of transcendence, especially in its historical manifestation. I think that in his theory of reality, and in the direction of his praxis, he remained ever faithful to the "more" that he always, inexorably, encountered in history, and to which he tried to respond and correspond: he was existentially incapable of turning away from the reality of a history always pregnant with "more." In this one sees the Zubirian idea "that reality can give more of itself" and the Ignatian "*magis*," "to the *greater* glory of God."

In his philosophical and theological writings, he analyzed conceptually this transcendence that he felt existentially. He greatly appreciated Zubiri's thinking about God, and he himself wrote a masterful philosophical article on faith.[5] Theologically, he understood historical salvation "as a greater presence of the ever-greater God."[6] In homilies and speeches he spoke naturally about God, and whenever he could he promoted pastoral work, especially among the poor and simple people, because of his conviction that faith in God gives one lucidity, strength, courage, and dignity. Ellacuría had no use for empty words, and never used God's name in vain; he wanted to say something real whenever he mentioned "God."

His words were even "less vain," if you know what I mean, when he spoke and wrote about Jesus of Nazareth. With existential pathos his words conveyed the conviction that the true human being was revealed in Jesus—*ecce homo, homo verus*—and that was why following Jesus was so absolutely central for him, as it was for the synoptics and St. Ignatius. He also had a conviction that Jesus revealed the true God, not the God we selfishly invent to fit in with our wishes and interests. As he wrote a little before Puebla, to explain the theological basis of the option for the poor, the true God is "the God who came down, who was poured out primarily for the poor."

Ellacuría talked a lot about Jesus, especially the historical Jesus, in order to advocate a praxis of justice and liberation—theologically and often polemically, in the way such things were debated in the Church and in the Company of Jesus in the 1960s. But that Jesus also had a powerful attraction for him. Certainly he felt the impact of Jesus' mission, the proclamation and building of the kingdom of God, the defense of the weak and marginalized, the denunciation of oppressors and powerful people of every kind—all of which he tried to reproduce in *orthopraxis*. But that was not all. It is less widely known that Jesus' way of being had an impact on him: his attitude toward life and death, his honesty toward the truth, his mercy, his steadfastness to the end, his active availability to God—to which he responded with what we have called *orthopathy*, the right way to be affected by Jesus.

But once he "let it show." He suddenly said in a theology class: "The point is, Jesus had the justice to go to the depths, and at the same time he had the eyes and heart to understand human beings." Someone who was there said later, "Ellacu fell silent, and then finished talking about Jesus with these words: 'he was a great man.'"[7] When he talked about Jesus, Ellacuría conveyed not just an enlightening idea, or even an inspiring ideal, but—like the New Testament—he conveyed good news: "the kindness and humanity of God our savior has appeared."

It was that Jesus of Nazareth, I think, with whom Ellacuría walked in history, telling himself and others what to be and what to do in this world: to eradicate sin, but only by bearing its burden; to hear a promise, but in the world of the poor; to save reality, but by turning history upside down; to redeem violence, but by taking it on in martyrdom; to seek joy, but to find it more in giving than in receiving. These things—each one made concrete and Christian by the "but"—are what Ellacuría used to call "the Christian aspect." "The Christian aspect" was the focus of his life, in largely verifiable ways.

But let us come back to "faith" in its strictest sense, to that reality which cuts across and is expressed in "the Christian aspect" but goes far beyond it: faith in the mystery of God. What echoes of that faith are to be found in Ignacio Ellacuría? I will answer with something that happened one day in 1983. Returning from his second exile in Spain, to a place where we Jesuits from the Central American University were on retreat (not to say in hiding), Ellacuría celebrated the eucharist and spoke about the "Heavenly Father." Later I wrote: "I was thinking to myself that Ellacuría, the critical, intellectually honest one, could not have used those words out of mere sentimentalism. If you said Heavenly Father, I told him, it was because you believed in him."

What Ellacuría's faith was like, or that of any other human being, we can only guess. Like many other people throughout history—Abraham, Jacob, Job, Jesus—he struggled with God, and it looked to me like God won.

Facing the Mystery of God with Archbishop Romero

The faith of those "challenging years," as I said earlier, was later challenged by something new: Archbishop Romero. When Ellacuría was 47 years old and had been working about ten years in the Central American University, Archbishop Romero "appeared" to him—and I use that word intentionally, to express the corresponding elements of surprise, confusion, and blessing.

It was not Ellacuría's first encounter with a person who would strongly influence his life. But I am convinced that for him, meeting Archbishop Romero was different from meeting other teachers. The difference is that he met Monseñor's faith. This doesn't mean, of course, that other teachers didn't touch his faith. Certainly Father Miguel Elizondo did in the novitiate, in 1949, by bringing him existentially to the figure of Jesus through the experience of St. Ignatius. Karl Rahner must have had a great impact on him during the years at Innsbruck, when at the height of his theological development, he was writing his masterful articles on God and the mystery, the incarnation, the trinity. Xavier Zubiri also had an impact with his philosophy of God and with Zubiri's own faith.[8] It also doesn't mean, of course, that it was only Archbishop Romero's faith that had an impact on him. Like many others, Ellacuría was deeply affected by Romero's prophecy, his hope, his incorruptible work for justice, and his closeness to the poor.

All this is true, but I want to insist on the specific, unique impact of Archbishop Romero's faith on Ignacio Ellacuría. To put it graphically, Ellacuría sincerely thought of himself as a "disciple" of his former teachers, but as the years went by, he also saw himself—rightly and without arrogance—as their "colleague." In principle he could put himself on their level with regard to theology, philosophy, even the interpretation of St. Ignatius. But that never happened with Msgr. Romero. Ellacuría used to say, with absolute sincerity, "Archbishop Romero was way ahead of us."

Of course Monseñor and Ellacuría were "companions" and "colleagues" in their dedication to truth and justice, but where "faith" was concerned, it was a different matter: Monseñor was always out in front. Ellacuría was impressed with his way of turning to God, not only in reflection and preaching, but in the deepest reality of his life. God was absolutely "real" for Monseñor, and it is that God who really made people and history human. Archbishop Romero's faith imposed itself on Ignacio Ellacuría. With that faith, the mystery of God that he had struggled with earlier took on a "new" and somehow "definitive" newness. That is why, at key moments when Ellacuría talked about Archbishop Romero he linked him directly with God, as if one could not adequately talk about Monseñor without mentioning God. And he did it in bold language.

I have told this story many times. In his homily at the eucharist we held at the Central American University three days after Monseñor's assassination, Ellacuría said, "with Archbishop Romero, God passed through El Salvador." Those were bold words, perhaps, but they were sincere, and I believe Ellacuría needed them to say clearly what he thought about Monseñor. They were a sort of public confession of what the good bishop and martyr meant to him. Archbishop Romero spoke to him of God, a God of the poor and martyrs, a liberating, demanding and prophetic God. In a word, Archbishop Romero spoke to him of the "here and now" in God. But he also spoke of the ineffable, never quite historicizable, "beyond" in God, of the bottomless and blessed mystery. And he not only talked to Ellacuría about God, but led him to God.

This is the most important part of what I want to say in this prologue, but perhaps we can make it a little clearer. A few months after that homily, the journal *Sal Terrae* asked Ellacuría to write an article about Archbishop Romero. He did, and using bold words again he titled it "Msgr. Romero, sent by God to save his people."[9] Everyone knows that for Ellacuría "people" and "salvation" were central values, but in relating them to Archbishop Romero, he added a primary emphasis on God. He said in the article:

> Archbishop Romero never tired of saying that political processes, no matter how pure and idealistic they are, are not enough to bring integral liberation. He understood perfectly what St. Augustine meant by saying that in order to be a man, one must be "more" than a man. For him, if history is merely human history and doesn't try to be more than that, it will not remain human either. Neither human beings nor history are complete in themselves. That is why Msgr. Romero always called us to transcendence. The theme came up in almost all his homilies: God's word, God's action breaking through human limits.[10]

One last quote. In 1985, five years after Archbishop Romero's martyrdom, the Central American University posthumously awarded him an honorary doctorate. On that occasion Ellacuría gave an important speech, from which I will emphasize two things. The first is that despite accusations to the contrary, the Central American University publicly acknowledged Archbishop Romero's importance and "superiority" in its own life and mission. Thus Ellacuría said:

> It has been said maliciously that Msgr. Romero was manipulated by our University. Now is the time to say publicly and solemnly that it was never true. Msgr. Romero asked our collaboration on many occasions; this was and always will be a great honor for us, both for his sake and for the things he asked us to do. . . . But in these collaborations there was never any question about who was the master and who the helper, who was the pastor setting guidelines and who carried them out, who was the encourager and who was being encouraged, whose was the voice and whose the echo.[11]

With these words Ellacuría confessed—with a humility that was not characteristic of him, and a sense of gratitude that was—how much the University owed Monseñor. But I also see in them a recognition of his deep personal debt to Monseñor. Moreover, in a key moment of the speech Ellacuría returned to the linkage between Archbishop Romero and "God":

> [Archbishop Romero's] hope rested on two pillars: the historical pillar was his knowledge of the people, to whom he attributed an inexhaustible ability to find ways out of the gravest problems, and the transcendent pillar was his belief that ultimately God is a God of life and not death, that the ultimate reality is good and not evil. That hope not only helped him overcome every temptation to discouragement, but encouraged him to go on working, in the awareness that no matter how short the time was, his effort would not be in vain.[12]

Carried by the Faith of a Crucified People

It is hard, and finally impossible, to get inside the faith of another person—especially a person like Ellacuría. But I have no doubt that Ellacuría was truly impacted by Archbishop Romero, in a different way than by a Rahner or a Zubiri. Monseñor entered into the depth of his person, the place where people choose what to do with themselves, without being able to delegate the choice; or more radically in terms of grace, where people accept—helplessly, gratefully, joyfully—being shaped by another or by The Other.

For Ellacuría, Archbishop Romero was like the face of God in our world, a face definitely more *fascinans* than *tremens*. Not only that; in Archbishop

Romero's presence he felt—unusual for him—small, with a smallness that does not humiliate, but enlarges and dignifies. Monseñor gave him, as he gave many others—with exquisite delicacy—what Monseñor had in abundance and the rest of us in more modest quantities.[13]

In conclusion, Ellacuría saw a man of God in Archbishop Romero, and saw God in that man. Truth and prophecy, mercy and justice, utopia and grace, all in limitless flower at the same time in Monseñor, as difficult as that is, made him present—helplessly present—to God. In Monseñor he saw, I think, that the universal desire was fulfilled: that God is good, and that it is good that there is God.

We have already said that for both Archbishop Romero and Ellacuría, the ultimacy of God did not detract from the ultimacy that belongs to historical realities. Archbishop Romero knew and communicated the truth that God radicalizes and empowers the important things in historical reality. Two historical realities were absolute for Ellacuría, even before his encounter with Monseñor, but Monseñor confirmed and empowered them. One was the suffering of the poor; the other, the call to serve them by bringing them down from the cross. In the letter I wrote to Ellacuría in 1990, I described the ultimacy of the poor this way:

> You were a faithful disciple of Zubiri, a philosopher and theologian of liberation, a theoretician of popular political movements, but you never fought for these theories as if they were a "dogma." Rather you were able to change your viewpoints—you, the inflexible one—and when you did, it was always for one reason: the tragedy of the poor. This is why I think that if you had one rock-solid "dogma," it was this: the suffering of the crucified peoples.

And that suffering of the poor is what moved Ellacuría to make service his ultimate calling. I wrote:

> Above and beyond everything else you were a man of compassion and mercy. The ultimate within you, your very heart, was moved by the enormous suffering of these people. That is what never left you in peace. That is what set your creativity in motion. Your life was never just service, but the specific service of "bringing down the crucified peoples from the cross." Those are your words, words that intelligence alone cannot invent, but only intelligence inspired by mercy. That is why you served in the University, but did not in ultimate terms serve the University. You served in the Church, but did not ultimately serve the Church. You served in the Company of Jesus, but did not ultimately serve the Company of Jesus. The more I came to know you, the more convinced I was that you were serving the poor in this country and the third world, and that it was this service that gave ultimacy to your life.

I have said that compassion and service were the ultimate things for Ellacuría, even before he met Monseñor. But once he met him, perhaps a different kind of ultimacy began to grow in him, more clearly expressed in the reality of his life than in his doctrinal writings: the ultimacy of gratuitousness. We have already alluded to it by beginning this analysis with the words, " Archbishop Romero *appeared* to him," came forward to meet him. But derived from that fundamental grace, there were other historical experiences and expressions of gratuitousness.

Perhaps it is useful here to recall Ellacuría's insistence on the ethical-praxic dimension of human intelligence: one must "take responsibility for reality," and also "bear the burden of reality," as burdensome as it is. In theory and practice Ellacuría led the way on this point, but I think also on the dimension of gratuitousness, which also can be described as "letting reality carry us"—or even more, as "carrying one another" in solidarity. So we may ask whether in fact Ellacuría "let others carry him," whether he was "willing to receive from others." The answer is that he let himself be carried by the faith of Archbishop Romero, and by the faith of the crucified people, which was also influenced by Archbishop Romero.

Monseñor used to say things like "the people are my prophet," and "with these people it is not hard to be a pastor." He acknowledged that the people were carrying him, and this must have given food for thought to Ellacuría. Whereas in most things Ellacuría had to lead the way and carry others, in his faith he felt he was being carried by others. I like to think he was living the reality of which Paul wrote: "For I am longing to see you . . . so that we may be mutually encouraged by each other's faith, both yours and mine" (Romans 1:11–12). Ellacuría saw in the crucified peoples a sacrament of the presence of that mysterious God in the world, and in their hope, their commitment, and their dignity he saw their faith in God. Faith cannot be delegated, but it can be shared in solidarity. In his awareness of being carried by the faith of others, Ellacuría experienced the element of gratuitousness that belongs to faith in God.

Let us say in conclusion that the faith of Archbishop Romero and the crucified people never turned Ellacuría's faith into "cheap grace," "cheap faith," but rather into "costly grace," "costly faith." Historically this led to his martyrdom—one of the characteristics of costly grace, according to Bonhoeffer—and in the meantime, it led him to walk in history. In that walk, I believe, he was always clear about "doing justice," as Micah says, but also about "walking humbly"; right down to the end he had to look God in the face.

What other people's faith is like, how they hold on to it down to the end, is a secret placed in God's hands. Ignacio Ellacuría has left us two texts, written shortly before his death. In both he speaks of faith and of God. The first is the speech he gave at the Barcelona city hall on November 6, when he was awarded the Alfonso Comín Prize. Although it was basically a political occasion, here too he spoke of faith and of God.

At the theologal level we advocate maintaining a tension between faith and justice. . . . [Both must be placed at the service] of the popular majorities and some fundamental values of the kingdom of God, which Jesus preached in utopian terms.[14]

The second text is his last theological writing, "Utopia and Prophecy," which ends with these words—a true synthesis of prophecy and utopia, of walking in history, in faith and darkness, and "discerning God."

A prophetic rejection of the Church as the old heaven of a civilization of wealth and empire, and a utopian affirmation of the Church as the new heaven of a civilization of poverty, is an irrefusable demand of the signs of the times and the soteriological dynamic of the Christian faith. That faith is lived in history by new men and women, who keep proclaiming a new future, firmly despite the present darkness, because beyond each successive historical future they can discern the saving God, the liberating God.[15]

One can only enter into another person's faith on tiptoes, quietly. Perhaps we have been too daring in this essay. But we hope that for those of us who have "stayed behind," it has been helpful to enter into the least visible but most real dimension of Ignacio Ellacuría. And we hope that those who have "gone ahead" will smile with understanding and forgiveness on our audacity.

—*Translated by Margaret Wilde*

Part Four

EPILOGUE

A Letter to Ignacio Ellacuría
(1990)

Dear Ellacu:

For years, I've thought about what I'd be saying at the Mass of your martyrdom. I've had the same feeling as I had about Archbishop Romero. His martyrdom was inevitable, too, and yet I never wanted to admit to myself that it would finally come. But your death was so likely that it was simply impossible for me to get the idea out of my head. And here are the two things that have most impressed me about you.

The first is that, while I was struck by your intelligence and creativity, it always seemed to me that these weren't your most specific traits. Even to you they were quite important, of course, but you didn't steer your life in the direction of becoming a renowned intellectual or prestigious college president. Here's an example. I remember how, in one of your exiles in Spain, you wrote a manuscript that would have made you famous in the world of philosophers. But you didn't ascribe all that much importance to it. You didn't even finish it when you came back to El Salvador. You had other things to do—more important things—from helping solve some national problem, to attending to the personal troubles of someone who'd asked you for help. For me the conclusion is really clear: Service was more important to you than the cultivation of your intelligence and the recognition it could have meant for you.

But service to what, and why? You served *at* the University of Central America, but ultimately not the University of Central America. You served *in* the church, but not ultimately the church. You served *in* the Society of Jesus, but not ultimately the Society of Jesus. The more I came to know you, the more I arrived at the conviction that you served the poor of this country and of the whole Third World, and that it was this service that gave your life its ultimacy. You were a faithful disciple of Xavier Zubiri, that philosopher and theologian of liberation, that theoretician of popular movements. But you didn't fight for his theories as if they were some kind of dogma. Instead,

Read at Mass, November 10, 1990. Originally published in *Carta a las Iglesias*, no 223 (1990), pp. 12–13. Reprinted from *The Principle of Mercy* (Maryknoll, N.Y.: Orbis Books, 187–189.

you changed your viewpoints. Inflexible you! And when you changed them, it was always for the same reason: the tragedy of the poor. So I think, if you were bound by any unshakable "dogma," there's only one thing it could have been: the pain of the crucified peoples.

This led me to the conclusion that, over and above everything else, you were a person of compassion and mercy, and that the inmost depths of you, your guts and your heart, wrenched at the immense pain of this people. That's what never left you in peace. That's what put your special intelligence to work and channeled your creativity and service. Your life was not just service, then: It was the specific service of "taking the crucified peoples down from the cross"—words very much your own, the kind of words that take not only intelligence to invent, but intelligence moved by mercy.

That's the first thing I'd like to mention. The second thing about you I recall—and this one is more personal—is your faith in God. Let me explain. Your contact with the modern philosophers—unbelievers, most of them, except for your beloved Zubiri; the atmosphere of secularization—in fact, of the death of God that prevailed at the time you were coming to your intellectual maturity; your own critical, honest intelligence, so disinclined to credulity; and the great God-question, which *in se* is the unjust poverty of Latin America—none of that made your faith in God easy. I remember one day in 1969, when you told me something I've never forgotten. Here's how you put it. You were talking about your great mentor, Karl Rahner. Suddenly you remarked, "He managed his own doubts very elegantly." I asked you what you meant. And you explained. You meant that neither was *your* faith anything obvious. It was a victory.

And yet I'm convinced you were a great believer. You certainly communicated faith to me. You did it one day in 1983. You had just come back from your second exile in Spain. You were saying Mass, and when the time came for you to speak to us, you talked about the "Heavenly Father." And I said to myself that if Ellacu the brain, the critic, the honest intellectual, used those words, then it wasn't just sentimentality. If you talked about the Heavenly Father, it was because you believed in the Heavenly Father. You communicated faith to me a great many other times, too, in what you said and wrote about Archbishop Romero and his God, or when you spoke so simply about the piety of the poor. And you communicated it to me in your way of talking and writing about Jesus of Nazareth. In your writings, you expressed your faith that, in Jesus, we've had revealed to us what we human beings truly are. But you also expressed in those writings, gratefully, your faith that, in Jesus, an "ever more" surrounds us all—the ultimate mystery and utopia that draws all things to itself. I don't know how much you wrestled with God, like Jacob or Job or Jesus. But I believe that God won the match, and that Jesus' Father gave your life its deepest direction.

Ellacu, this is what you've left us, or at least left me. Your exceptional capacities could dazzle, and your limitations could confuse. I think, Ellacu, that neither the one has bedazzled me nor the other obscured what, to me, is the rock-bottom thing you've left me: that there's nothing more essential than the exercise of mercy in behalf of a crucified people, and nothing more humane and humanizing than faith. These are the things I've had in my head for years now. Today, on the first anniversary of your martyrdom, I say them. With pain and with joy—but especially, with gratitude. Thanks, Ellacu. For your mercy, and for your faith.

Jon

—Translated by Robert R. Barr

Letter to Ignacio Ellacuría
(2001)

Dear Ellacu:

Another year of ventures and misadventures. The recent ones have been big. First the barbarity of the twin towers. Now a very poor country, Afghanistan, after twenty years of war, suffering, and poverty, is being bombed mercilessly—literally, "without mercy." It is on the verge of human disaster. Between six and eight million Afghans are facing a lack of food, which may cause the death of thousands of people, according to the United Nations High Commission on Refugees (UNHCR). And there is no end to the tragedy in sight. Are we looking at another Rwanda?

This is the misadventure. But we are all expected—in order to avoid being anathematized—to support it with pride, in the belief that this way we are doing good. Because in the last analysis, we have almost never been concerned about the fate—the life and death—of countries far away from our western tradition, not fully human as we are. We are arrogantly required to assist in the "globalization" of the barbarity of bombs, hunger, and cold—while we go on waiting for that other globalization, of justice, mercy, and truth.

We have firmly condemned the attack on the towers, but with regard to Afghanistan, I was immediately reminded of your bold analysis of the northern superpower and your boldness in telling the truth. In 1989 you said something that I've never heard anyone else say: "From my point of view—and this may be prophetic and paradoxical at the same time—the United States is much worse off than Latin America. Because the United States has the solution, but in my opinion it is the wrong solution, for them and for the rest of the world."

Then you went on with these equally bold, utopian words: "By contrast in Latin America there are no solutions, only problems. But as painful as it is, it is better to have problems than to have the wrong solution for the future of history." Is anyone paying attention to you today? Do people pay attention even when they are honoring you as a great thinker and effective negotiator?

Back to Afghanistan. Since we're in a chapel, I'll tell you that neither the Church as a whole nor the hierarchy has been up to the challenge. There have been exceptions, thank God, and we live by those exceptions: the condemnation by the Brazilian bishops, Pax Christi International, the Jesuits

222

of *America* magazine. . . . And there have been deep things, like the families of victims in the United States who rejected revenge and offered forgiveness.

Ellacu, I want to tell you that you, the martyrs that our civilization doesn't know what to do with, are alive and giving life in these acts. It is you who hold us up and redeem us from within, bearing the burden of this world's sin. You make it a little harder for the words of Scripture to come true: "Because of you, the western, Christian, and democratic world, the name of God is blasphemed among the nations."

I want to tell you a second thing. Now they are talking about a "new world order." But they don't say what the "order" is. Is it "a good arrangement of things in the world," "human harmony"—the good side of order—or is it simply the distribution of geographic, economic, military, ideological power among the same old people? They also don't tell us if "new" means the world is going to change, or if it will be more of the same: a few rich and powerful, the majority poor and helpless.

The current crisis is not helping to bring order out of disorder, nor is it challenging the "principle of greed" that has guided every previous reordering: the powerful dividing up power among themselves in order to assure the good life for themselves. The four billion poor—or more—still don't count when it comes to putting the world in order. No one cares or thinks about a humane and civilized world.

That is where I remember your prophecy, with the upside-down utopia that you described with true audacity. Right up to your death you insisted on the need to "turn history upside down," in a new world, the opposite of the present one. Now that the civilization of wealth—the one that is trying to protect itself in the new world order—has failed, you said we need a dynamism that can overcome it dialectically. You called that dynamism the civilization of poverty. You dreamed of it this way: "Then the spirit can flourish, the great spiritual and human richness of the poor and the peoples of the Third World, who today are suffocating in misery under cultural models that are developed in some ways, but not in the ways that would make them more fully human."

You said the world needs such a civilization of poverty: "A universal state of things which guarantees the satisfaction of fundamental needs, freedom of personal choice, and an environment of personal and community creativity that allows new ways of life and culture to appear, new relationships with nature, with other human beings, with ourselves, and with God."

The conditions are not favorable for that utopia, Ellacu. That is clear. They are not favorable in the western democracies, which are mainly trying to square the circle: to go on living well and better, without making others live badly and worse. They are not favorable even among Christians and followers of the poor Jesus. We have to look for it like a precious stone hidden in small communities, in the primordial holiness of poor people and victims, in men and women of inexhaustible solidarity, and maybe in an occasional thinker or politician who goes against "political correctness."

But your idea is essential if the world is to work. You offer a principle out of which the whole, the universal dimension can grow in a humane way. That principle is not power, or wealth, but the poor. From them and with them we can build a human universalism. Without them, all universalizing movements, from globalization to religious ecumenism, can offer nothing but clichés: to work for the common good, to promote the universal desire for peace, to come together around a single God or a human ideal. . . . That is all well and good, but it is not enough. Unless we make the poor central, there is no axis on which humanity can turn "humanly." Humanity for the most part will merely be a "species," with strong and weak members, and the strong eating the weak. With the poor as the axis, humanity would turn in a different way; it would turn as a "family."

That, Ellacu, is how I see the essence of your proposal. And I like the way you bring God into this utopia. We hear a lot of talk about God these days, and a lot of talk against the god of the religious fanatics. But President Bush is talking about God too; the powerful have always talked about "gods," and so do the secularized democracies—using other names. Certainly we are talking about God. Sometimes in sacred clothing (the gods of the religions), sometimes secular (gold, oil, uranium, strategic areas—like El Salvador, which was called the "back yard" of the empire and thus made into something ultimate, untouchable, that is, a god).

Ellacu, you talked about God, but not that way. In your last theological writing, you dreamed of a "new heaven" and wished for a new Church, "the Church of the poor," and "new men and women." You ended with a faith and a hope: "always despite the darkness [they can see] an ever greater future, because beyond each successive historical future they can discern the saving God, the liberating God." No one talks much today about that liberating God. Not only because of the prevalent secularism, but because that God is closely linked to prophecy against the empire with its wrong solution, linked to the utopia of the civilization of poverty.

History is made up of ventures and misadventures. These days the misadventures have been big. But there have also been the kind of ventures that supply love and set our out-of-kilter world turning on a new axis. And there is hope. From Jesus, from the little people of this world, from you the martyrs, a venturesome wind keeps blowing, a modest hope that encourages us to keep walking, to build a civilization of poverty. That is what will civilize us all.

Thanks, Ellacu.
Jon
November 10, 2001

—Translated by Margaret Wilde

Notes

4. From a Theology of Liberation Alone to a Theology of Martyrdom

[1] An example is I. Ellacuría, who was never naïve either about the harsh demands of reality, or about the real possibilities of the theology of liberation. I think it is important to emphasize this. Ellacuría used to say that the intellectual must be analytical, prophetic, realistic, and utopian, all at once. In other words, the intellectual's scientific approach must be drawn from and dedicated to reality; the intellectual must be realistic—as he showed in his own work as a mediator in the Salvadoran conflict—but also humane (and Christian), and therefore prophetic and utopian.

[2] Today there are many ecclesiastical and secular critics, who triumphantly proclaim that liberation theology is a thing of the past. "The storm is gone," they seem to be saying, "and everything is back to normal"; in other words, back to the right. But I am more surprised that some progressive intellectuals, European and North American, not only deny the value of liberation theology—which should be discussed with respect on both sides—but now deny, *a priori*, even its possibility, which is even more serious. They have in fact increased their critical warnings to the point of exaggeration, and sometimes fail to hide their eagerness to distance themselves from the theology of liberation, perhaps in order not to be mistaken for naïve (old-style) socialists. The problem here has nothing to do with the content of liberation theology, but rather with its presupposition: the situation of oppression in the world.

[3] The problems of indigenous religions and cultures, women, and the environment have not received sufficient attention in El Salvador—or it has not been given with the same dedication as in other places. But perhaps the main obstacle to understanding and acceptance of these reflections in other parts of the world has been the scope and radicality of the praxis of liberation and martyrdom in this country.

[4] In this case as in many others, historical experience, the people's faith, and the corresponding pastoral practice were ahead of theology in acknowledging the value of martyrdom. In theological terms, in 1983 the journal *Concilium* published a monographic issue on martyrdom, with several Latin American theologians collaborating as authors.

[5] The repression, the persecution of the Church, and the making of martyrs began in 1977, when the popular movements had barely begun taking action. It was in 1977, in fact, that Archbishop Romero asked me to write a first reflection on martyrdom: "Sentido teológico de la persecución a la Iglesia," in *Persecución de la Iglesia en El Salvador* (San Salvador, 1977, 39–75); ET in *The True Church and the Poor* (Maryknoll, N.Y.: Orbis Books, 1984), 228–252.

[6] Among many other words of Archbishop Romero, let us recall: "I rejoice, brothers and sisters, that our Church is persecuted, precisely because of its preferential option for the poor and because it tries to incarnate itself in the needs of the poor. . . . It would be sad if in a nation where people are being murdered so horribly, there were not also priests among the victims. They are the testimony of a Church incarnated in the problems of the people" (July 15, 1979; June 24, 1979).

[7]It was first published in a collection of essays, *Cruz y resurrección* (Mexico, 1978), 49–82. After his assassination we reproduced it in the *Revista Latinoamericana de Teología 18*, 1989, 305–333.

[8]This is not the time to explain the reasons for that shift in the New Testament, its positive meaning and its risks, or how it was moderated in the synoptic gospels. We mention it only to show the importance of the more recent movement, back toward a balanced emphasis on both martyrdom and liberation.

[9]Though it is common knowledge, we must remember Archbishop Romero's efforts to contribute to historical liberation in El Salvador with his homilies, speeches, and pastoral letters, as well as his intervention in the national dialogue, in the coup d'état of 1979, in the crisis of January 1980, etc.

[10]We remember his articles on such themes as poverty, the strike, the violence, etc., in *Concilium, Misión Abierta,* and *Sal Terrae* among other journals. More particularly, he wrote the following for the *Revista Latinoamericana de Teología:* "Historicidad de la salvación cristiana" (vol. 1, 1984, 5–45); "Aporte de la teología de la liberación a las religiones abrahámicas en la superación del individualismo y del positivismo" (vol. 10, 1987, 3–28); "La teología de la liberación frente al cambio socio-histórico de América Latina" (vol. 12, 1987, 241–263); and his last article, "Utopía y profetismo desde América Latina" (vol. 17, 1989).

[11]A. González, "Approximación a la obra filosófica de Ignacio Ellacuría," *ECA* 505–506 (1990), 980. In this quotation we have substituted *theology* where the author used *philosophy,* since the same is equally and even more true of theology; his theology reached the deepest, most Christian, roots of his person.

[12]We have discussed this subject more extensively in *Jesus the Liberator: A Historical-Theological View* (Maryknoll, N.Y.: Orbis Books, 1993).

[13]We have said it before: when they killed Archbishop Romero at the altar, people had to go far back in history—to the eleventh century—to find a parallel in the killing of Thomas Becket, archbishop of Canterbury. But there was a very important difference. Becket was assassinated for defending the freedom and legitimate interests of the Church; Archbishop Romero, for defending the poor.

[14]Not long ago in Europe, Teilhard called Christ "the omega point"; K. Rahner called him "the absolute bearer of salvation"; Bonhoeffer, "the man for others"; more recently, Ch. Duquoc has called him "free man." All these ways of naming Christ are important. By adding the name "liberator" we do three things at once: show his relevance for our time, see him in the context of his own life of service to the kingdom, and give a more absolute meaning to the name by which we call him today—Christ.

[15]Ellacuría said this in many ways. Eduardo Galeano remembered: "Ellacuría told the oppressors that they will see their truth in the oppressed. That is why he was assassinated."

[16]Among other representative works in this line see J.L. Segundo, *El dogma que libera* (Santander 1989; ET, *The Liberation of Dogma* [Maryknoll, N.Y.: Orbis Books, 1992]), and *La historia perdida y recuperada de Jesús de Nazaret* (Santander 1992). I. Ellacuría was also concerned with this topic, although he did not publish much on it. But see his foundational article, "Voluntad de fundamentalidad y voluntad de verdad: conocimiento-fe y su configuración histórica," *Revista Latinoamericana de Teología,* 8, 113–131.

5. Jesuanic Martyrs in the Third World

[1]"Dimensiones del martirio," *Concilium* 183 (1983), 323.

[2]Homily, September 23, 1977.

[3]There are other types of martyrs, which I have analyzed elsewhere. An enormous number of human beings (often children, women and the elderly) have been assassinated in great massacres; we still don't have an adequate way to describe them. My colleagues and I compare them to the "servant of Yahweh," who bears the sins of the world and

dies under their weight, ignominiously and anonymously. Archbishop Romero said that today the servant of Yahweh is "the suffering people" (Homily, October 22, 1979), which Ignacio Ellacuría analyzed theoretically in his article *"El pueblo crucificado,"* which was published in several places and posthumously in *Revista Latinoamericana de Teología* 18 (1989), 305–333.

[4] J.M. Castillo, "El martirio en la Iglesia," *ECA* 505–506 (1990), 959–965.

[5] Th. Baumeister, "Mártires y perseguidos en el cristianismo primitivo," *Concilium* 183 (1983), 312–320.

[6] This is worth remembering even today. It is well and good to promote such values as tolerance, dialogue, consensus, but that does not diminish the inherent conflictiveness of the Christian faith—which in the last analysis derives from the conflictiveness of reality: the active existence of idols, of the antikingdom. In other words, this conflictiveness is metaparadigmatic or transparadigmatic; it does not disappear with a paradigm shift.

[7] However, this definition is also evolving, precisely because there are Christians in the third world who are assassinated because they are defending justice.

[8] This was Rahner's interpretation of the usual concept of martyrdom, from the standpoint of dogma and fundamental theology (cf. *LthK VII*, p. 136). The emphasis is ours.

[9] *Catechism of the Catholic Church*, n. 2473. This paragraph is found in a section on "The eighth commandment," under the subheading "Witnessing to the truth."

[10] "Anyone who thinks of Maximilian Kolbe without preconceived ideas will look more closely at his death and his conduct in the concentration camp, than at his earlier life; they will then think of him as a martyr of selfless Christian love" (K. Rahner, "Dimensiones del martirio," *op.cit.*, 323). Indeed, Kolbe's statue now stands in Westminster Abbey as one of the ten great martyrs of the twentieth century. Kolbe's death also clearly stands in the Johannine line of death for love of the neighbor.

[11] Let us briefly note that a problem of power is also involved in these reflections. Those who define martyrdom (or holiness, conversion, happiness, etcetera) hold great power over the collective Christian conscience. That fact is clear, and requires the power to be exercised wisely.

[12] The day after the assassination of the martyrs of the Central American University (in El Salvador), when I was in Thailand, a young man asked me with a gesture of total incredulity: "In your country there are Catholics who kill priests?"

[13] To establish this resemblance it has also been important (and necessary) to understand Jesus' death historically, as a consequence of his life of service to the kingdom and against the anti-kingdom, rather than as the mere fulfillment of an abstract plan of God.

[14] "Reflexión sistemática sobre el martirio," *Concilium* 183 (1983), 326.

[15] Although in the synoptic gospels Jesus is condemned for blasphemy (*in odium fidei* of the true God, the God of Jesus), this passage is known to have been a later redaction. The true cause of Jesus' death was his repeatedly expressed intention to destroy the temple, the symbol of an unjust theocracy (*in odium iustitiae*).

[16] *ST II-II* q. 124. a 2. ad 2.

[17] "The dramatic denunciation that runs through the gospel [of John] is that one can so completely pervert the concept of God as to replace it with a principle of death and lying (in that order: death and lying)!" J. Barreto, "Seales y discernimiento en el evangelio de Juan," *Revista Latinoamericana de Teología* 40 (1997), 55.

[18] Reading some acts of the martyrs, one can only be moved by the great love of Christ that they express. Also, in many martyrdoms *in odium fidei* there is no need for the existential passion that comes from working for the kingdom, a passion that makes martyrdom "more bearable," as has also happened in some nonreligious martyrdoms; this may enhance the brilliance of those martyrs' love for the person of Christ. But on the other hand, let us remember that the "traditional" martyrs may have been more existentially aware than others were of the nearness of their reward: they would soon be with Christ. This only reaffirms our thesis: it is a complex matter, and in the last analysis impossible, to judge another person's subjective holiness.

[19]In our opinion, Jesuanic martyrdom has been forgotten because christology in general has forgotten the kingdom of God, Jesus' essential point of reference, and has concentrated instead on the person of Christ.

[20]Indeed, even Vatican II had little of importance to say about martyrdom, let alone about Jesuanic martyrdom. It only mentions persecution in LG 8 and martyrdom in AdG 42, as if in passing and in a generic way. It also said nothing important about the Church of the poor, except for a few allusions in LG 8, GS 1, and AdG 5. One must say that there is a quite logical relationship between these two absences. Until Medellín, the time simply was not ripe for these subjects.

[21]*El cuerno del jubileo* (Madrid, 1998), 7.

[22]*Todavía estas palabras* (Estella, 1989), 45.

[23]Cf. Jos M. Tojeira, "El martirio en la Iglesia actual. Testigos de Cristo en El Salvador," *ECA* 589–590 (1997), 1093.

[24]It follows that the Church should be very cautious in affirming, for example, "Archbishop Romero is ours"—a problem that is reappearing as the process of his beatification begins. See what we wrote in "El proceso de canonización de Monseñor Romero," *Revista Latinoamericana de Teología* 43 (1998), 12s.

[25]L. Boff, *op.cit.*, 330.

[26]*ST II-II*, q. 124, a 4, ad 3. He also affirms that those who die "defending the fatherland from the attack of enemies who work for the corruption of the Christian faith" can be called martyrs, *In IV Sent.* dis. XLIX, q. V, a. 3, quaest. 2, ad 11. The fundamental reason for these affirmations is that "not only those who suffer for faith in Christ, but also those who suffer for any work of justice, are suffering for Christ" (*In Ep. Ad. Rom.*, c. VIII, lect. 7).

[27]Cf. *Jesus the Liberator* (Orbis Books, 1993).

6. The Latin American Martyrs

[1]"Medellín ayer, hoy y mañana," *Revista Latinoamericana de Teología* 46 (1999), 79f.

[2]Homily, July 8, 1979.

[3]"Función liberadora de la filosofía," *ECA* 435–436 (1985), 50. Ellacuría was alluding to Heidegger's famous question in *Was ist Metaphysik?*: why is there something and not nothing?

[4]"Discernir el signo de los tiempos," *Diakonía* 17 (1981), 58.

[5]"Monseñor Romero, un enviado de Dios para salvar a su pueblo," *Revista Latinoamericana de Teología* 19 (1990), 5–10.

[6]In history there are rival, opposing gods: the God of life and the idols of death (the absolutization of economic, military, cultural, religious power). Similarly there are opposing mediations, forms of society: the kingdom of God, justice, and brotherhood on one side, and on the other, currently, societies shaped by neoliberal capitalism. Finally, there are opposing mediators: those who consciously or unconsciously have followed the cause of Jesus on one side, and on the other, the cause of financial systems, security councils, multinational enterprises, etc. In this context, the "cross" is what necessarily happens to a mediator struggling against an unjust mediation.

[7]Words at the awarding of an honorary doctorate in Political Science to the President of Costa Rica, Dr. Oscar Arias (mimeographed text, San Salvador, September 1989, 6).

[8]If in fact a canonical process holds grace in its hands, it needs to be infused by grace and let its procedures show it. And in so far as humanly possible, the process needs to keep sin and *hybris* to a minimum.

[9]For a more detailed treatment of this theme, see chapters III and V of *La fe en Jesucristo. Ensayo desde las víctimas* (San Salvador, 1999). Much of the following section is taken from those chapters.

[10]"Quinto centenario. ¿Descubrimiento o encubrimiento?" *Revista Latinoamericana de Teología* 21 (1990), 281f.

7. The Crucified Peoples

[1] I dedicate this article to Ignacio Ellacuría because he dedicated his life to the crucified people and in his death assumed their fate. He also made them the object of his theological reflection. See his article written in 1978: "El Pueblo crucificado. Ensayo de soterologia historica," *Revista Latinoamericana de Teología* 18 (1989), pp. 305–33, and "Discernir 'el signo' de los tiempos," *Diakonia* 17 (1981), pp. 57–59. On 1492, he wrote *Quinto Centenario. America Latina. ¿Descubrimiento o encubrimento?* (Barcelona, 1990).

[2] "The 'Crucified' Indians—A Case of Anonymous Collective Martyrdom," *Concilium* 163 (1983), 51.

[3] Ellacuría, "Discernir" (n. 1), 58.

[4] *La Voz de los sin Voz* (San Salvador, 1980), 208.

[5] Ibid., 366.

[6] Ellacuría, "Discernir" (n. 1), 58.

[7] Here I repeat much of what was said in "Meditacion ante el pueblo crucificado," *Sal Terrae* 2 (1986), 93–104; "Brief an Ludwig Kaufmann aus El Salvador," in *Bioteppe der Hoffnung* (Olten & Freiburg im Breisgau, 1988), 392–398. See also *The Crucified Peoples* (CIIR pamphlet), London, 1989.

[8] *Quinto Centenario* (n. 1), 11.

[9] Ibid.

[10] "The Kingdom of God and Unemployment in the Third World," *Concilium* 180 (1982), 91–96.

[11] *Quinto Centenario* (n. 1), 16.

10. The Legacy of the Martyrs of the Central American University

[1] See Jon Sobrino, and I. Ellacuría, *Companions of Jesus* (Maryknoll, N.Y.: Orbis Books, 1990).

11. Archbishop Romero and the Faith of Ignacio Ellacuría

[1] In this foreword I have reworked and expanded what I wrote in an earlier, more extensive essay: "Ignacio Ellacuría. El hombre y el cristiano," in I. Ellacuría, J. Sobrino, R. Cardenal, *Ignacio Ellacuría, el hombre, el pensador, el cristiano* (Ediciones EGA, Bilbao, 1994), 15–80. On Ellacuría's faith, see 53–61.

[2] "Monseñor Romero: mártir de la liberacion. Análisis teológico de su figura y su obra," *ECA* 377–378 (1980), 253–276.

[3] "El Padre Arrupe, hombre de Dios y hombre de los hombres," *Carta a las Iglesias* 227 (1991), 5. (Ed. note: Father Arrupe was the Superior General of the Jesuits.)

[4] Soon after his death there were attempts to manipulate Ellacuría as a way of justifying the violence of the ETA, although he had condemned it shortly before his death. See his essay, "Trabajo no violento por la paz y violencia liberadora," *Concilium* 215 (1988), 85–94. In El Salvador, former guerrilla fighters insist—selectively and manipulatively—on his realistic, pragmatic and diplomatic attitude and praxis; all of that is true, but it overshadows and ignores his prophetic and utopian attitude and praxis, thus impoverishing his memory.

[5] "Voluntad de fundamentalidad y voluntad de verdad: conocimiento-fe y su configuración histórica," *Revista Latinoamericana de Teología* 8 (1988), 13–131.

[6] "Liberación," *Revista Latinoamericana de Teología* 30 (1993), 226.

[7] *Carta a las Iglesias* 245 (1991), 10.

[8] His faith was such that Ellacuría told Zubiri, half seriously and half in jest, that he was so much a believer that it was causing difficulties for his philosophy.

[9] *Sal Terrae* 12 (1980), 825–832.

[10]Ibid. 830.

[11]"La UCA ante el doctorado concedido a Monseñor Romero," *ECA* 437 (1985), 174.

[12]Ibid.

[13]Ellacuría also felt the impact of Archbishop Romero's direct, effective and affective closeness to the poor, which he also appreciated in Rutilio Grande—perhaps because externally, that was not his way of being.

[14]"El desafío de las mayorías pobres," *ECA* 493–494 (1989), 1080.

[15]I. Ellacuría, J. Sobrino (eds.), *Mysterium liberationis: Fundamental Concepts of Liberation Theology* (Orbis Books, 1993).